The New
IRAs

and How to Make
Them Work for You

NEIL DOWNING

Dearborn™
Trade Publishing
A **Kaplan Professional** Company

Editorial Director: Donald Hull
Senior Project Editor: Trey Thoelcke
Interior Design: Lucy Jenkins
Cover Design: Scott Rattray, Rattray Design
Typesetting: the dotted i

Library of Congress Cataloging-in-Publication Data

Downing, Neil.
   The new IRAs and how to make them work for you / Neil Downing.
     p.   cm.
   Includes bibliographical references and index.
   ISBN 0-7931-5416-2 (pbk.)
    1. Individual retirement accounts—Law and legislation—United States—Popular works.   2. Tax planning—United States—Popular works.   I. Title.
KF3510.Z9 D69 2002
343.7305′233—dc21

                                  2002000372

Dedication

In memory of Dana R. Gagne, CFP

Contents

Foreword   ix
Preface   xi
Acknowledgments   xiii

1. Traditional IRAs   1

    What a traditional IRA is
    How a traditional IRA works
    The tax benefits for contributing
    Benefits for married couples
    Breaks for women
    A new tax break for saving
    Nondeductible IRAs

2. Managing Your IRA   23

    Understanding your rights
    Where to open an account
    Your investment options
    Flexibility of IRAs
    Avoiding fees
    Moving your IRA

3. Withdrawing Money from Your IRA   35

    When you're under 59½
    How the 10 percent penalty works
    Ways to avoid the penalty
    Drawing income from your IRA
    When you're between 59½ and 70½

4. **When You Must Make Withdrawals**   43

A five-step plan for required minimum withdrawals
Understanding the benefits of the new rules
When you turn 70½
Calculating your first withdrawal
Figuring future withdrawals
Withdrawals when you own more than one IRA
Withdrawing from a nondeductible IRA
Withdrawing from a SEP-IRA, SIMPLE-IRA
Withdrawing from a Roth IRA
Trusts

5. **IRAs and Estate Planning**   67

Naming a beneficiary
Working with beneficiary forms
An IRA check-up
Using a trust for beneficiaries
The Stretch IRA
IRAs and the Death Tax

6. **Inheriting an IRA**   81

What to do when you inherit an IRA
Rules for spouses
Rules for non-spouses
When there are multiple beneficiaries
Separate accounts, moving accounts
A tax break for beneficiaries

7. **Education Savings Accounts/Education IRAs (Part 1)** 97

What they are
How they work
Who may contribute
What can you contribute
For whom may you contribute
Where to open an account and invest

8. **Education Savings Accounts/Education IRAs (Part 2)** 115

Using your account for education
Taking advantage of tax breaks
Saving for private, public, or religious elementary or high school

Saving for college
How rollovers work

9. The Roth IRA   127

What it is
How the benefits work
How much you may contribute
Tax-free withdrawals
Avoiding the penalty
Roth IRAs and your estate

10. Roth IRA Conversions   145

What they are
How they work
The price of converting
The benefits of converting
Should you convert

11. SEP-IRAs, SIMPLE-IRAs, and SAR-SEP IRAs   153

Simplified Employee Pensions (SEPs)
Salary-reduction style SEPs (SAR-SEPs)
SIMPLE plans for small businesses
Tax consequences
A new tax credit

12. Rolling Over Your Retirement Plan at Work   167

Understanding your options
The drawbacks of cashing out
Lump-sum withdrawals
When your plan includes company stock
Rolling over directly to an IRA
Leaving money in your employer's plan

Appendix A   185
Appendix B   187
Appendix C   199
Bibliography   201
Index   203

Foreword

The new tax law and IRA distribution rules have made it easier for you to accumulate and retain IRA money. But Uncle Sam will only go so far to help you build your retirement savings and pass it on to your loved ones. Protecting your nest egg is up to you.

Even after the recent stock market decline, money in retirement accounts is at an all-time high. Where did all this IRA money come from? It wasn't from investing $2,000 a year in an IRA. It came from company retirement plans that were rolled over into IRAs. Then the stock market took over and supersized these accounts. If you are like many workers and retirees, your IRA may be or end up being the largest single asset you own. It may even dwarf your home equity.

You owe it to yourself to make sure that this money lasts for as long as possible and is withdrawn with the smallest possible tax bite. This process is known as IRA distribution planning and is one of the many important issues that this book covers.

The IRA distribution rules and the new tax law contain numerous provisions that allow you to accomplish this, but these tax rules are complicated and fraught with tax traps along the way. It's like a board game, where a mistake might cost you a turn or send you back to the beginning. But this is your life savings. You cannot risk missing a turn or going back to the beginning.

People spend a lifetime accumulating money that eventually ends up in an IRA, but then they drop the ball when it comes to the last line of defense—IRA distribution planning. The U.S. tax code offers very few second chances.

Whether you are working and still accumulating retirement savings, are retired and have an IRA, or have inherited an IRA, this book is for you. It deals with the complex world of IRA distribution planning, but the information you need to know is presented in easily digested, bite-sized nuggets.

You'll also find helpful information about the Education IRA (renamed the Education Savings Account), the Roth IRA, SEPs and SIMPLE plans, and lots more.

It's up to you to take advantage of every tax provision that helps you build and keep your IRA money tax deferred for as long as possible and to pass what's left after your death to your beneficiaries on the most favorable tax terms. All this can be accomplished by reading this gem by experienced business writer Neil Downing. Because Neil writes for the public and not for the IRS, his employer and his publisher force him to write in English. You don't have to know tax code to make the most of your retirement savings. That's why you bought this book. Neil Downing has translated the tax code for you.

Don't just sit there hoping the government will take care of things for you. You cannot afford to neglect your IRA. Doing so would negate all your years of hard work and saving. If you ignore your IRA—and IRA distribution planning—the IRS will get more of your money than you or your heirs, and they will get it in much less time than it took you to earn it.

This book lays it all out for you nice and easy, step by step. Take your time and go through the various chapters that apply most to your situation, and you'll see that keeping your IRA in the family is not so difficult after all.

Ed Slott, CPA, publisher of *Ed Slott's IRA Advisor*
December 3, 2001

Preface

For Individual Retirement Accounts (IRAs), it's a whole new ballgame.

A new federal tax law has expanded and enhanced IRAs. You may now save more money on your own, through a traditional and/or a Roth IRA. You may save more at work, through an employer-sponsored plan that may be tied to an IRA. You may also move money freely from a retirement savings plan at work to an IRA (and vice versa).

Under another new federal law, the Education IRA now has a new name, the Education Savings Account, and you may use it not only for college costs, but also for elementary and high school expenses.

In yet another development, new federal regulations have made required withdrawals from traditional IRAs easier to calculate and easier to understand.

These and other changes have made IRAs a lot more appealing but also a lot more complicated. To take advantage of all the benefits that IRAs offer while avoiding the penalties and other dangers, you need a clearly drawn roadmap, a plain-language guide.

Although you may decide to read this book from front to back, you can also choose a chapter that contains the information you need to know about right now, saving the other chapters for later. For example:

- If you're leaving your old job—either because you're retiring, moving to another job, or are being laid off—look to Chapter 12 to learn about the benefits (and drawbacks) of rolling over the money from your retirement savings plan at work to an IRA.
- If you've inherited an IRA and want to know what to do next, see Chapter 6.
- If you're 50 or older and want to know about the rules that let you contribute more money to a traditional IRA than younger people can, see Chapter 1. For the rules that let you contribute more to a Roth IRA, see Chapter 9.

- If you're 70½ or older and want to know how the new rules for figuring required withdrawals can cut your taxes and save you money, see Chapter 4.
- How can you use an Education Savings Account to buy a new computer for your child or pay for other expenses in elementary school, high school, or college? Flip to Chapter 7.

The point is that each chapter stands on its own and can be read independently of the others.

If you own a car, you need an owner's manual. If you have a computer, you need to know how to run it. If you have an IRA, you need an easy-to-read, easy-to-use guidebook to learn how your account works and how you can make it work best for you.

That's what this book is all about. I think you'll like it.

Acknowledgments

I am indebted to Marvin Rotenberg and Ed Slott, two nationally recognized experts on IRAs and retirement savings plans, for taking the time to review and comment on a number of chapters as I prepared the manuscript for publication. Mr. Rotenberg is the national director of retirement services at Fleet Bank's Private Clients Group, responsible for creating distribution strategies from IRAs and qualified plans for clients with substantial net worths. Mr. Slott is a CPA in Rockville Centre, New York, and the editor and publisher of *Ed Slott's IRA Advisor,* a monthly newsletter about IRAs. I am also grateful to Mr. Rotenberg's associate, Mark S. LaVangie, senior wealth strategist at Fleet, for sharing his considerable expertise and suggesting improvements.

I also appreciate the help and insights of Seymour Goldberg, a lawyer and CPA with Goldberg & Goldberg PC in Garden City, New York, who is also a nationally recognized expert on IRAs and retirement savings plans.

In addition, I am indebted to the staff of BISYS Retirement Services of Brainerd, Minnesota, a unit of BISYS Group, Inc., of New York, especially Thomas G. Anderson, executive vice president at BISYS; Roger Geraets; Mike O'Brien; Pamela S. O'Rourke; Jon Schloemer; Jonathan Yahn; and Karleen Schmidt as well as Mike Rahn and the staff of *The IRA Reporter* newsletter.

My thanks, as well, to Dick O'Donnell and the staff at RIA Group, Inc., of New York; Sue Floyd-Krause, Melissa Lande, and the staff at Lande Communications of Ambler, Pennsylvania; Mark Luscombe, Leslie Bonacum, Mary Dale Walters, and the staff at CCH, Inc., of Riverwoods, Illinois; and Dallas Salisbury and the staff at the Employee Benefit Research Institute of Washington, D.C.

Thanks, also, to Jordan E. Goodman, author of *Everyone's Money Book* (Dearborn) and America's answers man when it comes to personal finance; Robert Muksian, professor of mathematics at Bryant College in Smithfield, Rhode Island, who specializes in retirement and Social Security issues; Patricia A. Thompson, CFP, CFA, and tax partner with Piccerelli Gilstein & Co. of

Providence, Rhode Island; and Robert J. Glovsky and the faculty, staff, and students of the Boston University Program for Financial Planners.

I also appreciate the support and commitment to excellence of the officers, directors, and staff of the *Providence Journal,* including Howard G. Sutton, chairman of the board, publisher, president and CEO; Joel P. Rawson, senior vice president and executive editor; Carol J. Young; Thomas E. Heslin; Peter Phipps; John Kostrzewa; Bob Wyss; and the rest of the *Journal* staff.

My thanks, as well, to the readers throughout the country of my "Money-Line" newspaper column. Their questions and comments inspired sections of this book.

Without the guidance, faith, and support of Cynthia Zigmund, Don Hull, and the staff at Dearborn Financial Publishing of Chicago, this book would not have been possible. I also appreciate Dearborn's granting me permission to incorporate into this book certain key formulas and other information from my earlier book, *Maximize Your IRA,* which Dearborn published in 1998.

Mostly, I thank God for the love, patience, and support of my wife, Vicki-Ann, and our children: James, Andrew, and Caitlin.

1

Traditional IRAs

This chapter explains the basics of traditional IRAs and reviews key changes that have added to the IRA's appeal, such as higher contribution limits, higher income limits for contributors, a special break for some married couples, and a new break for low-income and moderate-income savers.

Somewhere along the line, the traditional IRA fell out of favor. Saddled with so many restrictions imposed by Congress, it lost its appeal.

There was a limit on how much you could contribute, and the limit was way too low.

Only people below a certain income level could get the traditional IRA's biggest tax break. Many who did qualify didn't bother contributing because they couldn't afford it.

Now things have changed. The traditional IRA has regained its luster. New benefits make the traditional IRA much more attractive.

You May Invest More in an IRA

For example:

- Under a new federal law, you can contribute more money each year to a traditional IRA. Under the old rules, the limit was $2,000 a year. Under the new rules, the limit is $3,000 a year through 2004, and it will keep rising thereafter.
- If you're 50 or older, you're now able to kick in an additional amount each year, more than you could otherwise: an extra $500 a year through 2004, for example. As a result, if you're 50 or older, you can now contribute a total of $3,500 a year through 2004, and more in later years.

A New Tax Break

What if your income is so low you can't afford to save in a traditional IRA? There's something new for you, too: a special tax credit known as the *saver's tax credit*. If you qualify, you can get a special tax break for every dollar you contribute to an IRA. This is on top of all the other tax breaks that come with saving through an IRA.

As you can see, the traditional IRA has a whole new look with a whole new set of enticements. Ignore them, and you might miss the chance to save a lot of money.

Before looking at these benefits in detail, let's see first what a traditional IRA is and how it works.

The ABCs of Traditional IRAs

The traditional IRA is a special tool you can use to save for your retirement. You open an account, put in some money, let it be, and watch it grow. After you retire, you start to take the money out.

In some ways, the IRA is just like any other savings account. So what's the big deal? IRAs offer some big tax benefits.

If you qualify for the tax breaks, IRAs are almost magical, with benefits that make them practically irresistible.

Skeptical?

Look at it this way. When you deposit money in a passbook savings account, for example, you get no tax break.

Sure, your money earns interest. But every January, the bank sends you a statement. It's called a Form 1099. It shows how much interest your account earned over the past year. You have to report that interest on your federal income tax return, and you'll probably pay taxes on it. The same thing happens the next year. And the next.

As long as your money is in a *taxable account*, such as a regular savings account at a bank or credit union or a money market mutual fund, all the interest you earn will be taxed. It will be taxed by the federal government. State and local governments may tax you, too, depending on where you live.

So think for a minute about what happens. Odds are that the money you deposit in a bank account has already been taxed. Maybe it came out of your paycheck or from some other place where taxes take the first bite.

When your account starts to earn you interest, the interest itself gets taxed. In other words, you get whacked twice.

Two Tax Benefits

Now look at the IRA. Instead of getting taxed twice, you may qualify for two tax breaks. This can save you money. Here's how it works.

Putting money into an IRA is known as a *contribution*. It's kind of like a deposit. (You can also transfer money to an IRA from a pension plan or another IRA, but that's a different matter, and it's the focus of a later chapter.)

When you contribute money to an IRA, odds are that you can use it to claim a *tax deduction*.

What does that mean? A deduction is, in effect, a reduction in the amount of income you report for tax purposes. This can lower your tax bill. It doesn't mean you actually earned less. It just means that you get to tell the IRS you earned less than you really did.

The government taxes you not on your actual earnings but on your reported earnings, after you subtract your deduction. Because the IRS taxes you on your reported earnings, not on your actual earnings, you get to save money in taxes.

Therefore, simply by contributing money to an IRA, you can tell the government you earned less than you really did. This means you pay less federal income tax than you ordinarily would. As you can see, an IRA contribution can help cut your tax bill.

THE VALUE OF AN IRA

If you make a fully deductible contribution to a traditional IRA, you can save money in federal income taxes—whether you're single or married.

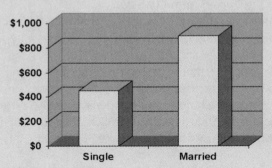

Amount of savings shown assumes a $3,000 deductible contribution if single, $6,000 if married ($3,000 per spouse), and a 15 percent federal income tax bracket.

Suppose you're single and have $22,000 in income. To keep things simple, let's assume that all the money came from your job. (We'll ignore for now any of the usual deductions, exemptions, and other items that are part of a typical tax return.)

For convenience, let's just say that the IRS might charge you about $3,300 in federal income tax on your $22,000 in earnings.

Suppose, however, that you put $3,000 into an IRA during the year. Let's also assume that your entire $3,000 contribution is deductible.

When it comes time to tell the government how much you earned for the year, you tell them you made $19,000, not $22,000.

So now the IRS may charge you only about $2,850 in federal income tax, instead of $3,300. That's a savings of $450. In other words, by saving $3,000 in an IRA (instead of in a regular taxable account, such as a bank savings account), you save yourself $450 in federal income tax.

Why? The government wants to encourage people to save for their own retirement, and it's willing to give up some tax revenue to help you do the job.

It's that simple.

If you are married, then you and your spouse can get the same sort of break.

It's not as if you lose the money you put into the IRA, or spend it, or gamble it away. It's still your money. You just choose to put it in an account marked *IRA*, where it will remain, and hopefully grow, until you need it. For this, you get a tax break.

Your IRA Can Grow Each Year

IRAs also offer another big tax benefit: the money your IRA earns for you each year doesn't get taxed immediately.

What's so special about that? Remember that with a bank account, as with lots of other types of taxable savings accounts, the interest you earn generally gets taxed every year.

IRAs don't work like that. The money your IRA earns isn't taxed each year. Instead, the tax bill is postponed; it typically doesn't come due until you take your money out, which normally happens after you retire. As a result, all the money that your IRA earns each year stays inside your IRA. All of your money can continue to grow, not just the part of it that's left after the annual tax bite.

Experts call this *the power of tax-deferred compounding*. Here's how it works.

Suppose you're paying federal tax at the rate of 15 percent, and you stash away $3,000 at the start of each year. Suppose, too, that your money earns a modest 6 percent.

HOW AN IRA CAN GROW

Because the money inside your IRA can grow each year without being taxed, you may end up with far more than you would by saving in an ordinary taxable account, such as a bank account.

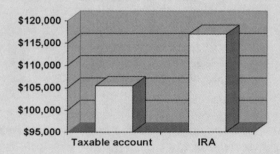

Assumes investor who is taxed at 15 percent puts away $3,000 at the start of each year for 20 years and earns 6 percent a year in both an ordinary bank account and an IRA.

If you put the money in a bank account or other taxable savings account, you might have $105,366 after 20 years.

If, however, you put your money in an IRA, you'd have $116,978 after 20 years.

In other words, simply by choosing an IRA as a place to save your money, you'd wind up with an extra $11,612 or so. Why? When you have a taxable account, less money is available to grow; a part of your stockpile is leaking out to pay taxes every year.

With the IRA, however, all your money is working for you, year-in, year-out. None of it trickles out of your account each year in taxes.

True, your IRA dollars will be taxed someday, when withdrawn. But odds are you won't withdraw your IRA money in a lump sum; you'll probably take out a little at a time, to help meet expenses in retirement. This means the rest of the money in your IRA can continue to grow, year after year, until withdrawn.

How Much You May Contribute

In 1981, Congress fixed the annual limit on IRA contributions at $2,000 per person. That's where it stood for the next 20 years. In that time, Congress neither raised the limit nor allowed it to rise with inflation through annual

HIGHER LIMITS

A new federal law means just about everyone may save more each year in an IRA.

Year	Annual limit
2002	$3,000
2003	$3,000
2004	$3,000
2005	$4,000
2006	$4,000
2007	$4,000
2008	$5,000

After 2008, the maximum annual contribution limit may increase with inflation in annual increments of $500.

cost-of-living adjustments. As a result, the true value of your annual contribution to an IRA got smaller and smaller as the years passed.

In 2001, however, all that changed. Congress approved a huge tax-cutting and pension-reform measure, the biggest in a generation, and President Bush signed it into law.

That law brought good news for savers. It not only raised the annual contribution limit for IRAs but also tied that limit to inflation in later years, so that it can keep rising with the cost of living.

For example, the new law set the contribution limit at $3,000 a year through 2004, $4,000 a year for 2005 through 2007, and $5,000 for 2008. After that, the limit may rise with inflation.

This means that savers finally get to stash away more money in their IRAs, and the result can be a boon. For example, if the old limit of $2,000 was still in place, and you saved that amount every year for 20 years (earning 10 percent a year), you'd end up with about $126,000.

However, if you saved $3,000 a year over the same period, earning the same amount, you'd end up with about $189,000.

That's $63,000 more for your nest egg. And that extra amount isn't just from the additional $1,000 you've saved each year in this example. Those added contributions come to only $20,000. The big boost—about $43,000 worth—comes from the interest that your money earns over that period.

Congress also tossed in a sweetener for the 50-and-older crowd, the opportunity to stash away even more in an IRA than younger people can, in the form of a *catch-up contribution.*

THE CATCH-UP

A new federal law lets savers who are 50 and older contribute an extra amount to their IRAs in the form of a *catch-up contribution.*

Year	Annual limit
2002	$ 500
2003	$ 500
2004	$ 500
2005	$ 500
2006	$1,000

A Break for Women

A Congressional report at the time put it this way: "The Committee understands that, for a variety of reasons, older individuals may not have been saving sufficiently for retirement. For example, some individuals, especially women, may have left the workforce temporarily in order to care for children.

OLDER WORKERS CAN SAVE MORE

A new federal law means you may save more each year in an IRA. If you are 50 or older, you may make an additional catch-up contribution for that year, allowing you to save even more.

Year	Annual limit (for everyone)	Catch-up (for age 50+)	Overall limit (including catch-up)
2002	$3,000	$500	$3,500
2003	$3,000	$500	$3,500
2004	$3,000	$500	$3,500
2005	$4,000	$500	$4,500
2006	$4,000	$1,000	$5,000
2007	$4,000	$1,000	$5,000
2008	$5,000	$1,000	$6,000

The maximum you may contribute in a given year is the amount listed above or your total taxable compensation for that year, whichever is less. You may contribute to a traditional and a Roth IRA for a given year, but your overall contribution cannot exceed these limits. After 2008, the maximum annual contribution limit that applies to everyone—$5,000—may increase with inflation (in annual increments of $500).

Such individuals may have missed retirement savings options that would have been available had they remained in the workforce. Thus, the Committee believes it appropriate to accelerate the increase in the IRA contribution limits for such individuals."

As a result, under the new law, if you're 50 or older in a given year, you'll be able to contribute a little something extra to your IRA for that year: an extra $500 a year through 2005, and an extra $1,000 a year for 2006 and later years.

This means that, if you're 50 or older, you'll be able to save a lot more in an IRA than you could before. By 2008, for example, you'll be able to save a total of $6,000—triple the limit under the old law.

Consider the impact. Suppose you turn 50 in 2008. If you'd saved $6,000 a year for 15 years, earning 10 percent a year, at the end of the period, you'd have about $209,700.

What if the limit were still $2,000? You'd end up with only $69,900. In other words, in this example, you'd be able to sock away almost $140,000 more by taking advantage of the higher limit and catch-up contribution.

Can You Open an IRA?

Who gets to open an IRA? Just about everybody.

It doesn't matter if you have a pension plan at work. It doesn't matter if you work for somebody else or if you work for yourself. You can set aside money in an IRA for a given year as long as you have what the IRS calls *taxable compensation* or *earned income.*

What does that mean? For most people, it boils down to this. If you've got a job, you can set up an IRA and contribute money to it. Don't worry: the government uses a pretty broad definition of the word *job.* Basically, it means you made money either from wages, salary, tips, or commissions. Alimony counts, too.

What doesn't count? Interest and dividend income, pensions and annuities, rental income, and items that you wouldn't normally consider earned income.

The amount of your taxable compensation comes into play in another way, too. Technically, the most you may contribute to an IRA in any given year is either the maximum dollar limit for that year (as outlined earlier in this chapter), or 100 percent of your taxable compensation, *whichever is less.*

What does that mean? Suppose that Doreen makes $30,000 from her job in 2004. The maximum dollar limit that applies to IRA contributions for that year is $3,000. Because Doreen's taxable compensation of $30,000 is greater than the maximum dollar limit that applies to contributions for that year ($3,000), she may contribute the full $3,000 to an IRA for that year.

CAN YOU OPEN AN IRA?

Whether you can set up and contribute to an IRA (traditional or Roth) depends mainly on whether you have earned income, or what the government calls *taxable compensation.*

What counts as taxable compensation:

- Wages
- Salaries
- Tips
- Professional fees
- Bonuses
- Commissions
- Self-employment income
- Alimony

What does *not* count as taxable compensation:

- Pension income
- Interest income
- Dividend income
- Rental income
- Social Security benefits
- Annuity income
- Deferred compensation
- Foreign earned income

Note: The IRS generally treats as compensation any amount listed in Box 1 of your Form W-2. If you're self-employed, *compensation* means the net income from your trade or business reduced by your deduction for contributions on your behalf to retirement plans, and by the deduction allowed for one-half of your self-employment taxes. *Alimony* means all taxable alimony and separate maintenance payments you receive under a decree. *Deferred compensation* means compensation payments postponed from a past year.

If, however, Doreen earns only $2,500 in taxable compensation for 2004, the most she may contribute to an IRA for that year in this example is $2,500.

This rule won't apply to most people, especially those who are employed full-time in the workplace. However, this rule does come into play for people who work part-time, and for children or teens who may work only part of a given year—a summer job, for example. (Keep in mind, too, that some IRA trustees or custodians do not allow minors to have an IRA.)

The Age Limit

Another limit that may spoil your plans has to do with your age. You can set up and contribute to an IRA as long as you haven't reached age 70½ by the end of the year. If you've reached the age limit, you still have the right to transfer money from one IRA to another, but you can't make annual contributions. This age rule applies to traditional IRAs, but not to Roth IRAs (which are discussed in detail later in this book).

Can You Claim a Tax Deduction?

Will you be able to claim a federal income tax deduction for the amount you contribute to an IRA? In the early 1980s—boom times for traditional IRAs—just about anyone could save money in a traditional IRA *and* claim a federal income tax deduction for the amount they contributed.

In 1986, however, Congress changed the rules. With the Tax Reform Act of 1986, Congress clamped down. Under that law, anyone who wanted to claim a deduction for making an IRA contribution first had to pass a two-part test.

Because the test was so strict, lots of taxpayers were no longer able to claim the deduction. Some who were eligible for an IRA deduction didn't bother with it because the two-part test seemed so complicated. As a result of Congress's crackdown, the national level of IRA contributions plunged.

The Rules Aren't as Strict

The bad news is that the two-part test still exists today. The good news is that the rules are looser now. As a result, more people may claim the deduction. Here's how the test works.

- If you are *not* covered by a pension plan at work (what the IRS calls an *employer-sponsored qualified plan*), then you may claim the full tax deduction on your federal return. In this case, the amount of the deduction you may claim is equal to the amount you contribute. For example, if you contribute $3,000 to a traditional IRA, you may claim a $3,000 federal income tax deduction.

- If you *are* covered by some type of retirement plan at work, you may still contribute to a traditional IRA. However, the amount of the deduction you may claim depends on how much you earn—your *adjusted gross income* (AGI).

Adjusted Gross Income

What is your adjusted gross income? This figure is on the front of your federal income tax return, toward the bottom. In general, it's your overall income, reduced by some business expenses and certain other items.

DO YOU TAKE PART IN A RETIREMENT PLAN?

If you're *not* an active participant in a pension or retirement savings plan at work, you may claim a full deduction for the amount you contribute to a traditional IRA. If you *are* an active participant, how much of a deduction you may claim generally depends on how much you have in adjusted gross income for that year. Here are some employer-sponsored plans that count.

- Pension, profit-sharing, stock bonus, money purchase, and Keogh plans
- 401(k) plans
- Union-sponsored plans
- Government plans (including 457 plans)
- 403(b) plans
- SEPs, SARSEPs, and SIMPLE plans

When Are You Covered?

- For *defined contribution plans* (such as profit-sharing and 401(k) plans), you're an active participant in the plan if money is contributed or allocated to your account for the plan year that ends with your tax year.
- For *defined benefit plans* (such as traditional pension plans), you're an active participant if you're eligible to take part in the plan for the plan year that ends with your tax year.

Note: In general, you're an active participant in an employer-sponsored retirement or pension plan if the Pension Plan box is checked on the Form W-2 wage and tax statement you get from your employer. Coverage under Social Security or Railroad Retirement Tier I and Tier II benefits doesn't count.

For the average taxpayer, adjusted gross income is just about the same as overall income. So, as a general rule, the more money you make from work each year, the less likely you are to be able to claim a tax deduction for the amount you contribute to a traditional IRA.

How much AGI is too much AGI? For many years, the dollar limit was fixed. It was generally $25,000 to $35,000 if you were single, $40,000 to $50,000 if you were married and filing a joint federal income tax return.

What did that mean? If your income fell below the range, you could claim a full deduction for the amount you contributed to a traditional IRA. If your income fell within the range, you could claim a partial deduction. If your income exceeded the range, you could not claim a deduction at all.

Nor did Congress give any special treatment for married couples. If you were married, filing jointly, with adjusted gross income above $50,000, and

CAN YOU DEDUCT AN IRA CONTRIBUTION?

If you're considered an *active participant* in a pension or retirement savings plan at work, your ability to claim a deduction for money you contribute to a traditional IRA depends on your adjusted gross income (AGI). If your income is below the range shown here, you may claim a full deduction; within the range, a partial deduction; above the range, no deduction.

For a Single Taxpayer

Year	AGI Phase-Out Range
2002	$34,000 to $44,000
2003	$40,000 to $50,000
2004	$45,000 to $55,000
2005 (and later)	$50,000 to $60,000

For Married Taxpayers (filing jointly)

Year	AGI Phase-Out Range
2002	$54,000 to $64,000
2003	$60,000 to $70,000
2004	$65,000 to $75,000
2005	$70,000 to $80,000
2006	$75,000 to $85,000
2007 (and later)	$80,000 to $100,000

Note: Separate—more liberal—rules apply for someone who is not an active participant in a plan at work but whose spouse is.

either spouse was covered by a pension plan, then *neither* spouse could claim an IRA deduction.

The two-part test remains, even today. However, because of a 1997 law, Congress finally eased the limits.

The income ranges will generally increase each year through 2005 for single taxpayers and through 2007 for married couples filing jointly.

One word of caution. Technically, you don't use your adjusted gross income to figure out how much of an income tax deduction you may claim.

You really have to use something called *modified adjusted gross income.* But this isn't as complicated as it sounds. In general, your modified adjusted gross income is simply your adjusted gross income before you take into account the amount of your IRA deduction and a few other items. (Details are in the instructions to your tax return.)

How the Income Range Works

What if your income falls between the limits? How much of a federal income tax deduction will you get by contributing to an IRA?

A formula is involved. Before you jump in, check the appropriate year in the table at left. There, check your filing status (single or otherwise not married, or married and filing jointly). Then find the year for which you want to make the contribution. On the same line, find the high end of the income range for that year. Then follow these steps.

- Subtract your modified adjusted gross income from the high end of the income phase-out range (as shown on the table) for that year.
- Divide your answer by $10,000.
- Multiply that result by the maximum contribution allowed for the year (including the catch-up contribution, if you're 50 or older).

The answer is how much you may claim as a deduction on your federal income tax return for that year.

Here's an Example

Suppose that Melissa, 25, is single and has modified adjusted gross income of $42,000 for 2003. The most she may contribute to a traditional IRA for 2003 is $3,000.

The income phase-out range for that year for a single person is $40,000 to $50,000, so the high end of that income range is $50,000. To find out how much of a deduction she may claim, she takes the following steps:

- She subtracts $42,000 (her modified adjusted gross income) from $50,000 (the high end of the income phase-out range for the year). The answer is $8,000.
- Next, she divides $8,000 by $10,000. The result is 0.80.
- She multiplies 0.80 by $3,000 (the maximum contribution allowed for the year—because she's 25 years old, she doesn't qualify for the additional catch-up contribution).

The answer is $2,400. That's how much Melissa may claim as a deduction for contributing to a traditional IRA for 2003. Melissa may contribute the full $3,000 allowed by law, but she may claim a deduction for only $2,400; the $600 balance is treated as a nondeductible contribution. (Keep in mind that, if you're a married couple filing jointly and you're trying to figure the amount of your deduction for 2007 or later years, use $20,000, instead of $10,000, in Step B in the formula.)

A Special Benefit for Couples

The law that loosened the rules for deductible IRA contributions also finally gave some married couples a break.

Under the old rules, if either you or your spouse took part in a pension or retirement savings plan at work, neither of you could claim a deduction for IRA contributions unless your income fell within or below the income phase-out range.

This was especially painful if your spouse worked but you didn't. In effect, the working spouse who took part in an employer-sponsored pension plan "tainted" the spouse who was at home.

Congress has changed that rule. Now, you won't be considered an *active participant* in an employer-sponsored pension plan just because your spouse is.

But here, too, there are dollar limits. If your adjusted gross income is below $150,000 for the year, there's no problem; you may claim a full deduction. If it's between $150,000 and $160,000, the deduction gets reduced or phased out, and above $160,000, no deduction is allowed.

Suppose, for example, that Walter takes part in a pension plan that's sponsored by his company. His wife, Thelma, isn't employed, and stays at home, raising their children. The couple's adjusted gross income for the year is $125,000. Both Walter and Thelma can contribute to IRAs. Walter's contribution isn't deductible because he doesn't meet the income limits for people who are active participants in an employer-sponsored plan. But Thelma's contribution *is* deductible—fully deductible, in fact—because the couple's income is below the special income range ($150,000 to $160,000).

A Special Tax Credit for Savers

Suppose your income is so low, you don't think you can afford to contribute to a traditional IRA.

Uncle Sam has an extra bonus for you. It's called the *Saver's Tax Credit*.

If you qualify, you may be able to claim a special break of up to $1,000 on your federal income tax return.

There is a catch. You may claim the credit only if you earn below a certain amount. However, if your overall income (from work and other sources) falls below that level (shown in the table below), you can claim the credit on your return. That's in addition to the deduction you may get for contributing to a traditional IRA.

HOW THE SAVER'S TAX CREDIT WORKS

If you contribute to a traditional IRA and your adjusted gross income falls below certain limits, you may be eligible to claim a special tax credit on your federal income tax return, the *Saver's Tax Credit*.

The dollar amount of the credit you may claim is tied to the amount of money you contribute to your IRA. The maximum credit you may claim is 50 percent of that amount.

For purposes of the calculation, the maximum contribution you may take into account is $2,000. For example, if you contribute $2,000 this year, and if—based on your AGI as outlined below—you're eligible for the maximum of 50 percent, you may claim a $1,000 tax break on your federal tax return (because $1,000 is 50 percent of your $2,000 contribution).

AGI if you're married filing jointly	AGI if you're filing as head of household	AGI if you're single	Credit Rate (as a percentage of your contribution, to a maximum contribution of $2,000)
up to $30,000	up to $22,500	up to $15,000	50 percent
$30,001 to $32,500	$22,501 to $24,375	$15,001 to $16,250	20 percent
$32,501 to $50,000	$24,376 to $37,500	$16,251 to $25,000	10 percent
Over $50,000	Over $37,500	Over $25,000	0 percent

Note: Credit is available only through 2006.

Who Qualifies?

This may be especially attractive if you're just starting out in the workplace and you're not quite sure whether you can afford to contribute to your plan. The tax break may provide just the extra boost you'll need.

You may use the credit to reduce your federal income tax, dollar for dollar. In other words, after you claim all the deductions and exemptions and other such stuff on your tax return, and after you calculate your tax based on the income that remains, *then* you apply the credit. It comes right off your tax.

For example, if your overall tax for the year is $1,200 and you qualify for a tax credit of $1,000, you can slash your overall tax to just $200. That can go a long way toward helping you afford the IRA contribution in the first place.

Both Spouses May Benefit

If you're married, both spouses may claim the credit, and the tax savings can quickly add up. Here's an example adapted from one provided by the IRS.

Suppose that John and Susan are married and file a joint federal income tax return showing $34,000 in AGI and tax of $3,000. In 2003, Susan contributes $2,000 to her 401(k) plan at work; John makes a $2,000 deductible contribution to an IRA.

As a result, they have reduced their AGI for that year to $30,000, down from $34,000. This brings an instant tax savings of $600.

They're also eligible to claim a saver's tax credit of $2,000 (50 percent of their $4,000 in retirement savings contributions). Total tax bill: $400. Total savings: $2,600.

Here's another way to look at it. Although they contributed a total of $4,000 to the 401(k) and IRA, it really cost them only $1,400, after taking into account the $2,600 in total tax savings. They still have that $4,000 socked away for their retirement as well.

Here are a few other points to keep in mind about the Saver's Tax Credit.

- To be eligible, you must be 18 or older, you can't be a full-time student, and you can't be claimed as a dependent on someone else's return.
- The maximum contribution you can take into account to figure out how much of a credit you might get is $2,000.
- If you're married and filing a joint federal return, either or both of you may claim the credit.
- If you have a retirement savings plan at work, such as a 401(k), and your employer is willing to kick in some money if you contribute, too, consider taking advantage. The Saver's Tax Credit applies to employer-sponsored retirement savings plans, as well as Roth IRAs.

- Bear in mind that this credit won't be around forever. It's scheduled to disappear after 2006. For more details on the credit, see the end of this chapter.

When You Should Contribute

The good news is that you don't have to contribute to an IRA by the end of the tax year. You can wait until April 15 of the following year to make a contribution. It will still be counted as a contribution for the previous year. (Keep in mind that you may contribute only cash to an IRA.)

This little twist in the rules can come in handy. Suppose you couldn't scrape together enough money last year to make an IRA contribution, but you will have a little extra coming in during the first few months of this year. If that's the case, you have until April 15 of this year to make an IRA contribution and still have it count on your tax return for last year. The outfit that holds your IRA for you is generally known as your *IRA trustee* or *custodian*. You'll have to let your trustee or custodian know exactly what year the contribution is for. Remember to note this down on your IRA form when making your contribution.

Bear in mind, too, that April 15 is the final deadline for making IRA contributions for the previous year. So suppose you plan to file your federal income tax return after April 15. You still must make your IRA contribution by April 15 to have it count for the prior year. (In some states, the filing deadline may be a few days after April 15.)

The Earlier You Save, the Better

Of course, the earlier you make your IRA contribution, the better off you'll be, because your money will have more time to grow. Even if you can't make the full contribution at the start of each year, try to make smaller contributions regularly to your account throughout the year. The point is not to wait until the last minute if you can help it, because you will have missed the opportunity for your money to grow.

What if you don't have the time or the discipline to set aside money in an IRA each month? Let your IRA trustee or custodian do it for you. If you have a checking or similar account at your bank, most IRA trustees or custodians will supply you with the necessary forms to let them debit your bank account automatically each month, making the contributions automatically for you. This can be a relatively painless way to save.

Keep in mind, too, that you aren't required to make the full contribution that's allowed for each year. If you've only got $500 to set aside, for example, do it, and the earlier you can invest it, the better.

Some Final Points

Here are some other points to keep in mind.

- If you're married and your spouse works but you don't, each of you may still contribute the maximum to a traditional IRA—and claim a deduction, too (assuming you meet the income limits described earlier in this chapter). For example, if John earns $40,000 this year, and his wife, Carol, is at home with the children, both John and Carol may make the maximum contribution allowed for the year and claim the deduction for each.
- Children or teens may contribute to traditional IRAs assuming that they have earned income from a summer job, a paper route, or baby-sitting, for example. Check with the IRA trustee or custodian first to find out its policy. Some financial institutions don't allow minors to open and contribute to an IRA; others may require special arrangements.
- If you have no job and your only income is from alimony, you may still contribute to an IRA. But remember: the only income that counts here is *taxable* alimony (and separate maintenance payments) you receive under an official divorce decree or a decree of separate maintenance.

The point is clear: the traditional IRA is an appealing way to save money for your retirement, and saving for retirement is important. Forget about all those debates on whether Social Security will still be around when you retire. Maybe it will, maybe it won't, or maybe it'll operate in a different way than it does today.

But so what? The real question is whether you'll have enough money to do the kinds of things you may want to do in retirement, whether you'll have some spare cash to help pay for "extras" such as traveling, dining out, going to shows, or attending to hobbies, things that add to the quality of your life.

How much you can do often depends on how much money you have. Social Security and pension benefits may take care of food, shelter, and your other basic needs, but having extra money stashed away in an IRA can add luster to your retirement years.

Remember that the government is willing to help you save by giving you tax breaks for putting your money in a traditional IRA. You may get an immediate income tax deduction for contributing to an IRA, and the money in your account can grow each year without being taxed. If you take advantage, you can cash in on both these tax benefits and watch your money really grow.

Nondeductible IRAs

Nondeductible IRAs are still alive and you need to know how they work, either because you already own one or because you plan to open one (after having exhausted all other options).

Technically, there's no such thing in federal law as a nondeductible IRA. In practice, however, people use the term to describe a traditional IRA that includes contributions for which you did not (could not) claim a federal income tax deduction.

Why bother with a nondeductible? Even though you get no immediate tax benefit, the money that's in your account will still grow each year without being pinched by taxes. In other words, with nondeductible IRAs as well as with deductible IRAs, your money grows through the magic of tax-deferred compounding.

Some people don't qualify for deductible IRAs because their income is too high. They have few other options available to take advantage of tax-deferred growth, so they've chosen to use nondeductible IRAs.

How the Rules Work

Fortunately, the rules for nondeductible IRAs aren't all that different from the rules for traditional deductible IRAs.

For instance, the most you can contribute each year is either the maximum amount allowed by law for a given year ($3,000 a year through 2004, more in later years) or the total of your earned income, whichever is less.

You have until April 15 to make a contribution to a nondeductible IRA for the previous year. But if you do make a nondeductible contribution, you've got to let the government know about it, in detail, by filing U.S. Form 8606 with your annual federal income tax return. (If you fail to file this form, you'll be subject to a federal penalty.)

If you keep your forms on file—and you should—you'll have a convenient starting point from which to figure out the tax consequences for your withdrawals. You'll also have plenty of ammunition to fight the IRS in case your tax calculations are challenged.

As with deductible IRAs, you can't leave your money in your account forever; the law generally requires that you begin making at least minimum annual withdrawals at about the time you reach age 70½.

A Different Formula

But the formula you use to figure out how much of each withdrawal will be taxed is different than the formula for deductible IRAs. You have to know a few important numbers—how much your account was worth before you made the withdrawal, how much in nondeductible contributions you made to the account over the years, and how much you're going to withdraw. Once you have these numbers, the calculation is fairly simple.

In essence, you use the numbers first to figure out what part of your account's overall value comes from nondeductible contributions. That percentage is the percentage of your withdrawal that will be tax-free.

How the Formula Works. Suppose, for example, that the total value of your nondeductible IRA is $20,000 before you make the withdrawal.

You made a total of $2,000 in nondeductible contributions to your account over the years. You now plan to withdraw $1,000.

What portion of that $1,000 withdrawal will be tax-free? What portion will be taxable?

Your total nondeductible contributions of $2,000 represent 10 percent of your overall account value of $20,000 ($2,000 divided by $20,000 equals 10 percent). As a result, 10 percent of your planned $1,000 withdrawal will be tax-free; the remainder will be subject to federal income tax at your marginal federal rate.

So, in this example, $100 of your $1,000 withdrawal will be tax-free to you (0.10 times $1,000 equals $100). The rest of your withdrawal—$900 in this example—will be taxed as ordinary income.

So, if your marginal federal rate is 15 percent, you'll owe $135 in federal tax for this withdrawal (0.15 times $900).

Here's another way to look at it. Of your $1,000 withdrawal, you'll wind up paying $135 in federal tax, and you'll be left with $865.

A Handy Sketch. The government supplies worksheets that you may use to figure out the tax consequences of withdrawals from a nondeductible IRA, but you can sketch it out yourself with a simple formula.

Nondeductible contributions divided by prewithdrawal account value times the amount of your withdrawal equals the tax-free portion of your withdrawal.

Using the numbers in our example, here's how the formula would look.

$$\$2,000/\$20,000 \times \$1,000 = \$100$$

This formula can get a bit more complicated if you've also made deductible contributions to the same account. To avoid the added complexity, you might want to have one IRA devoted entirely to nondeductible contributions and one or more additional IRAs devoted entirely to your deductible contributions. This can make the paperwork—and the calculations—a bit easier at tax time.

When a Nondeductible IRA Can Help

Although nondeductible IRAs require some extra paperwork and some extra figuring, they still have value. If you don't qualify for a fully deductible IRA contribution, remember that you can still make nondeductible contributions.

Suppose, for example, that you're covered by a pension plan at work. Suppose, too, that because you have a certain amount of adjusted gross income, you're allowed only a $1,500 deductible IRA contribution. In other words, the amount of deduction you may claim is phased out because of your income level.

If that's the case, keep in mind that your annual limit on IRA contributions overall is still $3,000 (assuming that you make it before 2005, when the maximum contribution jumps to $4,000). So in this example, you may still contribute a full $3,000 to your IRA for the year (assuming, of course, that you had at least $3,000 in earned income or taxable compensation for the year and that you're under age 70½).

But you'll get a federal income tax deduction only for $1,500 of the contribution; the remaining $1,500 will count as a nondeductible contribution.

Considering Your Options

If you're eligible to contribute to a tax-favored retirement savings plan at work, such as the 401(k) or 403(b) plan, do it. It's a much better option than a nondeductible IRA.

You get an up-front federal income tax deduction for the amount you contribute to 401(k) and 403(b) plans. Your money usually is set aside through payroll deduction, a convenient way to save. And your employer may kick in some money to your account as an incentive for you to save. You may also have the option to borrow against your account, depending on the plan and on your company's rules.

Among IRAs, the traditional deductible IRA beats the nondeductible IRA for most taxpayers. You get an up-front federal income tax deduction (depending on your income level), and your account grows tax-deferred.

The Roth IRA is also an attractive alternative. True, for Roth IRAs as well as nondeductible IRAs, you can't claim a federal income tax deduction for the amount you contribute.

With the Roth IRA, however, earnings grow tax-*free*. As long as you meet the rules, all your withdrawals are entirely free of federal tax. This is one reason it makes sense to convert existing nondeductible IRAs to Roth IRAs.

Some taxpayers are allowed only a partial contribution to Roth IRAs; some cannot contribute at all.

So if you cannot make a full annual contribution to a Roth and you still want to set aside some money in an IRA, look to the nondeductible IRA. It's still an option, but for a much smaller number of taxpayers than before.

For More Information ...

The Strong group of mutual funds. The Strong group offers several free booklets that outline how IRAs work and how the new tax law affects IRAs. For information, write: Strong Funds, P.O. Box 2936, Milwaukee, WI 53201, or call 1-800-368-3863, or visit the Web site: <www.strong-funds.com>.

The Internal Revenue Service. The IRS has published guidance—in English and Spanish—that you can use to help figure out whether you're eligible to claim the Saver's Tax Credit. (Details were listed in Announcement 2001-106.) For a free copy of this, or for an updated guide, visit your local IRS office, call the agency at 800-829-3676, or see its Web site: <www.irs.gov>.

Managing Your IRA

2

This chapter looks at how to manage your IRA, including how and where to invest your IRA dollars, how to keep fees to a minimum, and how to transfer or roll over money or other assets from one IRA to another.

So now you've decided to open an IRA. Congratulations! But what's next? You have to decide where to put it.

You can't just hide your IRA in a mattress. Somebody has to hold your IRA for you in safekeeping, in trust. That's because an IRA is technically a trust account, or custodial account. It's set up for your benefit or for the benefit of you and your beneficiary.

So a third party, usually a bank or some other financial institution, has to serve as your IRA's trustee or custodian. Their job is to make sure all the paperwork is in order, that the account meets all the rules, and that all the right forms get filed and reported to the IRS at the right time.

An Outline of Your Rights

Your IRA must have a written document that outlines the rules for your account as well as its terms and conditions. Your trustee or custodian *must* give you a copy of that document at about the time you set up your account. The document must show that your account meets all these requirements.

- Your account's trustee must be either a bank, a federally insured credit union, a savings and loan association (also known as an S&L, thrift, or savings bank), or some other outfit—such as a mutual fund company or insurance company—that has the IRS's stamp of approval to act as a trustee or custodian.
- The trustee can't accept contributions greater than the limit allowed by law. This annual dollar limit is higher if you're transferring—*rolling*

23

over—money from another IRA or from certain types of pension plans at work. (More on rollovers later. See the final chapter in this book.)

- You can only use cash, not property or other assets, to open an IRA. (For rollovers, other rules apply.)
- The document must show that you always have the right to withdraw all your money if you want to.
- In general, your trustee or IRA custodian can't mingle your account with other accounts; your IRA is yours, and the assets contained in your account generally must be kept separate from other accounts. (One exception: mutual funds.)
- Your trustee or custodian generally must see to it that you begin to make withdrawals from your IRA by April 1 of the year following the year in which you reach age 70½. (There are some exceptions.)

All these things are important, of course. But if you're just starting out, these are really just technical points. Most or all of them will be spelled out in the paperwork that you get when you open your account. You generally don't have to fret over these issues; the outfit that serves as your IRA trustee or custodian will notify you from time to time, usually by mail, about any technical matters that involve your account.

Where to Open an Account

Once you've chosen to open an IRA, your biggest decision is exactly where to open the account and exactly how to invest the money that's in your account. In other words, who's going to get your business?

Some people open IRAs at their local bank or credit union, mainly for convenience and perhaps out of a concern for safety. There's nothing wrong with that. Maybe your life is too busy and too complicated and you don't have a lot of time or energy to check out all the options. Or maybe you're just sick of having to make so many choices in your life each day. You want to open an IRA, put your money in a safe place, and forget about it.

That's okay. Just keep in mind that there are more places to open an IRA than banks, thrifts, and credit unions, and some of these options may suit you better.

Safety in Federal Insurance

True, by sticking your IRA dollars in a federally insured account at a bank, thrift, or credit union, you can be certain that your principal is safe, so long as the money that's in your account falls within federal insurance limits (generally $100,000 per depositor, per account category).

Yes, your money will grow, and the longer you keep it in your account, the more it will grow. But will it grow enough to give you the kind of nest egg you're hoping to build for your retirement? Might other places give you a better return in the long run and a bigger pile of cash at retirement?

Your Investment Options

You can invest your IRA dollars in a mutual fund, for example, or in stocks or bonds. History shows that, over the long haul, these investments are far more likely to outpace inflation than a typical bank account would. So you could wind up with a lot more money in the end.

But to get the higher returns, you have to be willing to assume some risk. That's the tradeoff. The value of stocks or of shares in a stock mutual fund, for example, can rise or fall over time, depending on market conditions and other factors. You can profit or lose money.

You've got to figure out how well, or how poorly, you tolerate risk. If you don't like risk, stick your money in a bank account and sleep tight. But if you can stomach some risk, if you can hang in there through the roller-coaster ride, if you've got the time and if you've got the patience, the rewards of investing in stocks (and stock mutual funds) can be enormous.

Mutual Funds

If you decide to press ahead, your choices are practically unlimited. You can choose from thousands of mutual funds and thousands more individual stocks.

For example, you can choose an investment company to hold your IRA. These companies pool people's money and use it to buy things such as stocks and bonds. These investment pools are known as mutual funds, and they're a popular place for IRAs.

Why so popular? Many investors like mutual funds because they offer what the experts call *professional management and diversification.*

Mutual funds typically hire professional money managers and support staff to manage the money that comes from you and thousands of other investors like you. By pooling investors's money, mutual funds can invest in a much wider variety of stocks and other securities than an individual investor could afford to do alone.

How do you go about picking a mutual fund that's right for you? Nowadays it's easy. Most major newspapers offer lots of stories about mutual funds, usually in their business sections.

How to Pick a Mutual Fund. Magazines such as *Money, Kiplinger's,* and *Consumer Reports* focus a lot of attention on mutual funds. Libraries and bookstores are packed with all sorts of books about mutual funds. To help in your selection, the reference section in your local public library probably keeps on file some guides—such as *Morningstar* and the *Value Line Mutual Fund Survey*—that are designed especially to help small investors choose and keep track of mutual funds. There's a ton of information; all you have to do is a little research, often at little or no expense.

Most of these reference tools will give you detailed information on each fund, including how it has performed, how much money you need to invest up front, and how to contact the fund.

Many funds are sold directly to investors; you just call the fund, usually through a toll-free number, and the fund mails you an application form along with its official offering document, known as a *prospectus.* The prospectus outlines all the details you need to know about what the fund is, how it works, its potential risks and rewards, and other items.

Once you read it, you mail back your completed application form along with a check, and you're all set. The fund keeps you informed with regular mailings and typically will send you an account statement quarterly, monthly, or whenever there's a transaction involving your account. Many funds also let you set up an automatic investment plan. With these plans, the fund automatically takes a certain amount out of your bank account at regular intervals, usually monthly. In this way, you don't have to plunk down your money all at once; you invest a little at a time.

Picking a Stock Brokerage

You can also open an IRA with a securities brokerage. Here, too, you have lots of options.

Magazines and other periodicals, such as the journal published by the American Association of Individual Investors in Chicago, publish articles once a year or more that compare brokerages by fees, services, and other standards.

Through a broker, you can set up an IRA and invest in such things as stocks, bonds, or mutual funds. But brokerages offer another option: you can set up what's known as a *self-directed IRA.*

With this type of IRA, you're the quarterback. Instead of letting a mutual fund's portfolio manager decide how to invest your money, *you* decide. You tell the broker exactly how your IRA dollars are to be invested. You can pick individual stocks, bonds, or other securities. You can sell some or all of the securities in your account when you want and buy others. The broker typically charges some sort of fee for each transaction within your self-directed

IRA, but this type of account also offers maximum flexibility for the do-it-yourself investor.

Also, some brokerages operate in part or exclusively on the Internet, allowing you to invest in mutual funds, stocks, or other securities, sometimes for only pennies per share.

Don't forget that insurance companies also offer IRAs. If you're already doing business with an insurance agent, your agent probably has lots of computer software available not only to help calculate how much life insurance you'll need, for example, but also to figure out your retirement funding needs. Adding an IRA to your portfolio of insurance and investment tools can be fairly simple for your agent. Also, if you do business directly with an insurance company, such as USAA Life in Texas, you may also set up an IRA with relative ease.

Investing Directly in Stocks

Do-it-yourself investors can also open IRAs with a growing number of companies that sell stock directly to investors.

These plans let you buy your first share—and every share—directly from the company itself, often for little or nothing in transaction costs. Bypassing brokerages in this way can save you money on commissions and other fees.

A small but growing number of these companies will even let you set up an IRA with them, or their agent; they'll hold the shares that you buy directly. (See the end of this chapter for more information.)

Even More Investment Choices

The 1997 tax law that radically changed the rules for IRAs also gives you more choices for exactly what your IRA dollars can buy. Are you fond of gold or other precious metals? The law now lets you invest your IRA dollars in platinum coins or in silver, gold, platinum, or palladium bullion (as long as the bullion is physically held by your IRA trustee, not by you). If you're interested, a bank or brokerage might be willing to serve as trustee or custodian for the precious metals in your IRA.

No matter which of all these options you choose, and no matter which outfit you pick to hold your IRA, remember that you've got to do some research first. Once you've decided to go beyond a bank, thrift, or credit union, and once you've compared all the various fees and other expenses involved, you should consider the risks and the investment choices that you should—and should *not*—make.

The price of precious metals can bounce around a lot. The price of gold, for example, soared in the early 1980s but then slumped. Are you sure you want your retirement money invested in gold or other precious metals?

Keep in mind, too, that no matter what type of IRA you choose, the money inside your IRA is going to grow without any immediate tax consequence. So it generally makes no sense to plunk your IRA dollars into an investment such as U.S. Treasury securities, municipal bonds, or mutual funds that invest in government bonds or in variable annuities.

IRAs Don't Stand Alone

If you wind up opening an IRA or if you already have one, please keep in mind a point that's worth repeating over and over. When it comes time to choose where to put your IRA dollars, remember that your IRA doesn't stand alone. It's part of your overall financial picture. So, when you're picking investments for your IRA, give some thought to where the rest of your money is invested, because your IRA is part of your overall financial plan.

Here's an example. Suppose you've got some sort of retirement savings plan at work that lets you choose how the money is to be invested, such as a 401(k), 403(b), or 457 plan, and all the money is invested in stock mutual funds.

Suppose, too, that you own some stock mutual funds directly, not connected with your workplace. Let's also say that you keep your spare cash to a minimum; you prefer to put all your money in mutual funds.

When you decide how to invest your IRA dollars, you certainly do not want them invested in stocks or stock mutual funds in this example.

Why? Because too many of your assets are already tied to the fate of the stock market. One of the keys to successful investing is to spread your money around, not have all or most of it concentrated in just one area.

It's like your mother or grandmother probably once told you: don't put all your eggs in one basket. The same is true for investments. Spread your assets among different types of investments, including stocks (and stock mutual funds), bonds (and bond mutual funds), and cash (or things that may be converted quickly to cash, such as money market mutual funds, short-term U.S. Treasury securities, Series I or Series EE U.S. Savings Bonds, and short-term bond mutual funds).

In this example, you probably have too much in stocks already. So you may use your IRA as a starting point to diversify your investment portfolio. Instead of investing your IRA dollars in stocks or stock mutual funds, you might put them in bond funds, for instance.

Look at Your Time Horizon

Here's another key point to bear in mind. If you've looked carefully at your overall investment picture and you think your IRA dollars should be invested in stocks or stock mutual funds, think about your time horizon first.

What does that mean? Well, remember what happened to stocks in the mid-70s? When the market lost nearly half its value? When stocks not only went down, but stayed down for about five years?

Suppose that were to happen again. Suppose, too, that your IRA dollars were invested in stocks or stock mutual funds. Suppose you had to withdraw some or all of your money from your IRA.

How much would you get? Maybe not as much as you had planned. Maybe even not as much as you had originally contributed, because the value of the stock market had declined so much.

The point is this. If you've got a long-term time horizon, if you won't need to tap your IRA for another 10, 20, or 30 years or longer, then stocks and stock mutual funds can be a sound investment choice. Odds are you'll have plenty of time to ride out the market's ups and downs in the meantime.

But if you have a shorter time horizon, then stocks and stock mutual funds probably aren't the place to invest your IRA dollars. If retirement is just a couple of years around the corner, for instance, and you'll need to withdraw some or all of your IRA at that time to help meet expenses, you'll probably want to put most or all of your IRA dollars into something conservative, such as a federally insured bank account, so you'll know the money will be there when you need it. The same holds true if you're planning to use some or all of your IRA dollars within a few years to help buy a house or pay for a child's college education.

As the old saying goes, sometimes the return *of* your principal is more important than the return *on* your principal.

Avoiding Fees

It began with just a few IRA custodians and trustees, but the practice soon became pretty much industrywide. To boost profitability, charge the IRA client $10 or $15 or $20 or more a year in annual fees.

Call them custodial fees, maintenance fees, administrative fees, or whatever other fancy name you want. The bottom line is that IRA owners might have been saving money in taxes each year, but they were getting whacked with fees.

For wealthy people with lots of money to invest, the fees were nothing but a small annoyance, a cost of doing business. But for the small or average investor, the fees could take a big bite out of annual earnings.

How Fees Reduce Your Return. Suppose, for instance, that you invest $3,000 in an IRA at the start of the year. The account grows by 8 percent so that one year later, your IRA is worth $3,240. That represents $3,000 from your original contribution, plus $240 in earnings.

But now suppose your account's custodian or trustee hits you with a $40 annual account maintenance fee. Suddenly, you've earned $200 for the year, in effect, not $240. Your percentage gain on the year is now down to about 6.7 percent, not 8 percent. In other words, in this example, the annual fee has eaten more than one full percentage point out of your earnings. Ouch!

You probably have the option to pay the fee out of pocket so that it isn't subtracted from the money inside your account. This way, more of your money remains in your account to grow tax-deferred through the years. Still, it's money you must pay, whether it comes out of your account or out of your pocket.

Most Don't Qualify for a Deduction. True, an annual IRA fee that you pay out-of-pocket may generally be claimed as a deduction from your federal income tax. But that's only if you itemize your deductions, and most taxpayers don't itemize, because they haven't enough expenses to qualify. They're stuck with the standard one-size-fits-all deduction.

Even if you do itemize, you may miss out on claiming a tax benefit for your IRA custodial fee. Why? The annual IRA fee falls under a category of expenses known as *miscellaneous itemized deductions.*

You get to deduct only that part of all your miscellaneous deductions that amounts to more than 2 percent of your adjusted gross income.

What to do? Lots of IRA owners have long complained about IRA fees, and the financial services industry has listened. As a result, some brokerages and other financial institutions have generally agreed to waive annual IRA fees altogether if the value of an IRA exceeds a certain amount (typically $10,000). Some mutual fund companies have generally waived annual IRA fees altogether or set the threshold low (at $500 or $1,000, for example). The bottom line? If fees bother you like they bother me, you can save money by shopping around.

It just so happens that IRAs are flexible enough so that you can move your money from one IRA custodian or trustee to another with relatively little problem and no tax consequences. There are two ways to do this.

Transferring Your IRA

You can transfer your IRA from one trustee or custodian to another directly with no tax impact. The Internal Revenue Service allows an unlimited number of such direct transfers each year. So if you're fed up with one trustee or custodian, you can transfer your account to another IRA custodian or trustee and pay no income tax or penalty.

What's more, some outfits will handle the transfer for you at no charge. You just contact the new IRA custodian or trustee, complete the application, and turn it in. The new custodian, trustee, or issuer will then arrange to have your account transferred, directly and automatically, with no additional steps required from you.

Just remember that the process may take some time. Your old trustee, custodian, or issuer may not be pleased to lose your account and may not make the transfer a top priority. Keep in mind, too, that your old IRA custodian or trustee may charge a fee for closing your account. Some brokerages, for example, levy stiff account-closing fees. To see if you'll be liable and to find out how much you may be charged, check the language in your original account contract.

Rolling Over Your IRA

Another way to move money or other assets from one IRA to another tax-free is through a *rollover*. In effect, you act as the go-between. As with a transfer, you can roll over some or all of the money (or other assets) from one IRA to the other.

In general, it works this way. You withdraw the money from your IRA, close your account, and get a check. You then move the money yourself—by mail, for instance, or on foot—to the new IRA trustee or custodian. But beware: You have only 60 days to complete the rollover. (Technically, you have to complete the rollover by the 60th day after the day you receive the money.)

Watch that Deadline. If you don't make the move in time, the amount you withdrew will be treated as ordinary income subject to tax. You could also be faced with a 10 percent *early withdrawal penalty* to boot.

What's more, the IRS allows only one rollover in every 12-month period. Some IRA owners use rollovers as short-term loans; they pull the cash out, use it to pay a bill let's say, then replace the money within 60 days. If you have the discipline for this, fine.

Just remember that you suffer big tax consequences if you don't meet the deadline. To avoid such problems, it's best to stick with direct transfers. They're cleaner, less bothersome, and don't risk tax consequences.

For information about rolling your retirement plan at work to an IRA, please see the final chapter in this book.

The Choice Is Yours

With IRAs, the sky's the limit. You get to pick from among almost any bank, thrift, or credit union or just about any mutual fund company, stock brokerage, or insurer. Having the ability to easily move your money from one IRA custodian or trustee to another is important not just because of fees but also because of performance.

Maybe you invested your IRA dollars in a certain high-flying mutual fund only to learn a few years later that the fund's well-regarded manager has jumped ship. Or perhaps you opened an IRA at your friendly neighborhood bank branch, only to find years later—or maybe just months later—that your community bank has been gobbled up by a national giant intent on closing branches and raising fees to meet shareholder demands. It's nice to know you're not locked in: you can move your IRA to another custodian or trustee with relative ease.

When IRAs Are Not the Best Choice

Keep in mind that moving money into an IRA from a pension or retirement plan at work isn't always the best strategy. In some instances, an IRA simply won't work for you or won't work out the best for you. (For more details, please see Chapter 12.)

For More Information ...

Fidelity Investments. The Boston-based mutual fund giant offers free kits with details on transferring, or rolling over, money to an IRA from a pension or profit-sharing plan at work. Much of this information is also available online. Call 800-544-4774 or write: Fidelity Funds, 82 Devonshire Street, Boston, MA 02109. If you have access to a computer, see the Fidelity Web site: <www.fidelity.com>.

The Investment Company Institute in Washington, D.C. A trade group for the mutual fund industry, this organization publishes a comprehensive listing of thousands of mutual funds. Its annual directory includes the name, address, and phone number for each fund. The Institute also publishes free brochures about the basics of mutual fund investing. For ordering information, write: Investment Company Institute, 1401 H Street NW, Suite 1200, Washington, D.C. 20005-2148. Here's the Web site: <www.ici.org>.

No-Load Stock Insider newsletter. This publication includes a master list of companies that offer no-load stock plans. For a free copy, write: *No-Load Stock Insider,* 7412 Calumet Avenue, Suite 200, Hammond, IN 46324. For more on no-load stocks (and dividend reinvestment plans), here are two related Web sites: <www.dripinvestor.com> and <www.noloadstocks.com>.

3

Withdrawing Money from Your IRA

This chapter looks at the tax and other consequences of withdrawing money from a traditional IRA: the 10 percent penalty for withdrawals before you turn 59½, how to avoid it, and steps to postpone withdrawals even after you reach 59½ so your account can continue to grow.

You were probably taught this as a child: Whenever you enter a building you haven't been in before, look around for the *Exit* signs, because you never know when you'll need them.

The same idea applies to IRAs. It's all well and good to save and save. But what happens when you need to take money out of your IRA to spend it? What are the rules? What will it cost you? Are there any alternatives? In other words, what will happen if you need to get your money and head for the door?

Three Main Exits

If you own an IRA, you typically have three main exits. The one that applies to you generally depends upon your age.

- The government discourages withdrawals from your IRA before you reach age 59½. If you do make an early withdrawal, you'll generally have to pay federal income tax on it, and you may have to pay a 10 percent federal early withdrawal penalty, too.
- If your age is between 59½ and 70½ and you withdraw money from your IRA, you'll generally have to pay federal income tax on it, but you won't be penalized.
- Once you turn 70½, you are *required* to start withdrawing money. Each withdrawal will generally trigger federal income tax, but it won't be penalized—if you withdraw enough.

Yes, the rules are a little complicated. And yes, you can't even take money out of your own IRA without getting caught in a tangle of rules and regulations.

Happily, the rules aren't all that complicated and they're a lot easier to understand if you look at them based on age.

Under 59½ Avoiding the Penalty

If you pull money out of your IRA and you haven't reached 59½, you'll have to mention this on your federal income tax return. In effect, you'll say, "I took some money out of my IRA!" and the government will say, "Great! Give us a piece of it! A great big piece!"

Why? The money in your account hasn't been taxed yet. You probably claimed a federal income tax deduction for the money you contributed. All the money that your account has earned over the years hasn't been taxed, either. It's been growing on a tax-deferred basis, year-in, year-out.

It gets worse. When you withdraw money from an IRA before you turn 59½, you'll also face a 10 percent *premature withdrawal penalty*. The penalty is applied to the amount you withdraw, and you must pay the penalty on top of any regular income tax you owe. That can be pretty painful.

For example, suppose you lose your job and have to withdraw $10,000 from your IRA to help meet expenses. You'll have to report the amount of the withdrawal as income on your tax return, and it will be treated as ordinary income, the same as wages and salary.

As a result, it will be subject to tax at your marginal federal tax rate. So, if you're paying federal tax at a rate of 30 percent, you'll pay $3,000 in federal income tax on your $10,000 withdrawal.

A Painful Penalty

In addition, you'll have to pay a 10 percent penalty. In this example, the penalty would amount to $1,000. So you can see how quickly the total tax adds up and how quickly the *net* amount of your withdrawal—the amount you get to keep after tax—can decline.

The tax and penalty could gobble up almost 40 percent of the amount you withdraw, not counting any state income tax that may be due. That stings!

But there is some relief. The government has gradually chipped away at the rules, easing restrictions.

Escaping the Penalty

As a result, you may now escape the penalty (but not regular income tax) if your withdrawal qualifies as a special exception, even if you haven't turned 59½.

These exceptions were once intended only for severe hardships, but Congress has added to the list of special exceptions. Here's how the situation stands right now. Early withdrawals incur no penalty if they're made under any of these circumstances (even if you're under 59½).

- *On account of your disability.* You have to show proof that you can't do any "substantial gainful activity" because of your physical—or mental—condition. A physician must determine that your condition can be expected to result in death or to be of "long, continued, and indefinite duration," the IRS says.
- *On account of your death.* If you die before you turn 59½, the money (or other assets) in your IRA can be pulled out by your beneficiary (or paid to your estate) without penalty.
- *Part of a series of payments.* This exception is often overlooked and little understood. You can avoid the penalty simply by making a series of withdrawals over a long period of time. But this exception is tricky, and it's easy to trip up because a lot of rules apply. For instance, the withdrawals must be part of a series of substantially equal withdrawals made at least once a year. These payments must be made over your life or the joint life expectancy of you and your primary beneficiary. (You may use government life expectancy tables, but there are other ways to calculate these payments and they can be tricky as well. Be sure to get professional help first.)

In other words, you can avoid the penalty if you agree to withdraw money in roughly equal annual installments for the rest of your life. These withdrawals must continue for at least five years, or until you reach 59½, whichever turns out to be the longer period. What does that mean? In effect, you may start withdrawing money from your IRA before you turn 59½, and you won't be penalized as long as the withdrawals are part of a regular series of withdrawals (made under an IRS approved method of calculation).

Once you turn 59½, you can stop the withdrawals if you want. How does that work? If you begin making withdrawals when you're 50, you'll have to continue them until you're 59½, when you can stop. But if you start the withdrawals when you're 57, you'll have to continue them until you're 62 and can stop then.

Remember the rule: Once you start your series of withdrawals, they must continue for at least five years or until you turn 59½, whichever is the *longer* period.

This exception to the 10 percent penalty isn't especially well known but could prove useful to people who need to tap their IRAs early.

- *Medical expenses.* The money you withdraw must be used to pay only for medical expenses. These are only expenses for which you haven't been reimbursed (by insurance, for example), and only those expenses that exceed 7.5 percent of your adjusted gross income. (You'd normally be able to include these medical expenses on Schedule A of your U.S. Form 1040, although technically you don't have to itemize your deductions to qualify for this exception.)

- *Health insurance.* You must be unemployed and use the money you withdraw to pay for medical insurance premiums for you, your spouse, and your dependents. You'll qualify for this exception only if you meet *all four* of these conditions.
  - You lost your job.
  - You received unemployment compensation for 12 consecutive weeks.
  - You make the withdrawal(s) during the year you received the unemployment benefits *or* the following year.
  - You make the withdrawals no later than 60 days after you've gotten another job.

- *College expenses.* The IRS says that you must use the money for *qualified higher education expenses* either for you, your spouse, or any child or grandchild of either you or your spouse. (You don't have to claim the child or grandchild as a dependent on your tax return.) The expenses include tuition at a "postsecondary educational institution," the IRS says, as well as any fees, supplies, books, and equipment required for enrollment or attendance at any eligible educational institution (such as a college, university, vocational school, or other postsecondary institution that's eligible to take part in student aid programs run by the U.S. Department of Education). The expenses also include room and board, if the student is enrolled at least half-time. The expenses can be for undergraduate and graduate study. But before you make any withdrawal, you'll first have to reduce the amount of education expenses by certain amounts you've already received, such as Pell Grants, tax-free scholarships, or tax-free educational assistance provided by an employer.

- *First-time homebuyer costs.* To qualify, you must use the money to buy, build, or rebuild a house that will serve as the "principal residence" for you, your spouse, or any child, grandchild, or ancestor (such as a parent or grandparent) of you or your spouse. The money may also be used to pay for any "usual or reasonable" settlement, financing, or other such closing costs, the government says. There's a 120-day deadline for using the money, and the clock generally starts ticking at the point of withdrawal. The money you withdraw under this rule can't exceed $10,000 over your lifetime.

Who, exactly, qualifies as a *first-time homebuyer?* The government is pretty loose on this point. In general, you don't have to be buying a house for the first time in your life. The IRS will consider you a first-time homebuyer as long as you—or your spouse, if you're married—haven't had an ownership interest in a principal residence during the two years before you acquire your next principal residence.

- *One more exception applies.* Money you withdraw from your IRA under an IRS levy to pay federal tax will escape the penalty.

Other Penalty-Free Moves

Some moves automatically avoid the 10 percent penalty. You probably know them all, but here's a quick summary of some other circumstances in which the 10 percent penalty is sidestepped.

- Money or other assets you transfer directly from one IRA to another, or from certain types of pension plans to an IRA
- Money or other assets you roll over from one IRA to another within the 60-day limit
- If you contribute after-tax dollars to an IRA, these contributions are known as *nondeductible contributions,* and if you withdraw them, they avoid penalty. But, if you withdraw any money from your account that your nondeductible contributions earned over the years, the earnings *will* be subject to the penalty—if you're under 59½ and you don't meet any of the main exceptions.
- Transfers made under a divorce decree or separate maintenance decree are generally considered tax-free and penalty-free (whether the name on an IRA is changed or assets from one spouse's IRA are transferred to the former spouse's IRA).
- *Timely withdrawals* of money you contribute to an IRA. Say you contribute $3,000 to your traditional IRA for a given year, but you claim no deduction for it, and you withdraw the $3,000—as well as any earnings it generated—before the due date of your tax return for that year. In this case, the $3,000 you withdraw won't be subject to either tax or penalty. (But any earnings that your $3,000 contribution generated will be taxed and generally will be subject to the 10 percent early withdrawal penalty if you haven't turned 59½.)

The Between Years of 59½ to 70½: Tax Consequences

Okay, so you've been stashing away money for your retirement, resisting time and again the temptation to spend. Perhaps now you choose to enjoy the money you've saved. No more scrimping, no more sacrifices. You decide to start withdrawing money.

Can you do it? Yes. Of course, it would be better if you could leave the money in your account as long as possible, so it could continue to grow, sheltered from taxes. But, if you really need to withdraw money between 59½ and 70½, it's nice to know you can get at it.

How do you go about it? Do you just take what you need and skip the details?

Some Tax Planning

Before you plunge ahead and start pulling your money out of your IRA, take a few minutes to think about the consequences. Some careful planning now can save you money in the future.

You won't be penalized. Remember that if you withdraw money from an IRA before you reach age 59½, the withdrawal generally is subject to a 10 percent federal penalty. If you withdraw money on or after you turn 59½, you won't be subject to this penalty at all. Congratulations!

However, any withdrawal you make must be included in your gross income for the year in which you make it. In other words, any withdrawal is going to be subject to federal income tax. If the withdrawal is large enough, it could wind up increasing your taxable income and bump you into a higher tax bracket.

Furthermore, a withdrawal from an IRA could boost your *provisional income,* making some part of your Social Security benefit subject to tax. (If some of your benefit is already taxed, an IRA withdrawal could mean a greater share of your Social Security benefit would be taxed.)

In addition, any money you withdraw from an IRA—even in retirement—won't have the chance to keep growing inside your account, sheltered from tax. So you lose the chance for more tax-deferred growth, not to mention the magic of compound interest.

Experts usually suggest that you delay as long as possible making any withdrawals from your IRA. But what can you do instead if you really need some money? Look to any other savings or investments you may have. Think about withdrawing the money that will have the least tax consequences.

Make the Most of Your Withdrawal

Say you need $1,000 to pay for a trip, to buy someone a gift, or just to go on a splurge, and you've got a few options. Here are some ways to get the money with the fewest tax complications.

- Withdraw first from a bank savings account or another taxable account, such as a bank money market account or a money market mutual fund. You've put after-tax dollars into these accounts, and the earnings have probably already been taxed. So you won't be taxed again when you make your withdrawal. What's more, of all your investments, these accounts may be generating the lowest yield for you.
- Consider cashing in shares of a mutual fund or selling some shares of stock. True, this step means tax consequences, too. But they're not as bad as they once were. Remember: The top federal tax rate on *capital gains* from the profit on the sale of stock, mutual funds, and similar assets used to be 28 percent. But the government changed the rules. Now, it's generally 20 percent (and some people in certain circumstances may pay only 8 percent).
- If you have more than one traditional IRA and you need to tap at least one of them, think about withdrawing from the one that's earning you the least.

Over 70½: When You *Must* Withdraw

A time will come when you must start withdrawing money from your traditional IRAs, even if you don't want to.

Calculating your minimum required withdrawals generally isn't a do-it-yourself deal, because it can be so complicated. If you plan to do the work yourself, or you just want to have an idea of how it's done, see the following chapter.

4

When You Must Make Withdrawals

This chapter explains the rules that require you to start withdrawing at least a minimum amount from your traditional IRA once you reach a certain age. We'll look at how these rules came about and how recent changes have made these rules more helpful to IRA owners and beneficiaries. We'll also walk you through an easy, five-step plan that lets you see how the rules apply to your personal situation and helps you calculate your own withdrawals.

It happened in Washington in the dead of winter. One president was getting ready to leave office; another president was days away from inauguration. That's when the U.S. Treasury struck.

In an official government publication, little noticed at the time, the Treasury took an extraordinary step. It cast away, in a single stroke, a set of outdated rules that had long confused and frustrated IRA owners, baffled beneficiaries, and bedeviled their advisors.

The Treasury's new rules are making a huge impact on just about everyone who owns or inherits a traditional IRA.

IRA owners are finding it easier than before to figure how much they must withdraw, at a minimum, from their traditional IRAs. They are also saving money—in some cases lots of money—in taxes. They are not the only ones to benefit, either. Just about anybody who inherits a traditional IRA profits, too.

An IRA Isn't a Vault

To understand the benefits of these changes, consider what IRAs are all about.

When created in 1974, the traditional IRA was not intended as a vault in which you could lock away your riches for eternity. Rather, it was designed as a way to help you save for your retirement, so that you could supplement your retirement income.

There's the rub. At some point, you must start taking money out of your account—at least a minimum amount, at least once a year. The magic age when you must start making these minimum annual withdrawals is 70½. (Technically, you need not make your first withdrawal until April 1 of the year following the year in which you turn 70½, but more on that later.)

As you might expect, that well-known division of the U.S. Treasury—the Internal Revenue Service—came up with a bunch of rules to govern exactly when and how you had to make these withdrawals. As you might also expect, the rules were extraordinarily complex.

A Peculiar Set of Rules

In effect, they required all IRA owners to solve an intricate puzzle made of what seemed a million pieces.

- You had to choose among a variety of complex and convoluted methods for making your minimum withdrawals. Make the wrong choice and you, or your spouse, could run out of money. The choice was also irrevocable: once you made it, you were stuck with it.
- If you were single and named no beneficiary for your account, you had to calculate your withdrawals based on your age alone. As a result, you had to make fairly substantial minimum withdrawals each year.
- If you named a beneficiary, you generally could calculate your withdrawals based on both your ages. This method typically resulted in somewhat smaller withdrawals. But you had to choose from among a variety of withdrawal methods, all of them based on perplexing rules with lots of tables and figures to pore over. That's not all. Whatever method you chose for withdrawals could have a lasting—and potentially punishing—impact on how your beneficiary calculated withdrawals after your death.
- You had the freedom to change your beneficiary later on if you preferred, but the change could make your calculations even more complicated—and even cost you more in taxes.

IRA Owners in Limbo

In short, it was a mess. To make matters worse, the IRS issued these rules as "proposed regulations" in 1987 and never got around to making them final. As a result, frustrated IRA owners, as well as their advisors and beneficiaries, were left to their own devices for nearly 14 years, struggling to understand this tangled web of rules.

> ## REQUIRED WITHDRAWALS
>
> This chapter focuses mainly on withdrawals you must make from your traditional IRA once you turn 70½. I generally refer to them here as *required withdrawals*.
>
> However, you may see them referred to elsewhere by their technical name, *required minimum distributions* (RMDs). Many financial advisors and official government publications also refer to them as RMDs.

New Rules

Thanks to the new rules that the Treasury published in 2001, however, your calculations are a lot easier. For most IRA owners, one simple method applies.

You'll face easier calculations; you'll get the chance to save money by paying less in taxes; you won't have to fear exhausting your account before you die; and you'll get to leave more money in your account for your beneficiaries. Your beneficiaries will also have the chance to stretch out their withdrawals over a longer period of time, giving the account a better chance to grow on a tax-deferred basis in the meantime.

Some Things Remain the Same

Although the new rules are helpful and a lot better than the old ones, you should keep in mind that some things haven't changed. For example:

- You still must begin making at least minimum annual withdrawals from your traditional IRA at about the time you turn 70½.
- If you don't withdraw enough money under the rules, you'll still be subject to a stiff penalty.
- Although the steps involved in calculating these withdrawals are a lot simpler now, you still must do some calculations yourself. True, your IRA trustee may do them for you. However, you should still be familiar with the rules and how they work. One reason is that your trustee may not be able to tell from its records exactly how the new rules fit your situation, and you may get a better deal—through smaller required withdrawals—by doing the numbers yourself.
- You should name one or more beneficiaries for your IRA(s), even before you turn 70½. The law doesn't require you to name one or more bene-

---

REQUIRED BEGINNING DATE

You must make minimum annual withdrawals from your traditional IRA starting with the year in which you reach age 70½.

However, you get a grace period for that first withdrawal only. If you decide to take advantage of the grace period, you must make that first withdrawal by April 1 of the year following the year in which you reach 70½.

This is what the IRS—and many tax professionals—refer to as your *required beginning date*. It's the final date by which you must make your first required minimum withdrawal. Miss it and you face a stiff penalty.

---

ficiaries; in fact, the law allows some beneficiary changes to be made for up to a year following your death. Nevertheless, you generally can avoid some adverse tax consequences (and other potential problems, such as squabbling among your heirs) if you name one or more beneficiaries as soon as possible, preferably as soon as you open your account.

The Dreaded Penalty

Why bother at all with making required withdrawals?

If you don't follow the required procedures, you'll have to pay, as a penalty, 50 percent of the difference between what should have withdrawn and what you actually did withdraw.

Suppose, for example, that according to the rules, you must withdraw $3,000 this year from your traditional IRA. Instead, you withdraw nothing. What happens? You'll be faced with a $1,500 penalty. Why? The difference between what you should have withdrawn ($3,000) and what you actually withdraw ($0) is, of course, $3,000. Fifty percent of that is $1,500. That's your penalty. (And you still must make the required withdrawal, too.)

What if you do make a withdrawal, but it totals only $2,000? You'll have to pay a penalty of $500. Why? The difference between what you should have withdrawn ($3,000 in this example) and what you actually withdrew ($2,000) is $1,000. Fifty percent of $1,000 is $500. That's your penalty.

The bottom line? If you're facing the deadline, make the withdrawal according to the rules so you can avoid the painful penalty; don't expect the government to bail you out.

A lot is at stake. A study issued in 2001 showed about $2.47 trillion in all IRAs, more than all of the money held in traditional pension plans and employer-sponsored retirement savings plans *combined*. IRA owners (and/or their beneficiaries) must withdraw that money at some point, and they need to know how the rules work to avoid a penalty.

The Nuts and Bolts of Withdrawals

Enough of the background. For now, let's get right down to the nuts and bolts of it all: how to figure your required minimum withdrawals. The government wants you to start making withdrawals from your traditional IRA at a certain point, and it wants you to calculate your withdrawals based on your life expectancy (or on the combined life expectancy of you and your beneficiary).

To do this, the government wants you to use tables that it has published. These tables are an attempt to reflect your life expectancy (or the joint life expectancy of you and your beneficiary). The tables don't really forecast accurately how long you'll live or how long you and your beneficiary will live. That doesn't matter, however, because you have to use the tables anyway.

Although the new rules make your calculations somewhat easier than they would have been, you still must do some calculations—using the government's tables to help ensure you don't make a mistake, which could trigger a nasty penalty.

A Five-Step Plan

Here's a five-step plan for making your required withdrawals.

Step 1: When Do You Turn 70½?

This may not occur as soon as you might think. In other words, you don't necessarily reach the magic age in the calendar year in which your 70th birthday falls. It may happen the following year, depending on when your birthday occurs.

If you were born early in the year, you'll obviously celebrate your 70th birthday early in the year, and you'll turn 70½ later that same year. As a result, you'll have to start thinking seriously about making a required withdrawal from your traditional IRA for the same year in which you celebrate your 70th birthday.

However, if you were born late in the year, you'll celebrate your 70th birthday late in the year, so you'll turn 70½ in the following calendar year. As a result, you won't have to start thinking seriously about making a required withdrawal from your traditional IRA until the calendar year following the calendar year in which you turn 70.

WHEN YOU'LL REACH THE MAGIC AGE

If you were born before July 1 in . . .	You'll turn 70½ in . . .
1932	2002
1933	2003
1934	2004
1935	2005
1936	2006
1937	2007
1938	2008

If you were born after July 1 in . . .	You'll turn 70½ in . . .
1932	2003
1933	2004
1934	2005
1935	2006
1936	2007
1937	2008
1938	2009

Confused? Here's an example.

Suppose you were born in February 1934. You'll celebrate your 70th birthday in February 2004. Six months later, you'll reach the magic age, 70½, that triggers the formulas used for figuring minimum withdrawals from traditional IRAs.

However, if you were born in August 1934, you'll celebrate your 70th birthday in August 2004. This means you won't reach the magic age of 70½ until February 2005. In that case, you won't have to make a withdrawal for 2004, the year you turned 70; you'll have to make one for 2005, the year you turned 70½. (See the chart above to determine when you reach the magic age.)

Step 2: When to Make Your First Withdrawal

In most cases, the answer is easy: by year-end. If you're 75, for example, you make your required withdrawal by December 31 of the year in which you celebrate your 75th birthday. If you're 76, you make your required withdrawal by December 31 of the year in which you celebrate your 76th birthday.

The only time this gets tricky is with your very first required withdrawal, the one that's triggered *for* the year in which you turn 70½.

The italics are there, in the previous sentence, for a good reason: you must make your first required withdrawal *for* the year in which you turn 70½, not necessarily *in* the year in which you turn 70½.

What does that mean? Technically, the government gives you a grace period. You aren't required to make your first withdrawal until April 1 of the year following the year in which you turn 70½.

Suppose, for example, that you were born in March 1935. You turn 70½ in September 2005. You must make your first required withdrawal *for* that year, 2005. However, you need not make it *in* that year; you may postpone it until early 2006, because that's what you're allowed by the grace period. You must make that first withdrawal by April 1 of the year following the year in which you turn 70½.

Benefits of the Grace Period. This grace period gives you some liberty in planning your money matters. For instance, you may be faced with a starkly different financial picture from one year to the next and appreciate the opportunity to time your IRA withdrawal for either year.

Suppose, in our example, you know you're going to inherit some money in 2005, which will supplement your retirement income. In 2006, however, there'll be no inheritance, and you know you'll have some major bills coming due—some renovations at home, for instance, or maybe a big purchase, such as a car. In this case, it's nice to know you can postpone your first withdrawal to a year in which you'll really need the money.

The grace period also can trigger all sorts of tax planning strategies—and complications. Suppose, in our example, you have a lot of income pouring in during 2005 but expect to have far less income in 2006. In that case, it may make sense—purely from a tax standpoint—to postpone your first required withdrawal until 2006.

However, if you have comparatively little income for 2005 but expect a sharp increase in income in 2006, taking your first required withdrawal in 2005 may make sense.

Taxes Are a Factor. You must also think about bunching. What is bunching?

Let's go back to our example. You must make your first withdrawal for 2005. (Even if you postpone it until early 2006, it still is counted as having been made *for* 2005.) You must also make one minimum required withdrawal for each year thereafter, and you must make it *in* each year thereafter.

In our example, therefore, your second minimum annual withdrawal would occur in 2006, and you'd have to make it by December 31, 2006. The grace period applies only to that first required withdrawal; all others must be made by the end of each calendar year.

FALLING FEDERAL INCOME TAX RATES

Year	27% rate drops to	30% rate drops to	35% rate drops to	38.6% rate drops to
2004	26 %	29 %	34 %	37.6 %
2005	26 %	29 %	34 %	37.6 %
2006	25 %	28 %	33 %	35.0 %

Congressional Conference Committee Report, 2001

Where, then, does bunching come in? Suppose, in our example, that you postpone that first withdrawal until March 2006. That takes care of the withdrawal you were supposed to make for 2005. Don't forget, however, that your next withdrawal is due by December 31, 2006. This means you'll wind up making two withdrawals in a single year—a single *tax* year. That's what bunching is all about: tax consequences.

Bunching may not necessarily be a bad thing. After all, the balance in your IRA may be fairly small, so the amount of each withdrawal may be fairly small, too. Therefore, the amount of each withdrawal may have a minor impact on your tax picture, even if you do bunch your first two withdrawals into the same year.

If you have a larger IRA, however, the amount of each withdrawal could be hefty, and two hefty withdrawals bunched in the same year could bump you into a higher income tax bracket.

That's not all. Don't forget that each withdrawal is also counted as income for purposes of figuring any tax that may be due on your Social Security benefits. Even if the amount of each withdrawal is fairly small, two such withdrawals bunched in the same year could be just enough to bump you into a higher tax bracket. They could also trigger a tax on your Social Security benefits for that year or subject a greater portion of your Social Security benefits to tax.

Furthermore, the money you withdraw gets added to your adjusted gross income (AGI) for tax purposes. Lots of tax breaks are tied to your AGI; the higher your AGI, the less likely you are to qualify for the tax break. For example, if you have medical bills, you generally may claim a federal income tax deduction only for that portion of your unreimbursed medical expenses that exceeds 7.5 percent of your AGI.

State income taxes may also come into play. Some states let you exempt, or exclude, a certain amount of retirement income. If you make two separate withdrawals—one in the year in which you turn 70½, another in the following year—you may be able to exclude both from your state's income tax. If you bunch both withdrawals in the same year, however, only a portion may be eligible for the state tax break; the rest may be taxable.

As you can see then, delaying that first required withdrawal until early the following year could have major tax consequences. Before you make the decision on when to make it, look at your overall tax picture, including the potential impact on your Social Security benefits. Also, consider seeking the advice of an accountant or other such professional, and be aware that federal tax laws are always changing and rates may change, too.

Step 3: Calculating Your First Withdrawal

Thanks to the new rules, withdrawals aren't very hard to calculate. You can do it yourself with only a little effort. There are some fine points to consider. For now, however, here's a straightforward snapshot, just enough to give you a general idea of how the process works.

You turn 70½, so you must withdraw at least a minimum amount from your account for that year. How do you calculate it? Like this:

- First, you check the balance of your account as of December 31 of the year before you are supposed to make your required withdrawal.
- Next, you find a certain figure that corresponds to your age in a government-published table. The key figure you'll find in the table is also known as a *divisor, multiple,* or *factor.* (A short version of that table appears on the next page; the complete table is in the back of this book, Appendix A.)
- Finally, you divide your year-end balance by the figure in that table. The answer is how much you must withdraw, at a minimum, from your traditional IRA.

Figuring by Example. Charlie was born in March 1935. He turns 70½ in September 2005, so he must make his first required withdrawal *for* that year, 2005. Although he may postpone that first withdrawal until early in 2006, he decides to make the withdrawal in 2005.

How does he do it? First, he checks the balance of his account as of December 31, 2004. Let's say it's $120,000.

Next, he checks the table to find the figure that corresponds to his age. In this example, it's 26.2. Why? That's the figure that corresponds to his age as of December 31 of the year in question. When you refer to the table in this example, use your age as of your birthday in the year you become 70½. Charlie turns 70½ in September 2005. As of December 31, 2005, Charlie is still 70 years

TABLE FOR FIGURING YOUR MINIMUM WITHDRAWALS

Your age	Your factor	Your age	Your factor
70	26.2	78	19.2
71	25.3	79	18.4
72	24.4	80	17.6
73	23.5	81	16.8
74	22.7	82	16.0
75	21.8	83	15.3
76	20.9	84	14.5
77	20.1	85	13.8

See Appendix A for complete table.

old; he won't celebrate his 71st birthday until March 2006. As a result, he uses the figure of 26.2 in his calculation, because that figure corresponds to his age for that year: 70.

Next, Charlie divides his year-end balance, which is $120,000, by the figure he found in the table, which is 26.2. The answer is $4,580. That's how much he must withdraw, at a minimum, from his IRA for 2005.

Easy, right? Well, almost. Here's where some of the fine points enter the picture.

For example, what if Charlie had waited until April 1, 2006, to make his first withdrawal? He'd calculate it in the same way, using the same dates and figures mentioned above. In other words, he'd still use his account balance as of December 31, 2004, and he'd still use the same figure from the table, 26.2.

However, what if Charlie had been born in November 1935? He'd turn 70½ in May 2006. He'd have to make his first required withdrawal by April 1, 2007. To calculate the amount of his first withdrawal, he'd use his account balance as of December 31, 2005. In checking the table, he'd look for the figure that corresponds to age 71, which is 25.3. Why age 71? Remember that in using the table to calculate your first withdrawal, you use your age as of your birthday in the year you become 70½. In this example, Charlie turned 70½ in May 2006 and celebrated his 71st birthday in November 2006. So he was age 71 in the year in which he turned 70½. As a result, in checking the table, he must use the figure that corresponds to his age for that year—age 71. This gives him a slightly smaller figure to use in his calculation: 25.3. Put another way, when making your calculation and referring to the table, use your attained age in the year for which you are making the withdrawal.

Had enough? There's more—a complication involving contributions. This probably won't affect you, but it's worth knowing about nonetheless.

USING PERCENTAGES

Calculating your minimum annual withdrawals means you must work with life expectancy factors from government-published tables. Confused? Look at the process instead from the standpoint of percentages.

Suppose that, in calculating your withdrawal for this year, your IRA balance as of December 31 last year was $35,000, and the key factor you're using from the government table is 26.2. This means you must withdraw $1,336.

To get a different perspective on the process, simply divide the number 1 by 26.2. Now you can look upon your required withdrawal as a percentage of your account balance. In this example, 1 divided by 26.2 is 0.03817. In other words, you must withdraw 3.817 percent of your prior year's balance.

Technically, you don't use your account balance when you calculate your first withdrawal; you use your *adjusted account balance*. For most people, the account balance will be the same as the adjusted account balance. There is an exception, however. It involves IRA contributions.

Suppose you were born in December 1934. You'll turn 70 in 2004. You'll turn 70½ in June 2005, so you must make your first required withdrawal for 2005.

What if you work during 2004 and make a deductible contribution to your traditional IRA in March 2005? (Technically, the rules say you can't contribute to a traditional IRA for the year in which you turn 70½. However, although you're making the contribution in March 2005, you're assigning that contribution to the year 2004—when you were 70. Your contribution therefore meets the rules.)

In this example, you'd normally calculate your first required withdrawal by checking your account balance as of December 31, 2004. In this case, however, you must add to that balance the amount you contributed in March 2005. This gives you your adjusted account balance, and you must use this figure in your calculation.

Confused? Let's say that Charlie was born in November 1934. He'll turn 70 in 2004 and 70½ in May 2005. As a result, he must make his first required withdrawal for 2005.

It turns out that Charlie worked throughout 2004 and decided to contribute the maximum amount allowed to his traditional IRA for that year, $3,500. (He made the contribution in March 2005 but took care to assign the contribution to 2004.)

To calculate his first required withdrawal, he notes down his account balance of $100,000 as of December 31, 2004. He adds to that amount the $3,500 he contributed in March 2005. Next, he checks the table to find the figure that corresponds to his age for that first distribution year. It's 25.3. (Remember that Charlie turned 71 in November 2005, so when he checks the table, he must use the figure that corresponds to someone at age 71.)

The bottom line? Charlie must withdraw $4,091. Why? He divided his adjusted account balance of $103,500 by 25.3.

When Your Spouse Is Your Beneficiary. All these examples show how Charlie would calculate his first required withdrawal. In other words, this is how Charlie would go about figuring his required minimum withdrawal for what the experts would call his *first distribution year*—the year in which he turns 70½.

Charlie would do the calculations this way if he had no beneficiary, one beneficiary, or more than one beneficiary.

There's one key exception, and it's a big one. It has to do with an IRA owner whose spouse is the sole beneficiary for the entire year and the spouse is more than ten years younger. In that situation, you do the calculations in much the same way, except that you use a different table. This will give you a different figure to use, and you'll end up making an even smaller withdrawal.

Why? The table that many IRA owners use is known technically as a *uniform table;* it applies to just about everybody. With this table, the government is giving you a break. In effect, the government is assuming that you have named a beneficiary for your IRA, even if you haven't. The government is also assuming, in effect, that your beneficiary is exactly ten years younger than you are, even if that's not true.

By building these assumptions into the table, the government is letting you use a larger figure in your calculations than you otherwise could. You get to make smaller required withdrawals than you otherwise would. As a result, your tax bill is smaller, and more money is left in your IRA—after your withdrawal—to continue growing on a tax-deferred basis.

However, what if your sole beneficiary is your spouse who is more than ten years younger than you are? You get to use another table that gives you an even greater break in your calculations. (Technically, this is known as the *Joint Life and Last Survivor Expectancy Table.* An excerpt appears on the next page, while the complete table is in Appendix B.)

Let's return to our example to see how this works. Suppose that Charlie was born in March 1935. He turns 70½ in September 2005, so he must make his first required withdrawal *for* that year, 2005.

His IRA balance as of December 31, 2004, is $120,000. He checks the uniform table to find the figure that corresponds to his age. In this example, it's 26.2. Charlie divides his year-end balance ($120,000) by the figure he found in the table (26.2). As a result, he must withdraw at least $4,580.

THE JOINT LIFE TABLE

Here is an excerpt from the table you'd use to help calculate your required minimum withdrawal if your spouse is more than ten years younger than you are. (The complete table is in Appendix B.)

Ages	55	56	57	58
70	29.9	29.1	28.4	27.6
71	29.7	29.0	28.2	27.5
72	29.6	28.8	28.1	27.3

For example, suppose you're 70 and your spouse is 55. Locate both ages on the table. The key factor you'd use in your calculation is located at the point where both ages intersect. In this example, the key factor is 29.9.

However, if Charlie's wife, Angel, is his sole beneficiary and is more than ten years younger than he is, he uses a different table and gets a break as a result. In that table, he finds a figure that corresponds to the actual ages of Charlie and Angel. This allows Charlie to use a larger figure in his calculations, one that lets him make a smaller withdrawal.

In our example, Charlie is 70 and let's say that Angel is 55. In the table, Charlie looks up his age and also looks up Angel's age. The point where both ages intersect is the figure that he must use in his calculations. In our example, the figure is 29.9. So he divides his $120,000 account balance by 29.9. The result—$4,013—is the amount he must withdraw, at a minimum, to meet the rules.

If Charlie used the uniform table in this example, he would have to withdraw $4,580. By using the other table, he gets to withdraw only $4,013. As a result, he can withdraw $567 less. He pays less tax and more money remains in his IRA.

Step 4: Calculating the Second Withdrawal

To calculate the amount of your second withdrawal, you generally follow the same process you did for your first withdrawal. Here, too, there can be some complications, but more on those later. For now, let's just take a straightforward look at how the process works for most people.

First, check your account balance as of December 31 of the preceding year. Next, go back to the table to find the factor that corresponds to your age. Remember to use your age as of your birthday during that year. Divide the account balance by the factor and you'll know how much you'll have to withdraw.

An Example. Maria was born in March 1933. She turns 70½ in September 2003, so she must make her first required withdrawal for that year, 2003. She makes it in November 2003, calculating it this way.

Her account balance as of December 31, 2002, was $120,000. She divides that by 26.2. As a result, she withdraws $4,580.

Now it's 2004. A second minimum annual withdrawal is due. Maria must make it by December 31, 2004. How does she know how much to withdraw? She checks her account balance as of December 31, 2003. It's $125,000. Remember that she must use the account balance as of December 31 of the year immediately preceding the year for which she's making a required minimum withdrawal.

She then checks the table to find the figure that corresponds to her age in 2004. Maria is now 71; the figure in the table that matches her age is 25.3. To calculate how much she must withdraw, at a minimum, by December 31, 2004, she divides $125,000 by 25.3. The answer is $4,941. She withdraws that amount and meets the rules.

Most people will calculate the amount of their second required withdrawal this way. They'll look for the account balance as of the previous December 31, and they'll refer once again to the uniform table.

What if your spouse is your sole beneficiary and is more than ten years younger than you? To calculate your second required withdrawal, you'd follow the same procedure outlined above, with one exception: instead of using the uniform table, you'd go back to the same table you used for your first withdrawal—the Joint Life and Last Survivor Expectancy table.

An Extra Complication. For most IRA owners, the calculation really is this simple. Some IRA owners, however, have one added complication. If you took advantage of the grace period for your first required withdrawal, you must now make an adjustment to your IRA balance before you can calculate the amount of your second withdrawal.

FINDING THE TABLES

To calculate the amount you must withdraw, at a minimum, from your traditional IRA, you must use a key figure that's published in official government tables.

You'll find these tables toward the end of this book, in the Appendix. Keep in mind, however, that the government updates the tables from time to time.

Make sure you have the latest version by visiting your local IRS office, calling 1-800-829-3676, or by using the IRS Web site: <www.irs.gov>.

Remember that your first withdrawal is *for* the year in which you turn 70½. You don't necessarily have to make it *in* the year in which you turn 70½. Technically, the first withdrawal must be made by April 1 of the year following the year in which you turn 70½. If you took advantage of that grace period for your first required withdrawal, and you're now trying to figure the amount of your second required withdrawal, your calculation has one key twist: subtract the amount of your first withdrawal from your account balance.

Here's a comprehensive example to show how all of this fits in.

Karen was born in November 1933. She turns 70½ in May 2004, so 2004 is her first distribution year; she must make a required withdrawal for 2004. She decides to take advantage of the grace period, so she makes her first required withdrawal in March 2005.

To calculate the amount of her first withdrawal, she checks her account balance as of December 31, 2003. (She must use the balance as of the end of the year that immediately precedes her first distribution year.) Let's say the balance as of that date is $125,000.

Next, she looks in the uniform table to find the key factor that corresponds to her age. She's married, and her spouse is the same age as she is, so she uses the uniform table. Because she turned 71 in 2004, her first distribution year, she uses the key factor that corresponds to someone who's 71. The key factor is 25.3. Therefore, she calculates the amount of her first withdrawal by dividing $125,000 by 25.3. The answer is $4,941, and that's the amount she withdraws in March 2005.

Now it's early December of 2005. Karen has until December 31, 2005, to make a required withdrawal for that year, which is officially her second distribution year. How does she do it?

She checks her account balance as of December 31, 2004. It's $131,000. Next, she checks the uniform table to find the key factor that corresponds to someone who's 72. (Remember that Karen is 72 as of the end of 2005.) The answer is 24.4.

She's now ready to calculate the amount of her second required withdrawal. From her $131,000 account balance as of December 31, 2004, she subtracts the $4,941 that she pulled out in March 2005 to cover her first required withdrawal. The answer is $126,059. She divides that by 24.4. The answer is $5,166. That's how much she must withdraw by December 31, 2005, to meet the rules for her second minimum annual withdrawal.

Step 5: Calculating Future Withdrawals

In future years, the process is fairly routine, and you probably know it by heart now. You check the balance of your IRA as of December 31 of the preceding year. Next, check the table for the key figure that corresponds to your age (as of the end of the year for which you're making the withdrawal). You then divide the account balance by the key figure you find in the table. The answer is the amount you must withdraw, at a minimum, from your IRA for that year.

Keep in mind that you need not make your required minimum annual withdrawal in a single lump sum. You can withdraw money in installments—twice a quarter or every month, for example, or even more frequently—as long as all the money you withdraw for a given year equals the amount you're required to withdraw for that year. (You can also withdraw more than the minimum required; you just can't withdraw less than the minimum required.)

How the New Rules Help

What about those new rules that the Treasury put in place in 2001? The rules that were supposed to be so beneficial to IRA owners? They're built right into the formula you use for calculating your required withdrawals (and they're built into the examples in this chapter).

One key benefit is that, under the new rules, you can't outlive your IRA (assuming that you have favorable investment results over time). No matter how old you are, the table always gives you more time to make withdrawals and still keep money in your account to grow on a tax-deferred basis.

Here are a few examples.

- If you're 70, you use a key factor of 26.2 from the table. In effect, this means that you must withdraw only 1/26th of your account for that year; the rest remains in the account to provide for your later years.
- If you're 90, you use a key factor of 10.5 from the table. In effect, this means that you must withdraw only about one-tenth of your account for that year.
- Even if you're 115, the table tells you to use a factor of 1.8. You must withdraw only about half of your account for that year, and you may leave the rest for later years—however many remain.

The Impact in Dollars and Cents

How do the new rules help in dollars and cents? Suppose in our example that you're single, you're making your first withdrawal (for the year in which you're 70 as of December 31), and you have no beneficiary. Your account balance is $120,000 as of the previous December 31.

If the old rules were in effect, you'd have to use the single life table (in Appendix C) to find the key figure that corresponds to your age. It would be 16.0. As a result, you'd have to withdraw $7,500.

Under the new rules, however, you'd use the uniform table (in Appendix A) to find the key factor corresponding to your age: 26.2. As a result, you'd have to withdraw $4,580 from your account for that year.

In other words, in this example, you get to withdraw $2,920 less than you would under the old rules.

Other Benefits from New Rules

The new rules also assume that you have a beneficiary—even if you don't. As a result, you get to use a bigger key factor than you otherwise would. This means you get to make smaller withdrawals, cut your taxes, and leave more money in your account for later years.

Under the old rules, if you changed beneficiaries after you started taking required minimum withdrawals, the change could have required you to make larger withdrawals each year. That's because your withdrawals were generally based on the combined ages of you and your oldest beneficiary.

Therefore, if you added an older beneficiary, you might have had to use a smaller key factor in your calculations, prompting you to make bigger withdrawals. Under the new rules, you can change beneficiaries as often as you like, and it doesn't matter how old they are.

However, if you name a spouse as your beneficiary, and your spouse is more than ten years younger than you are, you get to use a larger key factor from the tables—and make smaller withdrawals.

Special Situations

Now you pretty much know how to calculate your required minimum annual withdrawals. Next we'll look at how the rules for minimum withdrawals pertain to some special situations that may apply to you.

When You Own More Than One IRA

First, the bad news. You may have to do a separate calculation for each of your traditional IRAs. The government generally says that you must figure out the minimum amount of money that must be withdrawn from each account. The amount may be different for each of your traditional IRAs.

Now the good news. Although you may have to do a separate calculation for each IRA, you need not make a minimum annual withdrawal from each; you can just make one big withdrawal. You simply add up all the amounts that you're supposed to withdraw from each of your traditional IRAs, then withdraw the total from just one account.

For example, suppose that Tina owns three traditional IRAs. The first is at a bank, from which she's required to withdraw $1,000. The second is at a credit union, from which she's required to withdraw $750. The third is at a mutual fund company, from which she's required to withdraw $500.

In this example, Tina can simply add up the amount of each required withdrawal—they total $2,250—and withdraw the entire $2,250 from just one account (from the bank, perhaps).

You May Not Need a Separate Calculation

Here's another key point. Remember that I said earlier you *may* have to make a separate calculation for each IRA you own. In many cases, however, you won't; you'll simply be able to add up all the amounts in all your accounts and use that sum to figure how much you must withdraw for a given year.

How can this be? After all, when you have more than one traditional IRA, aren't you required to make a separate calculation for each account? Technically, yes. However, under the government's new rules for required minimum withdrawals, many IRA owners are allowed to consult just one table—the uniform table (see Appendix A)—to figure out how much they must withdraw.

You use that uniform table in nearly all cases: whether you're single or married and whether you have one beneficiary, more than one beneficiary, or no beneficiary at all.

You may be able to add up the balances of all your traditional IRAs, refer to the uniform table to find the key figure or factor that corresponds to your age, and divide the total of all your IRA balances by that key figure. You can then decide from which IRA or IRAs you want to make that withdrawal.

An Exception for Spouse

There is just one exception. If your sole beneficiary for the entire year is your spouse, who is more than ten years younger than you are, you use a separate table—the joint life table (see Appendix B)—to figure out how much you must withdraw.

For example, suppose you have one traditional IRA at a brokerage, naming your spouse as your sole beneficiary. You also have a traditional IRA at a bank, naming your daughter as beneficiary. In this case, you'll have to calculate the required minimum withdrawal for each account. That's because you'll use different tables (and different key factors) to determine the minimum amount you must withdraw from each: the joint life table for the brokerage IRA in which your spouse is sole beneficiary, and the uniform table for the bank IRA in which your daughter is the sole beneficiary.

If you have more than one traditional IRA, here are the general rules.

- If your spouse is the sole beneficiary for the entire year on at least one of your accounts, and is more than ten years younger than you are, and you have another beneficiary—or no beneficiary—on your other IRAs, you can't lump them all together. Instead, you must make separate calculations for each account to determine the amount you must withdraw from each. You don't have to withdraw from each account; you may make just one giant withdrawal from one account to cover yourself.
- If your spouse is a beneficiary on at least one of your traditional IRAs, but is not more than ten years younger than you are, you can lump together all the balances in all the accounts to figure how much you must withdraw. Here, too, you needn't withdraw money from each IRA; you may make just one big withdrawal from one account.

A Note of Caution

Be careful about this "lump together" feature, however. Only certain people with multiple IRAs have the ability to make just one withdrawal from just one account and still meet the rules for required minimum withdrawals.

For example, you can't lump together (or *aggregate*) your minimum required withdrawals if you own one IRA and hold another as beneficiary. You must calculate the minimum withdrawal for each account.

Likewise, you can't lump together your minimum required withdrawals if you own an IRA and a retirement savings plan, such as a 403(b) account or 401(k) account.

Nondeductible IRAs

What if your traditional IRA includes nondeductible contributions? In other words, what if it includes original contributions for which you did not claim a federal income tax deduction? In that case, only a portion of each withdrawal will be taxable; the rest will be tax-free. The experts call this a *tax-free return of your basis in the account*.

Because you made these contributions with after-tax dollars, they cannot—and should not—be taxed again.

To make sure you won't be subject to double taxation, you'll have to do a little extra work. Go over your records to see how much in nondeductible contributions you made. Then do a basic calculation to see how much of each required minimum withdrawal will be taxed—and how much will escape tax.

You'll need three basic pieces of information:

1. How much in nondeductible contributions you made to the account
2. The value of your account before you make the withdrawal
3. How much you're going to withdraw

All you're really after is this: your nondeductible contributions make up how much of your IRA? Whatever the answer is, that's how much of your withdrawal will be tax-free. The rest will be subject to federal income tax (and perhaps state and local income tax, too, depending on where you live).

Here's an example that shows how the simple formula works.

Over the years, you made a total of $10,000 in nondeductible contributions to your IRA. Today, your IRA is worth $125,000. So your nondeductible contributions make up 8 percent of your IRA ($10,000 divided by $125,000 equals 0.08). This means that 8 percent of each withdrawal you make will be free of tax; the remaining 92 percent will be taxed.

If you withdraw $1,000, for instance, $80 will escape tax, while the remaining $920 will be taxed.

Applying the Rule to Required Withdrawals

Now let's see how this simple formula works when you have to make a required minimum withdrawal from your IRA and the IRA includes nondeductible contributions.

Suppose you turn 70½ in December 2003, and you make your first required withdrawal that month, too. The value of your IRA as of December 31, 2002, was $125,000 (which includes $10,000 of nondeductible contributions). The figure you must use from the uniform table is 26.2. Therefore, you withdraw $4,771 as your first minimum required withdrawal.

How much of that withdrawal is tax-free? Only $382. Why? Your $10,000 in nondeductible contributions make up only 8 percent of the value of your account (assuming that the account value on the date of withdrawal is still $125,000). As a result, only 8 percent of your $4,771 withdrawal is tax-free (0.08 times $4,771 is $382).

Annuities

Before you turn 70½, you may choose to receive annuity-style payments from your IRA. This might happen when an insurance company (or an insurer's intermediary) converts your IRA to an annuity and you begin receiving regular payments, probably monthly. For example, you may use the money in your account to buy a *joint-and-survivor annuity*, for you and your spouse, so that you'll receive regular payments over both your lives.

Must you worry about the rules for required minimum withdrawals? No. If you've used the money or other assets inside your traditional IRA to purchase an annuity (directly from an insurance company or through a middleman), and your annuity payments have begun by the time you turn 70½, you generally don't have to worry about the rules for making required withdrawals. Your annuity payments typically satisfy the rules automatically.

This assumes that your annuity meets the rules, and they're not hard to meet. For example, you must start receiving your payments before April 1 of the year following the year in which you turn 70½, the payments must be made at least annually, and the arrangement must be irrevocable (meaning the terms generally cannot be changed once the payments begin).

To make sure your annuity meets the rules, contact your insurer or its representative.

SEPs, SIMPLEs, and Employer-Sponsored Plans

Certain types of plans for small businesses (including the self-employed) may be linked to IRAs. These include the Savings Incentive Match Plans for Employees (SIMPLE plans); Simplified Employee Pensions (SEPs); and a type of SEP in which employees set aside part of their salary on a pretax basis, known as salary-reduction SEPS, or SAR-SEPs. (By law, you can't create a new SAR-SEP, but many such plans still exist, grandfathered under law.)

In most cases, the money that's saved in these plans on an employee's behalf goes into what is, in effect, a traditional IRA, not into a full-blown employer-sponsored plan. (That's one of the things that makes these plans so simple, especially from a record-keeping standpoint, for employers.) As a result, the rules for minimum required withdrawals from SEP-IRAs and SIMPLE-IRAs, for example, are the same as those for traditional IRAs.

For purposes of required minimum withdrawals, the IRS views these small business plans as if they were traditional IRAs.

[handwritten notes: Bill Murray / groundhog day for WEDS!! / add black binder & scott certif to powerpoint]

Roth IRAs

With Roth IRAs, there's no need to worry about required withdrawals. While you're alive, you never have to withdraw money from your Roth IRA. Period. Assuming you can afford it, you can keep the entire amount in your account, no matter how old you are.

This is one feature that makes Roth IRAs so attractive. It's also one reason why owners of traditional IRAs—even people who are already retired—think about converting their traditional IRAs to Roth IRAs.

If you inherit a Roth IRA, however, you must generally follow the withdrawal rules for traditional IRAs.

Trusts

[handwritten notes: Bob... copies of P&R requiring o/o & individuals I.D. in beneficiary designation]

Another benefit of the new rules for calculating minimum withdrawals has to do with naming a trust as the beneficiary of your IRA. The new rules clarify a key point: you can name a beneficiary of the trust to be the *designated beneficiary* of your IRA for purposes of calculating your required annual withdrawals.

In effect, this means that when you calculate your required withdrawals, you can "look through" the veil of the trust to identify one or more beneficiaries of your IRA.

This is an important point. In general, a beneficiary of your IRA must be an individual. That way, withdrawals following your death can be stretched out over a long period of time—over a beneficiary's lifetime, for example. The longer it takes to withdraw the money in your IRA, the more money that can remain in the IRA, growing on a tax-deferred basis.

However, if the beneficiary of your IRA is not an individual—if it's your estate, for example, or a charity—withdrawals must occur much sooner.

The new rules clarify that if you name a properly drafted trust as the beneficiary of your IRA, it can be treated as an "individual," allowing withdrawals to be stretched out over a longer period. That's because, under certain circumstances, you can "look through" the trust to use, as your designated beneficiary, the names of one or more people who are beneficiaries of the trust.

You (or your legal advisor) must make sure, however, that the trust meets all of the rules to qualify for this special treatment.

For example:

- You must provide your IRA trustee or custodian with documentation to show who, specifically, are the underlying beneficiaries of the trust. In other words, you've got to show the identities of the trust's beneficiaries.

- The trust must be a *valid trust* under state law.
- The trust must be an irrevocable trust (or become irrevocable after your death).
- Trust beneficiaries must be individuals.

Other Points on Required Withdrawals

Here are some other points to keep in mind about required minimum withdrawals.

Withdrawing in Advance

What if you withdraw money ahead of time? In other words, suppose you withdraw money from your traditional IRA before you're required to—before you turn 70½?

That's fine, but that won't give you any extra advantage for purposes of calculating your required minimum annual withdrawals. You still must withdraw at least a minimum amount, at least annually, starting for the year in which you turn 70½, and you still must use the IRS-approved methods.

Required Withdrawals May Not Be Required

It's worth emphasizing here that you'll be subject to the rules for required minimum withdrawals only if you turn 70½ and still have money in your traditional IRA.

You may avoid the rules for required withdrawals (which are still complex, even after the Treasury issued new and simpler rules) simply by withdrawing all the money in your account by the time you reach the magic age.

In other words, the rules for required minimum withdrawals don't apply to everybody who owns a traditional IRA; they apply only to those people who can keep at least a portion of their traditional IRA intact until they turn 70½.

For More Information ...

Ed Slott's IRA Advisor. The rules for IRAs are constantly being challenged and are often revised. These changes may come in response to proposals from lawyers representing IRA owners and beneficiaries, as well as from the financial services industry and others. To keep up with these changes—especially if you have a lot of money at stake—read *Ed Slott's IRA Advisor,* a monthly newsletter devoted to IRA issues. An annual subscription costs $79.95. To order, call 800-663-1340 or write: *Ed Slott's IRA Advisor*, 100 Merrick Road, Suite 200E, Rockville Centre, NY 11570. Also see Slott's Web site: <www.irahelp.com>.

Seymour Goldberg. A lawyer and CPA with Goldberg & Goldberg PC, in Garden City, New York, he is a nationally recognized expert on IRAs, including IRAs and trusts. He has written several books on these subjects, including *Estate Planning With Retirement Assets* and *How the Income in Respect of a Decedent Rules Work,* both published by IRG Publications. He also oversees a Web site that focuses on IRA and retirement plan topics for financial professionals: <www.goldbergreports.com>.

Brentmark Software, Inc. This Florida company, which creates software and other services for financial professionals, also maintains a Web site devoted to the new rules for required withdrawals. It includes links to the regulations themselves, news articles on the subject, and studies by experts in the field. This Web site is an excellent resource not only for the consumer but also for financial professionals: <www.NewRMD.com>.

Two experts on the subject of required minimum withdrawals. Slott and Goldberg have written *A Consumer's Guide to the Retirement Distribution Rules,* which explains the new rules and how they may apply to your situation. The Internet version costs $19.95, the print version $24.95. For information, see: <www.guidetorules.com>.

IRAs and Estate Planning

What happens to your IRA after you die? Don't leave its fate to chance. By making careful plans in advance, you can reduce taxes and make life easier on your beneficiaries. This chapter looks at some ways to integrate your IRA into your estate plan. We look at the importance of naming a beneficiary, some beneficiary options, the "stretch IRA" strategy, and the impact of federal estate taxes on your IRA.

Although traditional IRAs offer a lot of tax benefits while you're alive, they can trigger some tax and other complications after you die. That's why it's important to plan ahead, so that you can avoid—or at least reduce—the impact for you and your beneficiaries.

Naming a Beneficiary

If any money is left in your IRA when you die, who gets it? That's up to you. That's one of the neat things about IRAs: you get to name your own beneficiary. So in this respect, an IRA can be a helpful tool for planning your estate.

You don't necessarily need a complex trust agreement, and you don't necessarily need to hire a lawyer. You just choose the person to whom you want the money to go. When you die, the assets in your IRA then become the property of the beneficiary you named in the official beneficiary documents you filed with the financial institution handling your account.

What your will says doesn't matter. In fact, it doesn't matter if you have no will. An IRA is a kind of "will substitute." In other words, your IRA generally doesn't have to go through the *probate process*. Probate is the procedure by which your will is "proven" in a court; your assets are then distributed under the court's supervision.

If you have no will, the court oversees the distribution of your estate's assets according to the terms set by your state's laws.

The assets in your IRA, however, will pass automatically to your beneficiary, under terms of the IRA contract in much the same way that a life insurance policy's death benefit goes directly to the beneficiary upon the policyholder's death.

So with an IRA, beneficiaries can avoid the potential delays, expense, and publicity that can accompany the probate process in some states.

You can name whomever you wish as your beneficiary. It doesn't have to be your spouse. It doesn't have to be a relative. The point is that you get to choose.

Don't Forget the Beneficiary Form

With that freedom comes responsibility. Some IRA owners may repeatedly change their wills but forget to file beneficiary forms for their IRAs. This can be a big mistake. So don't forget about your IRA; it may be your single biggest asset. Before you do any detailed planning of your estate, complete a beneficiary form for your IRA. Be sure to name not just a primary beneficiary, but also a *contingent beneficiary,* sometimes called a *successor beneficiary.* This person can inherit the IRA if the primary beneficiary dies first.

There are important practical and financial reasons for taking these steps.

For example, if you fail to name a beneficiary, odds are that your IRA will become part of your probate estate and will have to be processed through a probate court. (This will also happen if you name your estate as the beneficiary of your IRA.) This can result in unwelcome tax and other consequences.

The point here is to name a beneficiary. Sure, the rules have changed. Under new regulations published by the U.S. Treasury, you as the IRA owner don't even need a beneficiary to calculate your required minimum withdrawals once you turn 70½; you still get to use the same table used by most IRA owners who have beneficiaries.

Nevertheless, you need to designate a beneficiary on the official form issued by your IRA trustee or custodian to ensure that the IRA doesn't go to your estate and instead goes directly to the beneficiary. (After consulting a lawyer who's familiar with the rules, you may also want to draw up a customized beneficiary form, one that best suits your needs.)

An IRA Check-Up

It's also a good idea to give your IRA a check-up from time to time, at least annually, to make sure the beneficiary form correctly reflects your wishes and is up to date.

For instance, an IRA owner who gets divorced may forget about the beneficiary form for her IRA and may accidentally leave the ex-spouse on the form as a beneficiary.

Another need for change occurs when a beneficiary or contingent beneficiary dies since your last check-up. In that case, you'll need to name a new one.

A periodic check-up can also let you know whether your IRA custodian or trustee still has a copy of your beneficiary form on file.

Remember that about 44 million households in America have some type of IRA. That's a lot of paperwork to keep track of. Remember too that financial institutions that serve as IRA trustees and custodians are merging all the time, so there's a greater chance of losing or misplacing IRA beneficiary forms.

For this and other reasons, you should ask the bank, credit union, brokerage, mutual fund company, insurance company, or other institution that handles your IRA for a copy of the beneficiary form. If you get a copy, and your beneficiary designation is current, all is well. However, if your IRA trustee or custodian can't find the form, ask for a blank and fill it in.

If the form your IRA trustee or custodian has doesn't suit your needs, you may want to shop around among IRA trustees and custodians until you find one with a beneficiary form and beneficiary policy that best suits you.

For example, suppose a bank serves as the trustee or custodian of your IRA. Under the bank's rules, you may name only one beneficiary. However, you'd prefer to have the option to name more than one beneficiary. You propose to file a customized beneficiary form with the bank, but it refuses to accept it. In that case, you may want to do some comparison shopping until you find another financial institution that either has a form you find acceptable, or will accept a customized form prepared by you in consultation with your lawyer.

Another potential problem may arise when a financial institution's beneficiary form allows you to name multiple beneficiaries but requires that if one of those beneficiaries dies, the account will be distributed *per capita* (to the remaining beneficiaries) instead of *per stirpes* (to the children of the deceased beneficiary).

For example, suppose that Sandra has three sons: Peter, John, and James. Peter dies, leaving John and James as beneficiaries. Sandra doesn't update her beneficiary form. When Sandra dies, the account is split between John and James—even though Sandra may have preferred that Peter's share of the account should have gone to Peter's children.

It's also possible that the financial institution that serves as your IRA trustee or custodian won't let a beneficiary name his or her own beneficiaries. Instead, the institution may require that the money in the account be paid out in full when the original beneficiary dies.

For these and other reasons, make sure that you complete a beneficiary form and check periodically that it's current and reflects your wishes as to how the account will be disposed upon your death. Also, consult a lawyer about the possibility of creating a customized beneficiary form, one that accurately reflects your wishes and will be accepted by the financial institution that handles your account.

No matter what the circumstances, be sure to keep copies of your important documents—including your IRA beneficiary forms and other estate planning paperwork—in a safe place so that your loved ones (and advisors) will know where to look when the time comes.

Changing Beneficiaries

Another point to keep in mind is that you, as the IRA owner, may change your beneficiary selection even after you turn 70½. Under the old rules, you had this option, but with strings attached.

Under the new rules, changing beneficiaries after you turn 70½ generally won't affect the amount you must withdraw, at a minimum, from your traditional IRA. Knowing this, you can change your beneficiaries as late as you want. This option may be especially important if you want to stretch out the life of your IRA as long as possible, so that the account not only generates a steady stream of income for you and your beneficiaries over time, but also builds up substantial wealth. If you originally named an older beneficiary, for example, you can switch to a younger beneficiary—without impacting the calculation of required withdrawals while you're alive—and have the account last longer after you die. That's because the new (younger) beneficiary, after inheriting your account, will be able to stretch out withdrawals based on a longer life expectancy.

If you have multiple beneficiaries, you may want to establish separate IRAs while you're alive, naming a separate beneficiary (and contingent beneficiary) for each. This may make things more convenient for the beneficiaries after your death: each beneficiary can choose, separately, what to do with an IRA. One may want to withdraw all of the money, another may want to withdraw in several annual installments, and another may want to stretch out withdrawals over a lifetime.

If you're married and have more than one beneficiary, creating separate IRAs while you're alive can also be convenient and helpful to each beneficiary after your death. For example, if your spouse is the sole beneficiary on one of your IRAs, your spouse may get to roll over the IRA and treat it as his or her own, postponing withdrawals until age 70½, without regard to what the other beneficiaries do with their accounts (they may want to commence withdrawals sooner, for example).

Still, it's helpful to know that even if you don't create separate accounts while you're alive, your beneficiaries have the right to do it by December 31 of the year that follows the date of your death.

State Law

Remember that if you live in one of the states that has community property or marital property laws, you may have to get your spouse's consent before you name, or add, a beneficiary who is not your spouse. Check with your IRA trustee or custodian—and your lawyer—to see how the laws of the following states may affect your beneficiary decision: Arizona, California, Idaho, Louisiana, Nevada, New Mexico, Texas, Washington, and Wisconsin.

Using a Trust

Although you can name your own beneficiaries for your IRA, and your IRA can pass directly to them after you die, in some instances you may be better off naming a trust to receive your IRA assets instead.

If you want your IRA assets to pass to children who are minors, for example, a trust can ensure that the assets are properly managed until the children are old enough to make decisions for themselves. (The trust can make payments to the person who oversees a custodial account for the minor.)

In fact, if you use a trust and name the right people as trustees, you can have some comfort knowing that the assets you've accumulated inside your IRA will be properly managed for all of your beneficiaries—whether they're minors or adults.

When the owner dies, the financial institution that serves as the custodian or trustee of your IRA can distribute funds to the trust, which in turn can issue payments over time to the trust's beneficiaries.

If the trust is set up in the right way, the payments to a trust beneficiary can be stretched out over the life expectancy of that beneficiary. In other words, the payments needn't be made in a lump sum, so the tax impact of each payment is reduced and more money remains to grow on a tax-deferred basis.

New rules published by the U.S. Treasury in 2001 clarify that if you name a trust as the beneficiary of your IRA, it can be treated, in effect, as an individual, allowing withdrawals to be stretched out over a longer period of time. That's because, under certain circumstances, you can "look through" the trust to use, as your designated beneficiary, the names of one or more people who are beneficiaries of the trust.

A Trust Must Meet Rules

You (or your legal advisor) must make sure, however, that the trust meets all of the rules to qualify for this special treatment.

Using a trust also gives the trustees the flexibility to speed up payments if the beneficiary needs more money.

Another advantage involves protection from creditors. Keep in mind that creditor protection for IRAs varies from state to state. For example, some states shield IRAs from the claims of creditors; other states have restrictions. If your IRA holds a substantial amount of assets, keep in mind that a trust may be able to shield those assets from creditor claims against your beneficiaries after you die.

In weighing these and other potential benefits of a trust, you must also consider the legal and other costs associated with creating and maintaining the trust. You'll have to pay to set one up and pay someone (or a financial institution) a fee, perhaps annually or more frequently, to administer the trust.

However, if you think a trust may suit your needs, be sure to consult a lawyer who is familiar not only with trust rules, but also with how trusts interact with IRAs. This is not a do-it-yourself matter; you need professional legal advice.

The Stretch IRA

When a hot new fashion trend sweeps the country, a major department store chain typically places an advertisement in the *New York Times* about the garment. "It's the latest thing. Of course we have it!" the ad proclaims.

So it is with the stretch IRA. Lots of financial advisors trumpet this as the latest new trend in the world of IRAs. It isn't new. In fact, technically, there's no such thing in federal tax law as a stretch IRA.

What the financial advisors—and their backers—are promoting is simply a strategy to take full advantage of the existing rules so that you may stretch your IRA over the longest possible period of time. As a result, the IRA can benefit not only you but also your beneficiaries—and their beneficiaries, too.

The stretch IRA concept essentially assumes that you'll take only the minimum required withdrawals from the IRA while you're alive, and that your beneficiaries will do the same. All the while, the investments inside the account will generate handsome returns. As a result, the IRA will not only generate a steady stream of income for you and your beneficiaries, but will also build up a potentially huge reserve of wealth, to be passed from generation to generation.

Keys to the Stretch

How? Here's the key. Because only the minimum amount is withdrawn each year, more money can remain in the account. Because the account can survive for decades, the investments inside it can grow and grow, all on a tax-deferred basis, like magic—and it's legal.

When the U.S. Treasury issued new rules in early 2001 for minimum required withdrawals from IRAs, the agency gave a boost to the stretch IRA strategy. That's because the new rules let most IRA owners and their beneficiaries make smaller withdrawals than before. As a result, even more money can remain in the account to enjoy tax-deferred, compounded growth.

Look at it this way.

You've got a big rain barrel in the backyard. You drain off only a few ounces a year. In the meantime, the barrel keeps filling up, every time it rains. After many years, the barrel may be filled to overflowing.

The possibility of stretching your IRA over generations—providing income for beneficiaries and building wealth inside the account all the while—can make IRAs a more appealing place to park your retirement savings.

This is especially so if you've built up wealth in your retirement savings plan at work, in a 401(k), 403(b), 457 governmental plan, or other such arrangement. Under a new federal law, you may move your money more easily from the plan you have at work to an IRA. So if you want to employ the stretch-out strategy, an IRA may be the only place to be; your employer-sponsored plan simply may not give you this chance.

With an IRA, however, you get a lot of flexibility and the chance for a stretch-out to boot. For example, suppose that Tony, the IRA owner, dies. His wife, Karen, rolls over the account and treats it as her own. It continues to grow, tax-deferred, until she turns 70½, when she starts withdrawing only the minimum amount each year. When she dies, the beneficiaries (her children) withdraw only the minimum amount over their life expectancies (which can be 40 years or longer). If the children die before their payout period has ended, *their* beneficiaries can withdraw over however many years are left. All the while, the account keeps growing in value: each generation of beneficiaries drains out only a little water at a time, while the rain barrel keeps filling up from every passing shower.

It's easy to see how the IRA can provide quite a legacy.

With proper planning, and *if* things turn out as forecast, this strategy can work to your advantage.

Beware of Sales Pitches

Many financial advisors are well aware of the potential benefits of this strategy and can help you take the steps you'll need to take full advantage.

Just be careful. In their sales materials regarding the stretch IRA strategy, some advisors use unrealistic assumptions in an attempt to lure your business.

Remember that financial advisors may benefit by having your IRA under their umbrella. That IRA can generate a steady stream of annual income for them, too, in the form of various management fees and expenses. There's nothing wrong with that, of course; everybody needs to get paid for the services.

However, when considering where best to place your IRA and how a stretch IRA strategy may benefit you, you should first take a careful look not only at the fees and other expenses a financial advisor may charge, but also at the underlying assumptions the advisor uses to attract your business.

For example, while the stretch IRA strategy may well prove helpful to you and your beneficiaries, it may not generate the enormous wealth that some financial advisors or institutions promise, according to an investor alert issued by NASDR, Inc., a branch of the National Association of Securities Dealers that oversees all U.S. stockbrokers and brokerage firms.

In some cases, sales presentations for stretch IRAs give hypothetical examples showing how much the IRA will generate in income over the years and, more importantly, how much value can be built up inside the IRA over that time—sometimes for periods of up to 90 years. Remember, however, that such huge dollar values depend on a lot of assumptions, and those assumptions may not be practical.

If the sales presentations you review don't make sense for someone in your circumstances, ask the salesperson to use more realistic assumptions. After the salesperson changes the figures based on assumptions that you feel are more realistic, check whether the new projected results are in line with your goals.

Even if the representative of a financial institution knows all about the stretch IRA strategy and how to put it to work for you, the financial institution that stands behind the advisor may have roadblocks in place that could cripple this strategy after you die (overly restrictive beneficiary forms, for example).

For these and other reasons, enlisting the help of a lawyer, accountant, or other trusted advisor who is familiar with the rules and how they may apply to you is a good idea.

The advisor can request that a financial institution adapt its policies to your needs, or can draw up a customized beneficiary form that you and the financial institution find acceptable. By taking these and other steps, the advisor can help ensure that your stretch-out strategy is not only implemented but also maintained after you die.

The Death Tax

Although your IRA will bypass probate court when you die, it may not escape federal estate taxes, sometimes called *death taxes.*

If your estate is large enough, the assets in your estate—including your IRAs—will be subject to the federal estate tax. The balances in your IRAs will be added to your estate for purposes of figuring any estate tax that's due.

That's not necessarily something to worry about. Most taxpayers don't have enough in assets even to have to think about the estate tax, as we'll discuss in a moment.

If the value of your estate exceeds the threshold, you can reduce it—and reduce or eliminate the tax—by earmarking some of your assets for charity. (Charitable donations escape the estate tax.)

Also, if you're married, any assets that are passed to your spouse, including your IRAs, will also escape the tax. In fact, if you earmark all your assets for your spouse, your estate will avoid the tax entirely in most cases. (Check with a lawyer to see if your spouse qualifies.) This is one reason you may want to name your spouse as your beneficiary.

The problem is that your spouse's estate may be taxed in the future, depending in part on its size, how the assets are arranged, and whether your spouse remarries.

PHASING OUT THE DEATH TAX

Whether your estate will be clipped by the onerous federal estate tax (also known as the "death tax") generally depends on the value of your estate in the year in which you die. Because this threshold is scheduled to rise in future years, fewer estates will be subject to tax:

Year	Estate-tax threshold	Top tax rate
2002	$1.0 million	50%
2003	$1.0 million	49%
2004	$1.5 million	48%
2005	$1.5 million	47%
2006	$2.0 million	46%
2007	$2.0 million	45%
2008	$2.0 million	45%
2009	$3.5 million	45%

Even if the value of your estate exceeds the threshold in the year you die, the estate may escape the death tax under certain conditions (if all your assets pass to your surviving spouse who's also a U.S. resident, for example, or if they all pass to charity). The estate tax is scheduled to be repealed in 2010, but may return in 2011.

Source: U.S. Congress

The point to keep in mind here is that the death tax is still around. All that talk you may have heard about estate tax repeal is hogwash. Congress frequently tries to abolish this unpopular tax—and frequently fails.

Estate Tax Relief

In its latest attempt in 2001, Congress approved legislation, later signed into law by President Bush, that provides extensive estate tax relief. Under part of this law, the amount of assets that may pass free of the estate tax has increased and will keep on rising. The law set the threshold at $1 million for people who die in 2002 and 2003; $1.5 million for 2004 and 2005; and higher after that, until the death tax is repealed for people dying in 2010.

What happens after that? The estate tax will return, like Dracula in a B movie. (So too will other provisions of the 2001 tax-cutting law.) Therefore, unless Congress takes action beforehand, the death tax will be back. Even if Congress and the White House can agree to make repeal stick beyond 2010, you still need to be concerned about the tax. After all, 2010 is a long way off; who knows what will happen before then?

There's also no telling how big your IRA may grow. It may be big enough already to trigger the tax despite the higher thresholds. And even if your IRA isn't enough, on its own, to trigger the tax, your estate may still be subject to the tax when the value of your IRA, your house, other retirement accounts, stocks, mutual funds, and other assets are taken into account.

If your estate is likely to be taxed (or if your spouse's will after you die, and if you plan to pass your assets on to your spouse), you'll need to consult a financial planner, estate-planning lawyer, or other professional advisor to help you map out some tax-saving strategies.

Planning for Liquidity

If you've got the bulk of your assets tied up in IRAs or other retirement savings plans, you'll also have to make sure the rest of your estate has enough in liquid assets—cash or assets that could be quickly converted to cash—so that sufficient funds will be available to cover tax, legal, administration, funeral, and other expenses that will come due at your death. (Your lawyer, planner, accountant, or other advisor will also help you plan for any estate or inheritance taxes your state may levy.)

Keep in mind, too, that your beneficiary must also be prepared to pay some income tax, either immediately upon inheriting your account or some years down the road. Why? Unlike some other assets, IRAs don't enjoy a *stepped-up basis* upon the owner's death, as do stocks and other such assets.

No Basis with IRAs

If you have a traditional *deductible* IRA, there is no tax basis in your account. So the entire value of the account, including your original contributions plus any earnings, will be subject to tax, either when you withdraw the money or when your beneficiary withdraws money after you die.

If you have a traditional *nondeductible* IRA, your account will have a basis for tax purposes, equal to the amount of after-tax dollars you contributed. But when you die, that basis will be carried over to your beneficiary; it won't be stepped up to the value of the account at your death.

So, if a wife contributed $5,000 in after-tax dollars to a traditional nondeductible IRA, and the account is worth $85,000 at her death, her spouse beneficiary will have a carryover basis of $5,000.

He won't have to pay income tax on the original $5,000 in contributions. But he will have to pay tax on any earnings the account has generated over the years. As a result, if he withdrew the entire $85,000 after the wife's death, he'd have to pay federal income tax on $80,000.

This point is important to keep in mind for your estate-planning purposes. In general, the money in your traditional IRA will be taxed at some point, either when you withdraw it or when your beneficiary does. So while IRAs offer some tax benefits during your "wealth-accumulation years"—either through tax deductions for your contributions, tax deferral on your account earnings, or both—any withdrawals made by you, or by your beneficiary after you die, won't be eligible for favorable capital gains tax treatment.

They'll be taxed as ordinary income. It's also possible that the assets in your IRA may wind up being taxed twice, according to two different tax systems. If your estate is large enough, your IRA could be subject to the federal estate tax. Then the person who inherits your IRA will eventually wind up paying federal income tax on any withdrawals (although the beneficiary may be eligible for a special tax break in such a situation).

It's vital to keep in mind that, if your IRA is your chief asset, your beneficiary may be forced to make withdrawals—and suffer income tax consequences—if no other cash is available to pay funeral and burial expenses, legal bills, final medical costs, and any other expenses that may typically arise as a result of your death—including the federal estate tax (and any state death tax that may be triggered).

For these and other reasons, it's a good idea for you to get expert help to put together a sound estate plan that can resolve thorny tax, legal, and other issues in advance of your death. Make sure, too, that your plan includes enough liquidity—enough cash or assets that can be converted quickly to cash—to cover expenses so that the IRA won't have to be tapped to pay these costs.

If your IRA is your chief asset and it's big enough so that estate tax will be triggered, consider establishing an irrevocable life insurance trust. If the trust is properly arranged, the proceeds from the policy can be used to pay the estate tax, leaving the IRA intact.

Using Your Exemption

Here's another estate-planning point you'll need to consider.

If you die and have enough assets to trigger the federal death tax, remember that a portion of your estate can escape the tax altogether. This *exemption amount,* or *threshold amount,* changes from time to time. For 2002 and 2003, for example, it's $1 million. With careful advance planning, you can choose which of your assets will qualify under this exemption. Your IRA? Your stocks? Your mutual funds? Whatever you decide, it's important not to waste this opportunity.

For example, suppose Harold dies, leaving his entire estate to his wife, Maude. He dies in 2002, and the value of his estate is $1.9 million, including $1 million IRA and other assets. Because he passes his entire estate to Maude, no estate tax is due (assuming that Maude qualifies for this break, and most surviving spouses do). Let's also assume that Maude dies in 2003 and that the value of the estate remains at $2 million. All the money is supposed to go to Harold and Maude's children, which is what the couple had planned on. In this example, however, Maude's estate will be slapped with the federal estate tax. As a result, a chunk of her estate—potentially thousands of dollars—will have to be paid out to cover the death tax; her heirs get the leftovers. Indeed, the beneficiaries may have to tap their IRAs, withdrawing a far larger amount than they had planned on, to pay the tax.

How can the death tax be avoided in this example? There are lots of potential strategies. Under one such plan, Harold names the children as beneficiaries of his $1 million IRA. When he dies, in 2002, the children get the IRA. (They were going to get it anyway; Harold simply decides to give it to them immediately upon his death.) The remainder of the estate—$900,000—goes to Maude. When Maude dies, no estate tax is due, because the value of the estate—$900,000 in this example—is less than the $1 million death tax threshold in effect for 2003. The children inherit the $900,000 free of estate tax. In this example, the children inherit the $1 million IRA and the $900,000 in other assets—all free from estate tax.

The point to remember here is that, with a little advance planning, you can reduce the impact of estate and other taxes on your heirs. Just make sure you hire a qualified lawyer (and other financial advisors) to get the job done.

Gifts to Charity

If you're inclined to give a portion of your estate to charity, consider donating your IRA instead of other assets in your estate, such as stock. Why? Remember that your beneficiaries won't qualify for the stepped-up basis on an inherited IRA. In addition, each dollar your beneficiaries withdraw from a traditional IRA will be subject to federal income tax, at their highest applicable rate. As a result, the IRA may wind up being the most heavily taxed asset of your estate.

However, your beneficiaries will be eligible to claim a stepped-up basis on stock or other securities they inherit. This benefit is especially valuable if the stock has appreciated in value over the years (you acquired it decades ago, and its value today is far higher than it was back then). Normally you might be tempted to give the stock to charity, fearing that, otherwise, capital gains tax will be owed on profit when the stock is sold. However, if you give the IRA to charity and the stock to your beneficiaries, they'll get the stepped-up basis, and the profit they realize when they eventually sell the stock will be taxed at more favorable capital gains rates. (Keep in mind, too, that until Congress changes the law, you can't give an IRA to charity while you're alive; you must first withdraw the money, pay taxes on it, then give it to charity.)

For More Information . . .

Marvin Rotenberg. Based in Boston, he is the national director of retirement services at Fleet Bank's Private Clients Group, responsible for creating distribution strategies from IRAs and qualified plans for clients with substantial net worths. For more information, see his company's Web site: <www.fleet.com>.

Seymour Goldberg. A lawyer and CPA with Goldberg & Goldberg PC in Garden City, New York, he is the author of *Estate Planning with Retirement Assets* (IRG Publications), *How the Income in Respect of a Decedent Rules Work* (IRG Publications), and *J.K. Lasser's How to Protect Your Retirement Savings from the IRS* (John Wiley & Sons). He also speaks nationwide to lawyers, accountants, and others on these subjects, and he oversees a Web site that focuses on IRA and retirement plan topics for financial professionals: <www.goldbergreports.com>.

Natalie Choate. A lawyer in Boston, she is the author of *Life and Death Planning for Retirement Benefits* (Ataxplan Publications). She is a nationally recognized expert on estate planning for IRAs and retirement plans and is especially knowledgeable about the use of trusts in receiving IRA distributions. For more information, see her Web site: <www.ataxplan.com>.

NASD Regulation, Inc. This organization publishes an Investor Alert about stretch IRAs entitled "Stretch IRAs—Too Much of a Stretch for You?" To read it see the organization's Web site: <www.nasdr.com>.

National Association of Securities Dealers. To obtain the disciplinary record of a registered stockbroker or brokerage firm, call the organization's regulatory branch toll-free at 800-289-9999.

6

Inheriting an IRA

This chapter shows what steps you should take when you inherit a traditional IRA. It explains the differences between inheriting a traditional IRA directly (from the owner) and indirectly (through the owner's estate). You'll find out how your options differ as a beneficiary depending on whether or not you're the IRA owner's spouse, what happens when there's more than one beneficiary, and a special tax break you may claim if the IRA owner's estate was subject to the federal estate tax.

You've just inherited an IRA. What should you do? What *must* you do?

These are important questions. Unfortunately, they may arise at exactly the wrong moment. Inheriting an IRA means that an IRA owner has died and you're a beneficiary. In other words, it means that, in all likelihood, a loved one has passed away and left you some or all of the assets in an IRA, and you've got to figure out what to do next.

The problem is that you're also probably still in mourning, still dealing with a loss in your life, still working your way through the grieving process. There may be dozens or even hundreds of tasks to tackle first, all associated with the death of a loved one—and now this.

So what will you do? Fortunately, things aren't quite as complicated as they used to be. Early in 2001, the U.S. Treasury published new regulations that make your choices, and your obligations, clearer and easier to understand. You still have some hurdles to jump, but not quite as many as before.

In general, your choices depend on exactly how you inherited your IRA and what your relationship was to the owner. This chapter outlines your options. Scan through the headings, pick which one applies to you, then read it to find out where you stand.

Keep in mind, too, that you're not alone. Billions of dollars are locked away in traditional IRAs. Many of these IRAs hold money that the account owner originally saved at work, through 401(k) or similar employer-sponsored retirement savings plans.

Now the money has been passed along to you. The bank, credit union, brokerage, or other IRA trustee or custodian may not be familiar with all the rules regarding inherited IRAs. Don't be surprised or discouraged about this. The rules can be fairly complicated, and the people who oversee your inherited IRA have enough to do simply keeping up with the changes that occur so frequently.

So it's worth knowing yourself what the rules are and how they work to protect yourself, maximize your opportunities, and minimize your taxes.

Inheriting through the Owner's Estate

The first thing you must determine is exactly how you've inherited the IRA from the account's original owner. There are two main possibilities.

1. You may have inherited the IRA directly, via the IRA's official beneficiary form as filed with the IRA's trustee or custodian. In other words, the IRA owner may have designated you as the beneficiary of the account on the IRA's official paperwork, so that the IRA passed directly to you without having to go first through the IRA owner's estate—and be processed through a probate court.
2. You may have inherited the IRA indirectly, through the IRA owner's estate. This generally means that the IRA did not pass directly to you as a result of being named on the account's official beneficiary form. Instead, the IRA passed to the IRA owner's estate, and you inherited after it was processed through probate.

How You Inherited Affects Your Options

This distinction is important. If the proper steps are followed, some assets don't have to go through probate. In other words, they don't have to be included as part of the decedent's probate estate. This means they don't have to pass to heirs according to terms of the decedent's will (or according to state law, if there is no will). As a result, beneficiaries of these assets may not have to deal with the potential delays, expenses, and publicity often associated with the probate process.

Instead, ownership of these assets can pass directly—and almost immediately—to the named, or *designated,* beneficiaries. The trustee or custodian of these assets may simply require that you show a death certificate to claim the assets.

As you can see, the key issue to resolve right up front is how you wound up with the IRA. The answer affects how much you must withdraw from the account and how soon you must withdraw it.

Stretch Out Limited

If the IRA was included as part of the decedent's probate estate, you won't be able to stretch out withdrawals over your lifetime. As a result, your options are severely restricted.

Even in this case, however, there is some relief. Under the old rules, if the owner's IRA passed to an estate and you were a beneficiary of that estate, the money in the IRA in many cases had to be withdrawn promptly, triggering a potentially huge tax bill.

Under the new rules, however, you may be able to stretch out withdrawals a bit longer. How long? The answer depends on exactly when the IRA owner died in relation to the owner's *required beginning date*. The required beginning date is April 1 of the year following the year in which the IRA owner turned—or was to turn—70½.

None of this matters if you just want to get your hands on all the money as soon as humanly possible. If that's the case, you'll face a huge tax bill, and you won't be able to stretch out the IRA by withdrawing only the minimum amount required each year over a number of years (allowing the money that remains in the account to keep growing on a tax-deferred basis).

How the Rules Work

However, what if you would like to withdraw only the minimum required amount, and you'd like as much money as possible to keep growing within the IRA tax shelter? In that case, assuming that the IRA owner died without naming a beneficiary and the IRA went directly to the estate, the rules work like this.

- If the IRA owner died before the required beginning date, the money must be withdrawn within five years. The experts call this the *five-year rule*. (Technically, it must be withdrawn by the end of the fifth year following the year of death.)
- If the IRA owner died on or after the required beginning date, you may withdraw the money over whatever remains of the IRA owner's single life expectancy.

The first option is fairly straightforward.

The second option requires some explanation. For example, if the IRA owner died at age 82, you must look up a government-published table known as the Single Life Expectancy Table. (You'll find it in Appendix C. It's also available in IRS Publication 590.)

In our example, the table shows that the IRA owner had a single life expectancy of 8.4 years. As a result, in this example, you'd have to withdraw the balance in the IRA within 8.4 years.

If the IRA owner in our example died last year, and the IRA's balance as of December 31 last year was $100,000, you'd simply divide that by 7.4 (the lower factor reflects that a year has passed). The answer is $13,514. That's how much you'd have to withdraw from the account, at a minimum, this year. You'd stick with this procedure in following years, subtracting the number 1 from the key figure you used in the previous year. For next year, for example, you'd divide the account balance as of December 31 this year by 6.4.

Bear in mind throughout this chapter that if you intend to stretch out withdrawals, withdrawing only the minimum required amount each year, you must be careful to calculate the correct amount. Otherwise, you face a punishing penalty of 50 percent. The penalty is equal to half of the difference between what you actually withdrew and what you should have withdrawn.

A Spouse Inherits Directly from IRA Owner

What if it turns out that the IRA owner completed a beneficiary form and named you as beneficiary? What are your options, and how do you calculate withdrawals?

In general, the answer depends on whether you were or weren't the IRA owner's spouse.

As the spouse beneficiary, you get the maximum flexibility—the most options.

Treat It As Your Own

For example, you as the spouse beneficiary can choose to roll over the inherited IRA and treat it as your own. This move is probably the best for most spouses who inherit an IRA. It means that you need not begin making minimum required withdrawals until *you* reach the magic age (April 1 of the year following the year in which you turn 70½).

From the IRS's standpoint, it's almost as if nobody had owned the account beforehand, as if you had owned it all along. In other words, it's your account.

You become subject to the usual rules regarding required minimum withdrawals. So you can postpone withdrawals until April 1 of the year following the year in which you turn 70½—no matter how old the IRA owner was at the time of her death.

If you, as the spouse beneficiary, have already reached 70½ at the time you inherit the IRA, you can start withdrawals in the following year, based on your own age.

Whatever the case, your very first step should be to name your own beneficiary or beneficiaries.

When a Spouse Remains a Beneficiary

A spouse doesn't have to roll over. Instead of rolling over the inherited IRA and treating it as your own, you can remain the beneficiary of the deceased IRA owner's account.

Why choose this option? Suppose you're a young spouse—under 59½. If you roll over the inherited IRA, treating it as your own, and you want to withdraw money, your withdrawals will not only be taxed but also could face a 10 percent penalty (because you're under 59½).

If, however, you remain as the beneficiary of the account and you need to withdraw money, it will be taxed, but you won't be slapped with the 10 percent early withdrawal penalty. Why? Under the rules, withdrawals made by a beneficiary from an IRA as a result of the IRA owner's death escape the 10 percent penalty.

When it comes time to calculate the amount of your minimum required annual withdrawal, use the government-published table, the Single Life Table. (See Appendix C, or IRS Publication 590.) In that table, find the key factor that corresponds to your age. Then divide the account balance by that key factor. The result is how much to withdraw, at a minimum, from the IRA.

For example, suppose that Rudy dies this year and leaves his IRA to his wife, Marlene. As of December 31 this year, the account balance is $100,000. Next year, Marlene turns 45. She checks the Single Life Table to find the key factor that corresponds to her age. It's 37.7. As a result, she divides $100,000 by 37.7. The answer is $2,653. That's how much she must withdraw, at a minimum, from the inherited IRA (which remains in Rudy's name, for the benefit of Marlene as beneficiary).

The next year, Marlene turns 46. She goes back to the table to find the key factor that corresponds to her age. It's 36.8. Suppose, for convenience, that the account balance as of December 31 of the prior year has stayed the same, at $100,000. Marlene divides $100,000 by 36.8. The answer is $2,717. That's how much she must withdraw, at a minimum, from the IRA that year.

She repeats this process year after year. In the year she turns 47, for example, she goes back to the table to find the factor that corresponds to someone who's 47. The factor is 35.9. She divides the account balance—as of

December 31 of the prior year—by 35.9 to find out the minimum amount she must withdraw.

There's one other twist to the rules. Marlene need not make any withdrawals. Assuming that Rudy died before his required beginning date, and Marlene remains as the beneficiary and doesn't need the money, she can postpone withdrawals until December 31 of the year in which Rudy would have been 70½.

As you can see, you as the spouse beneficiary have a lot of flexibility. There's no need to withdraw the money quickly, in a lump sum, and face unwelcome tax consequences. You can either roll over your spouse's IRA and treat it as your own or remain as the beneficiary on the account. Either way, you can stretch out or postpone withdrawals, reducing the tax impact of your withdrawals and allowing as much money as possible to remain in the account and grow on a tax-deferred basis.

Although you have many options, you should weigh each one carefully before you make your decision. Don't rush, and consult an accountant or other professional who's familiar with the rules and who can spell out the impact of each option and which option might best suit your needs.

Nonspouse Inherits Directly from Owner

If you are a nonspouse beneficiary, you can withdraw the entire amount in a lump sum if you so choose. However, you'll face huge tax consequences, and miss out on the chance to keep the IRA growing inside the IRA tax shelter.

Your best bet, then, is to postpone withdrawals as long as you can and to keep those withdrawals to a minimum.

Before we get to the calculations, there are some vitally important points to keep in mind regarding the technical aspects of running the account once you've inherited it.

You Can't Roll It Over

As a nonspouse beneficiary (you're the account owner's child, for example), you don't have the option to roll over the inherited IRA and treat it as your own. A spouse beneficiary has this option; you don't. If you do roll it over, the IRS will view the rollover as a *distribution*—a withdrawal—and the entire amount will be subject to tax and possible penalty.

Instead, you must maintain the account as a beneficiary account for the rest of your life. In addition, the name of the deceased IRA owner must remain on the account forever.

This point is crucial to keep in mind. You can't make the IRA your own as a nonspouse beneficiary. You can't put the money in your own IRA. Instead, be sure to have the inherited IRA renamed, or retitled, so that it reflects these two key points: it remains in the name of the deceased IRA owner, and it's for the benefit of you as beneficiary.

Suppose, for instance, that Arlen Jones dies and leaves his traditional IRA to his son, Derek. Derek cannot transfer or roll over the account into his own IRA. If he does, all sorts of tax trouble will arise. Instead, Derek instructs the IRA trustee or custodian to rename, or retitle, his father's IRA this way: *Arlen Jones IRA (deceased 4-20-02), FBO Derek Jones, beneficiary.*

This identifies the inherited IRA as a beneficiary IRA.

One key change: the account will carry the son's Social Security number, not the father's, because withdrawals will be taxed to Derek.

Keep It in the Name of the Deceased Owner

It's crucial, however, to keep the account in the name of the deceased IRA owner, registered for the benefit of the beneficiary. In taking care of the deceased IRA owner's estate, the executor or administrator (or lawyer or other professional) may try to do something different. Don't allow this, however. Just show him this chapter and have him consult a professional who understands how the rules work for inherited IRAs.

Remember that an IRA is a special asset; it requires special attention and has to be handled with sensitivity. The person who's handling the estate—an executor, administrator, lawyer, or accountant, for example—cannot simply make wholesale changes to the way the IRA is registered, as is possible with most other assets in the estate, such as stocks, bonds, and real estate.

Changing Investments

What if you want to change the way the money inside the IRA is invested? You can. As the beneficiary of an inherited IRA, you have the right to change the investment mix. You can do this either at the same place that was holding the IRA while the IRA owner was alive, or you can have the IRA transferred directly to another IRA trustee or custodian of your choosing.

However, you can't simply pull the money out and walk it down the street to a new trustee or custodian. The minute you withdraw the money, it will be treated as a fully taxable event. You'll have to pay tax—and possibly penalty.

Instead, do what's called a *trustee-to-trustee transfer.* This transfer allows you to move the money directly from one IRA trustee or custodian to another

IRA trustee or custodian without tax consequences. You can't touch the money in between.

Some financial institutions that serve as IRA trustees or custodians may give you static about this option. For example, the IRA owner may have had his IRA at a bank, invested in CDs. Upon the owner's death, you inherit the IRA and want to move it to a brokerage or mutual fund company where you have more investment options. The bank may say you can't do this. The truth is that you can. However, out of caution (and perhaps a lack of understanding of how the rules work in this area), the bank may advise you against such a move, or it may require you to sign a statement that indemnifies the bank against future legal problems in this regard.

If you encounter such resistance, contact a lawyer who is familiar with how the rules work and who can advise the bank or other trustee or custodian that what you plan to do is fine. (You may still end up having to sign a form indemnifying the original IRA trustee or custodian against future legal problems.)

Calculating Your Withdrawals

Now for the calculations. You are the designated nonspouse beneficiary, so named on the account's official paperwork filed with the IRA trustee or custodian. You have inherited the IRA directly from the owner. You've carefully followed the steps outlined earlier, so that the account is registered properly (it remains in the name of the deceased owner, for the benefit of you as beneficiary).

You've decided you want to withdraw only the minimum required amount each year, so you can stretch out withdrawals as long as possible. How do you figure out the amount of each withdrawal?

You get to stretch out withdrawals over *your* remaining single life expectancy. You measure it in the year after the IRA owner's death, then subtract one for each year thereafter. You start with the government-published table known as the Single Life Expectancy Table. In the table, find the key factor that corresponds to your age. You divide the account balance as of December 31 of the previous year by the key factor that you find in the table. That's how much you must withdraw, at a minimum, from your inherited IRA.

For example, suppose that Henry died last year. On the official beneficiary form for Henry's IRA, he named his daughter, Christine, as the designated beneficiary.

As of December 31 last year, the account was worth $200,000. Christine turns 40 this year. By checking the Single Life Expectancy Table, she finds the key factor that corresponds to her age of 40 this year. The key factor is 42.5.

To find out how much she must withdraw, at a minimum, from the account by the end of this year, she divides $200,000 by 42.5. The answer is

$4,706. That's how much she withdraws. Assuming, for convenience, that the amount in the account stays the same, there will be about $195,294 left in the account after she makes her withdrawal, so that amount can continue to grow on a tax-deferred basis until her next withdrawal is due.

How does Christine calculate the amount of next year's withdrawal? For convenience, let's assume that the account's value as of December 31 this year is $195,294. Christine doesn't return to the Single Life Expectancy Table to find a new key factor; she simply subtracts one from the key factor she used in the first year, which was 42.5. As a result, in this example, she divides the account balance of $195,294 by 41.5. The answer is $4,706. That's how much she must withdraw, at a minimum, next year.

More Than One Beneficiary

What if there are multiple beneficiaries? Here, the new rules give you a break, allowing you to stretch out withdrawals over a longer period of time.

Under the old rules, if one IRA had multiple beneficiaries, you had to use the age of the oldest beneficiary in your calculations. This caused problems. For example, if one of the beneficiaries was 82, another was 75, and another was 50, each beneficiary had to use the key factor corresponding to the age of the 82-year-old to calculate withdrawals.

Because an 82-year-old has a life expectancy of only 8.4 years (according to the government tables), the entire amount in the account had to be withdrawn in just 8.4 years, and the amount of each withdrawal had to be fairly big (triggering big tax consequences).

Under the new rules, however, each beneficiary can use his or her own life expectancy. As a result, using our earlier example, the 82-year-old can withdraw based on her own age over a period of 8.4 years; the 75-year-old can stretch out withdrawals longer, over a period of 12.5 years (because that's the key factor in the table that corresponds to this person's own age); and the 50-year-old gets to stretch out withdrawals the longest, over 33.1 years.

Separate Accounts

To take advantage of this favorable treatment, however, who gets what from the account must be clearly indicated. In other words, the account's paperwork must show what portion of the account goes to each beneficiary. For example, if there are three beneficiaries, the account's official paperwork must specifically show that each beneficiary gets a one-third share; or that one gets 60 percent, another gets 25 percent, and the third gets 15 percent, for example.

This can allow for maximum flexibility. The inherited IRA can be carved up into separate accounts, one for each beneficiary. In other words, each beneficiary can manage a separate account in the way that each sees fit.

One beneficiary may want to withdraw the entire share in a lump sum, perhaps to buy a house. Another may want to invest the money in short-term certificates of deposit and withdraw portions of the share in large chunks spread out over a few years, to meet income needs.

Still another beneficiary may want to invest more aggressively, mainly in stocks or stock mutual funds, for example. This beneficiary may withdraw only the minimum required amount each year and stretch out withdrawals over the longest possible period allowed under the rules.

Another reason to split an inherited IRA into separate accounts is to give a spouse beneficiary maximum flexibility. Suppose Mike names three beneficiaries for his IRA: his wife, Lauren, and their two children, Violet and Neil.

When Mike dies, Lauren can't roll over her portion of the IRA and treat it as her own, because that option is allowed only if the spouse is the sole beneficiary. In this case, there are multiple beneficiaries: Lauren, Violet, and Neil.

However, if the beneficiaries take careful steps to ensure that the inherited IRA is split into separate accounts, Lauren then has the option to roll over her share and treat it as her own. Remember that the splitting of accounts should occur no later than December 31 of the year following the year of the IRA owner's death.

Register the Account Properly

However, if multiple beneficiaries of a single inherited IRA each want to have separate accounts, each should take care to register his or her separate account properly.

Suppose, for example, that Terry O'Neill owns an IRA and lists on the account's official beneficiary form the names of his three daughters: Ashley, Allie, and Anna. He files the form with his IRA trustee or custodian, keeps a copy for his own records, gives a copy to his lawyer and financial advisor, and gives copies to his three daughters. On that form, he indicates that each will inherit one-third of his account.

Upon his death in 2003, the daughters want to have separate accounts. They want to withdraw money according to their own plans. In that case, they would direct the trustee or custodian of the IRA, in writing, to register or title each separate account in this way.

- Terry O'Neill IRA (deceased 6-30-03), FBO Ashley O'Neill (Social Security # 000-00-0001)

- Terry O'Neill IRA (deceased 6-30-03), FBO Allie O'Neill (Social Security # 000-00-0002)
- Terry O'Neill IRA (deceased 6-30-03), FBO Anna O'Neill (Social Security # 000-00-0003)

The point is that each of the separate accounts will be maintained in the name of the deceased IRA owner, for the benefit of a certain beneficiary.

A Grace Period

Keep in mind that the new rules governing required minimum withdrawals give beneficiaries a kind of grace period during which they can resolve, or clean up, some issues to make IRA management go more smoothly.

Suppose, for example, that Colleen is single and names three beneficiaries for her IRA: her son, Dean; her son, Riley; and a charity.

Colleen dies before her required beginning date. (In other words, she dies before April 1 of the year following the year in which she turns 70½.) Suppose, too, that, by December 31 of the year following the year of Colleen's death, the beneficiaries haven't established separate accounts under the detailed terms described earlier in this chapter. In this example, because one of the beneficiaries is not a person, the entire account will have to be withdrawn within five years. This could result in unwelcome tax consequences.

However, if the portion of the account that's supposed to go to the charity is actually paid to the charity by December 31 of the year following the year of Colleen's death, then Dean and Riley can stretch out required minimum withdrawals over a potentially much longer period. They'll use the single life expectancy of whoever is the oldest, Dean or Riley.

In this example, if Colleen dies on or after her required beginning date and all the other conditions apply, with the charity remaining as a beneficiary, then the money must be withdrawn over whatever is left of Colleen's life expectancy. If, however, the charity is paid out in time, Dean and Riley can stretch out withdrawals over the life expectancy of the oldest—Dean or Riley.

What if Dean is much older than Riley? In that case, the account will have to be drawn down over a fairly short period (Dean's life expectancy). However, if Dean *disclaims* the benefits he's supposed to get from the IRA—in other words, if he properly executes the legal paperwork required to effect an official disclaimer, in a timely manner—then the account can be stretched out longer, over Riley's life expectancy (which is longer than Dean's, because Riley is younger than Dean).

Another option in this example is simply to have Dean withdraw his portion of the account by December 31 of the year following the year of Colleen's death. That leaves Riley as the sole beneficiary, and he can stretch out the inherited IRA by taking minimum required annual withdrawals over his— longer—life expectancy.

If you're planning to use a disclaimer involving IRAs, be sure to consult a lawyer who is familiar with how the rules work. Disclaiming assets can be a tricky business; it's not a do-it-yourself project.

Inheriting an Inherited IRA

For convenience, a beneficiary of an inherited IRA may in turn name beneficiaries. That may seem a strange idea at first glance, but think of it. If you inherit an IRA and you die, who inherits that IRA? In other words, who inherits an inherited IRA?

Financial institutions have different policies on this point. Some may allow the beneficiary of an inherited IRA to name beneficiaries; some may not. This issue may be important for your peace of mind.

No matter what the financial institution says, this much is clear. The people who inherit an inherited IRA cannot stretch out withdrawals over their lifetimes; they can withdraw only over what's left of the original beneficiary's withdrawal period. (After all, the government doesn't want IRAs to stretch out to infinity; the government wants to get its tax cut sooner.)

Nevertheless, you—as the beneficiary of an inherited IRA—may want the comfort of knowing that your inherited IRA can pass directly to your own beneficiaries without having to go through your estate. In that way, your beneficiaries won't have to face the potential delays, expenses, and publicity that are often associated with the probate process. Instead, they can, in effect, step into your role as the new beneficiaries of the inherited IRA and continue making withdrawals under the same schedule you used.

Check with your financial institution (the outfit that serves as custodian or trustee of the inherited IRA) to see if it permits this option. If it doesn't, and the issue is important to you, see if you can get the policy changed. Otherwise, arrange to have the account transferred to another financial institution that allows for this option.

A Special Tax Break

If you inherit an IRA, or part of one, you may be able to claim a special tax break on your federal income tax return. Whether you're eligible depends on whether the IRA owner's estate had to pay the federal estate tax (also known as the federal death tax). If part of that tax was levied on the value of

PHASING OUT THE DEATH TAX

Whether your estate will be clipped by the onerous federal estate tax (also known as the death tax) generally depends on the value of your estate in the year in which you die. Because this threshold is scheduled to rise in future years, fewer estates will be subject to tax.

Year	Estate tax threshold	Top tax rate
2002	$1.0 million	50%
2003	$1.0 million	49%
2004	$1.5 million	48%
2005	$1.5 million	47%
2006	$2.0 million	46%
2007	$2.0 million	45%
2008	$2.0 million	45%
2009	$3.5 million	45%

Even if the value of your estate exceeds the threshold in the year you die, it may escape the death tax under certain conditions (if all your assets pass to your surviving spouse who's also a U.S. resident, for example, or if they all pass to charity). The estate tax is scheduled to be repealed in 2010, but it may return in 2011.

Source: U.S. Congress

the IRA you inherited, you may be able to claim a kind of offsetting tax break on your federal income tax return when you make withdrawals from the IRA.

Perhaps this seems a bit too complicated to bother with. Don't be fooled, however. If you're eligible to claim this tax break, it can help offset the tax you pay on the money you withdraw from your inherited IRA.

Don't assume, either, that the IRA owner didn't have enough in assets to trigger the federal death tax. Even if someone has relatively few assets, the owner may have salted away a tidy sum in an IRA—perhaps by investing regularly over the years in a 401(k) or other retirement savings plan at work, then rolling over the balance into an IRA. In some cases, the IRA may hold so much, it's enough all by itself to trigger the federal estate tax.

A Break That's Often Overlooked

So don't pass up this vital tax break, often overlooked by IRA beneficiaries. It's well worth your time to find out if the IRA owner's estate had to pay a federal death tax and how much of an income tax break you might be able to claim as a result.

This shouldn't be too difficult. Just call or write the person who served as the executor or administrator of the IRA owner's estate. Even if the executor or administrator can't help you (for whatever reason), he or she should be able to steer you to the lawyer, accountant, or other professional who was responsible for preparing and filing the various tax returns and other documents related to the IRA owner's estate.

Once you have that information in hand, use an accountant or other professional to see how much you may be able to deduct on your federal income tax return each time you make a withdrawal from the IRA you inherited. You may be pleasantly surprised; you may be enjoying this tax benefit year after year.

How the Break Is Figured

Here's how it works.

When an IRA owner dies, the executor or administrator of the IRA owner's estate generally must add up the value of all the things owned by the IRA owner: bank accounts, stocks, bonds, mutual funds, land, house, retirement accounts (including IRAs), life insurance policies, and such.

The executor or administrator then deducts certain amounts, such as outstanding mortgage debt, funeral expenses, the cost of administering the estate, and other items. If the value of the IRA owner's estate at that point exceeds a certain amount ($1 million in 2002 and 2003; $1.5 million for 2004 and 2005; higher in later years—see the previous page), it may be slapped with a federal estate tax. The tax rate can be as high as 50 percent, depending on which year the IRA owner died.

In effect, the IRS says that the IRA owner had a right to the money inside the IRA at the time of death, so it should be taxed (even though the IRA owner didn't withdraw it).

The problem comes when a beneficiary starts withdrawing money from the inherited IRA. Remember that when you withdraw money from a traditional IRA, it's subject to federal income tax. In general, every dollar you withdraw gets hit with income tax.

Avoiding a Double Tax

If you inherit all or a portion of an IRA that has already been hit with the federal death tax, the government acknowledges that the money inside the IRA shouldn't also be slapped with federal income tax when the beneficiary withdraws it. That would amount to double taxation, and it wouldn't be fair.

As a result, the government lets beneficiaries claim a tax break on their federal returns for the year or years in which they withdraw money from the inherited IRA. This tax break is what the experts call a deduction for "income in respect of a decedent," or the *IRD deduction.* In effect, it lets the beneficiary offset the impact of the death tax that was levied on the IRA in the first place.

Suppose, for example, that your Aunt Maria dies. She has an IRA valued at $100,000. You're the sole beneficiary. Maria's estate gets slapped with the federal death tax. Out of the total death tax paid, $50,000 is attributable to Maria's IRA.

What happens? If you withdrew the entire $100,000, you'd have to report the entire amount as income on your federal tax return and pay tax on it. As a result, you might owe about $30,000 in federal income tax (depending on your tax bracket and other factors).

In this example, however, you may be able to claim a $50,000 deduction on your income tax return (because Maria's estate paid $50,000 in death tax attributable to the IRA).

As a result, instead of paying tax on the full $100,000 you withdrew, you'd pay tax on only $50,000. In other words, instead of having to pay about $30,000 in federal income tax, you might wind up paying only about $15,000 (depending on your tax bracket and other factors), thanks to that special deduction. That's enough to pay for the cost of this book—and then some!

What if you decided not to withdraw the entire $100,000 in a lump sum but instead spread your withdrawals out in installments over time? You'd be able to spread the special tax break out in installments over time, too.

Other Points about the Tax Break

Here are a few other points to keep in mind.

- Calculating the amount of the federal death tax attributed to an IRA can be very tricky. In general, you must figure the estate tax one way, including the effect of the IRA, then figure it another way, without the effect of the IRA. The difference between those two figures gives you the amount of federal death tax that can be attributed to the IRA. This is easier said than done, however. You must learn an entirely different tax system—the federal estate tax—and learn how to apply the rules in calculating the tax. This calculation is best left to a professional.
- The calculation can become more complicated when the IRA has more than one beneficiary. In that case, each beneficiary may be entitled to a partial deduction related to IRD. In general, it's equal to the portion of the IRA that a beneficiary inherited.

- The calculation can be even more complicated when other items are included in the IRA owner's estate, subject to federal estate tax. These include such items as interest that's accumulated on U.S. Savings Bonds; amounts the decedent owned in employer-sponsored retirement savings plans, such as 401(k) plans; royalties from the sale of books; and amounts due under installment sales.
- To claim the deduction related to IRAs, you must itemize your deductions. In other words, you must list your deductions item by item instead of taking the lump sum "standard" deduction on your tax return.

For More Information . . .

Ed Slott. A CPA in Rockville Centre, New York, he is a nationally recognized expert on IRA distribution and tax planning. He edits and publishes *Ed Slott's IRA Advisor*, a newsletter that focuses on a variety of topics related to IRAs. It's published monthly and costs $79.95 a year. For subscription information, call 800-663-1340. Slott also oversees a Web site that includes detailed information on IRAs, including a public discussion forum that includes more than 800 questions and answers: <www.irahelp.com>.

7

Education Savings Accounts/Education IRAs
(Part 1)

This chapter shows whether you're eligible to save money in an Education Savings Account, how much you may save in any given year, when you may contribute, for whom you may contribute (including details for special needs beneficiaries), and where you should invest your money.

I take it back. All my carping about the restrictions on Education IRAs I hereby rescind. All my faultfinding about its limitations I do hereby utterly and completely revoke.

For the plain truth is that the Education IRA has been born again, and it's a lot better than it used to be.

An Education IRA is a kind of mini trust fund, or custodial account. You set it up at a bank, credit union, mutual fund company, or other financial institution and name a child or other minor as beneficiary.

You don't get a tax deduction for the amount you contribute, but the money the account earns isn't taxed each year, and the earnings escape tax altogether if they're used for the beneficiary's education expenses.

More People May Contribute More Money

Under a new law, the contribution limit is higher now, so you can set aside more money in the account every year.

The income limit on contributors has also been raised, so more people will be eligible to chip in.

You can now use the account to help pay expenses not only at college, but also at private and public elementary schools and high schools. You can even use the account to help buy computer equipment.

If that's not enough to convince you, consider this. The Education Savings Account even has a new name—the Education Savings Account.

Whatever you call it, you should check it out, because if you're saving for a child's education, this is a great choice. It need not be the only thing you use; there are plenty of other vehicles out there, including the souped-up Section 529 plan. Still, the Education IRA/Education Savings Account is worth considering, even if it's just one of the ways you have in which you save.

More People Will Save on Taxes

Will all these changes make these accounts more attractive to savers? Congress thinks so. In fact, when it approved the changes, Congress reckoned that far more people would take advantage of the tax-saving features of these accounts—so much so that the U.S. Treasury would pass up millions more in tax dollars as the years went by. By the government's own reckoning, the tax savings reaped by people using ESAs will start out at about $203 million in the first year the changes take hold, in 2002 (see below).

After that, the annual tax savings will grow steadily. By 2010, taxpayers who take advantage of these accounts will save themselves more than $1.13 billion, according to estimates by Congress's Joint Committee on Taxation. (Tax rules may change after 2010.)

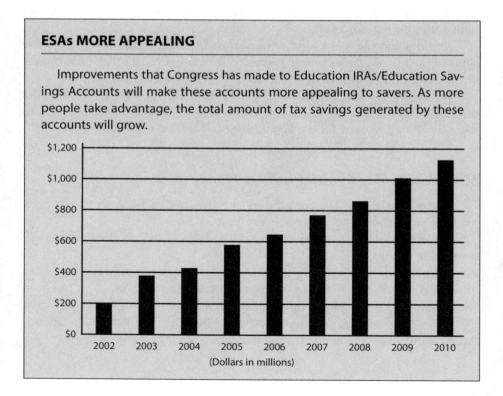

ESAs MORE APPEALING

Improvements that Congress has made to Education IRAs/Education Savings Accounts will make these accounts more appealing to savers. As more people take advantage, the total amount of tax savings generated by these accounts will grow.

(Dollars in millions)

Accounts Were Hobbled at First

What happened? When Congress created the Education IRA in 1997, it was hampered from the outset.

For example, the most you could contribute was $500 a year. That may be a lot of money to some people, but in the world of higher education, it's chump change—enough to buy a year or two of textbooks, if you're lucky.

That wasn't the only problem. Congress rejected proposals from some of its own members that would have allowed parents to use the account to help pay for private school tuition and other expenses.

Congress also limited the number of people who could take advantage of these accounts by setting income ceilings on contributors. In effect, Congress said, you could contribute only if you earned below a certain amount.

New Law Makes Improvements

Thanks to new legislation that Congress approved and President Bush signed into law in 2001, however, things have changed—really changed. For example:

- The contribution limit is now $2,000 a year—four times higher than the old limit. This means you'll be able to save a lot more. You still may not be able to cover all of a child's education expenses, but you'll at least get a pretty good start.
- The old law generally said that a single person could contribute only if income was less than $110,000; a married couple could contribute only if their income was less than $160,000. In other words, Congress built a marriage penalty into the formula. Two people living together would, in effect, be subject to an overall income limit of $220,000, but a married couple would face a stricter limit: $160,000.

    The new law eliminates the marriage penalty on Education Savings Accounts. The income limit for a single person remains at $110,000, but the limit for a married couple is now $220,000 (exactly twice that for a single person).
- Under the old law, any earnings you withdrew from the account would escape federal income tax and penalty only if you used the money for higher education expenses such as tuition, fees, and books at a college or university. Under the new law, however, your withdrawals may also be free of tax and penalty if you use the money to pay for education expenses at an elementary or high school—whether a private, public, or religious school. The old law talked solely about *higher education* expenses; the new law allows simply for *education* expenses.

- You can qualify for tax-free and penalty-free withdrawals for all sorts of education expenses—including the cost of a computer, connecting to the Internet (through an Internet service provider such as America On-line or the Microsoft Network), and computer software and games (so long as they're educational in nature).
- You can make tax-free withdrawals *and* claim other federal income tax breaks in the same year—through the HOPE and Lifetime Learning credits (assuming you're eligible)—as long as they're not all used for the same education expenses in the same year. The old law generally prohibited you from claiming these breaks in the same year.
- Contributions can be made in the same year for the same beneficiary to both an Education IRA/Education Savings Account *and* a state-sponsored college savings plan, also called a Section 529 plan. The old law generally penalized you for contributing to both.

Honoring Congressman Coverdell

Those are the highlights. Before we get into the details, there's something you should know first. When Congress created these accounts, it called them Education IRAs (even though these accounts had nothing to do with retirement).

In 2001, Congress made a lot of improvements to these accounts but kept the name the same. Shortly afterward, however, President Bush signed another piece of legislation changing the name of the accounts to Coverdell Education Savings Accounts. They are named for the late U.S. Sen. Paul Coverdell,

Sen. Paul Coverdell
(1939–2000)

a Republican from Georgia who long campaigned for tax-free accounts for education. Coverdell died in 2000 from a cerebral hemorrhage.

His name is now part of the law:

> The term *Coverdell education savings account* means a trust created or organized in the United States exclusively for the purpose of paying the qualified education expenses of an individual who is the designated beneficiary of the trust. . . .

Throughout this book, I occasionally use the old name—Education IRAs—mainly because some people opened these accounts before the name changed. However, I also use the term *Education Savings Accounts* (ESAs) because this is, after all, the new name, and the new name is starting to catch on with financial institutions and savers alike.

Now for the details.

Who May Contribute?

Just about anybody may contribute to an Education Savings Account. If you're saving for your child's or grandchild's education, that's fine. However, you may also contribute for somebody else: your niece, nephew, cousin—or your neighbor's newborn child.

The point is that the beneficiary need not be related to you in any way; as long as you meet the income limits (more on that in a moment), you can open an account and start saving.

In fact, a beneficiary may even contribute on his or her own behalf. (If you're the beneficiary and saving for yourself, however, you must make all your contributions before you reach age 18.)

You just contact a financial institution that deals in Education Savings Accounts, such as a bank, credit union, mutual fund company, brokerage, or insurance company. You then open an account on a beneficiary's behalf.

Before you sign up, make sure you read the plan agreement and disclosure statement carefully (the financial institution must give you copies), so that you'll understand fully any fees or other expenses that may be involved. Remember that fees and expenses can reduce the amount that your account earns, so shop around for reasonable terms.

When you sign up, you'll name—or designate—the beneficiary of the account and provide a Social Security number and date of birth. In other words, you'll write down the name of the child who'll benefit from the account.

You'll also name a *responsible individual*. This is generally the person who's in charge of the account and who decides how the money will be invested (after you make the initial choice). This person will also approve withdrawals from the account and decide whether to transfer the account to another member of the beneficiary's extended family should the need arise. The responsible person listed on the account will probably be you, although the financial institution may allow you to name someone else, such as the child's parent or guardian.

You'll also name a contingent beneficiary—someone who'll inherit the account should the designated beneficiary die. For example, you might simply list the name the designated beneficiary's brother, sister, niece, or nephew. If the contingent beneficiary—also called the *death designated beneficiary*—is under age 30 at the time the designated beneficiary dies and is a member of the designated beneficiary's extended family, that person can step in as the new designated beneficiary of the account. Otherwise, the assets in the account will simply pass to this person, who'll be responsible for paying tax on the earnings.

Keep in mind that you're free to contribute to an Education Savings Account even if you don't have earned income (generally money from a job) and even if you also contribute to another type of IRA or to a Section 529 college savings plan or prepaid tuition plan.

However, there are income limits. That's one thing that makes these accounts somewhat unusual. Some other types of education savings vehicles, such as the state-sponsored Section 529 plans, have no such restriction (although they have other limits).

Income Limits on Contributors

The income limits for Education Savings Accounts apply to the person or persons who are contributing the money, not to the beneficiary. The income limits are set fairly high. Still, they're out there, and they're a bit complicated. So, if your income is fairly high, and you're wondering whether you're eligible to contribute, you should know something about the limits and how they work.

There isn't just one limit that applies to everybody; there are various limits. Which limit applies to you depends on the filing status you use when you fill out your federal income tax return. For instance, one set of limits applies if you're single, while another applies if you're married and filing a joint return.

The rules would be easier if the limit was a fixed dollar amount depending on whether you were single or married. Unfortunately, they're more complicated than that. The limits involve ranges of income.

If your income falls below the range, you may contribute the maximum.

If your income falls within the range, you may make a partial contribution but not the full amount.

If your income falls above the range, you cannot make a contribution at all.

The Limits in a Nutshell

- If you're single and your adjusted gross income (AGI) is below $95,000, you may contribute the full amount: $2,000. If your AGI is at or above $95,000 but less than $110,000, you may make a partial contribution. If your AGI is at or above $110,000, you can't contribute anything.
- If you're married, filing a joint return, and your AGI is below $190,000, you may contribute the full $2,000. If your AGI is at or above $190,000 but below $220,000, you may make a partial contribution. If your AGI is at or above $220,000, you can't contribute anything. (Under the old law, the range for married couples was set far lower, between $150,000 and $160,000.)

These *phase-out ranges* are exasperating. Congress's Joint Committee on Taxation has repeatedly urged the full Congress to get rid of them.

Let's look at an easy strategy you may use to sidestep these silly rules (and complicated calculations) altogether.

How to Avoid the Income Limits

If you can't make a full $2,000 annual contribution to an Education Savings Account—because either your income falls within the phase-out range or exceeds the range—why not simply give $2,000 to someone who can?

Here's an example.

Fernando and Maria are married and want to contribute a full $2,000 to an Education Savings Account this year on behalf of their daughter, Felicity. However, because their income this year will total $225,000, they can't contribute anything; their income is too high.

What to do? They can skip this year's contribution, of course, but they'd waste a year. They could scramble between now and year-end to put in place all sorts of cunning steps to lower their income just enough so that they'll be eligible to contribute at least something.

Why bother? Instead, they give $2,000 to their trusted friend, Teresa, who's single and whose income of $50,000 is well below the limits. Teresa immediately places the $2,000 in an Education Savings Account, naming Felicity as beneficiary.

If you choose this route, just make sure that you don't accidentally trigger any federal gift tax complications. In general, the most you may give outright each year to any one individual is $11,000. If you're married and your spouse approves, you may give a combined $22,000 a year to any one individual. If you exceed these limits by a big enough margin, you could trigger problems under the federal gift tax system, and eventually you may have to pay an actual gift tax.

To avoid this problem, just make sure the money you give to a relative or trusted friend to place in an Education Savings Account won't, when combined with gifts you've made to that person, exceed the annual gift tax dollar limits. (Also, keep in mind that the annual limit is scheduled to rise with inflation over time. As of 2002, the limit was $11,000 for a single donor, $22,000 for married donors.)

Another option is simply to ask your employer to make the contribution instead. The law now allows employers, such as corporations and nonprofit organizations, to contribute to Education Savings Accounts, and they aren't subject to an income limit.

What Can You Contribute?

You may now contribute up to $2,000 per year per beneficiary in an Education Savings Account. That's a big change. Under the old law, the annual contribution limit was just $500. A new law enacted in 2001, however, provided a fourfold increase in the limit.

SAVING MORE IN AN ESA

Because the new law lets you invest more in an Education Savings Account each year, you can end up with more over time. For example, if you invested the maximum $500 a year under the old law, you'd wind up with $15,270. But if you invested the maximum $2,000 a year, as the new law allows, you'd end up with $61,078.

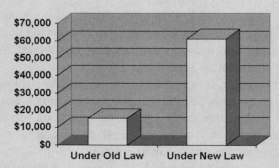

(Assumes you invest maximum amount each year for 19 years, earning an average of 5 percent a year.)

In a committee report that accompanied the 2001 law, Congress said, "Education Savings Accounts were intended to help families plan for their children's education. However, the Committee believes that the [old] limits on contributions to Education Savings Accounts do not permit taxpayers to save adequately. Therefore, the Committee bill increases the contribution limits to Education Savings Accounts."

What does this mean to you? Suppose that, under the old law, you invested the maximum amount allowed each year, $500. Assuming you invested for 19 years (starting with a child's birth) and earned an average of 5 percent a year, you'd wind up with about $15,270.

However, if you invest the maximum allowed each year under the new law, $2,000 (again assuming you invest over 19 years and earn 5 percent a year), you'd end up with about $61,078.

Higher Cap Means More Savings

In other words, under the new law, you might wind up with about $45,800 more in savings—thanks to the increase in the annual contribution limit.

That still may not be enough to cover the cost of four years (or more) at a public or private college or university, but you should be able to make a bigger dent in the overall bill than you could under the old law. Here's another way to look at it. Because you're able to save more, your child (or other beneficiary) may not be as burdened with loans upon graduation.

I've pointed out earlier, the Education Savings Account shouldn't be the only tool you use to save for college. You should also consider other savings vehicles—state-sponsored college savings plans, for example. Nevertheless, although it may be just one element of your overall savings plan, the Education Savings Account is a lot better than it once was.

Keep in mind that you may only contribute cash to an Education Savings Account; stocks, bonds, mutual fund shares, or other noncash items aren't allowed by law.

Limit Applies Per Beneficiary

Here's another key point to remember: the annual $2,000 contribution limit applies per beneficiary. No matter how many people may want to kick in each year—parents, grandparents, uncles, and aunts, for example—no more than $2,000 overall may be contributed in any single year for one beneficiary.

Here's an example. Tony and Karen live in Massachusetts and contribute $1,000 to an Education Savings Account this year on behalf of their daughter, Emily.

Emily's aunt, in Illinois, also kicks in $1,000 this year—either to the same Education Savings Account or to another for which Emily is the beneficiary. Emily's uncle in California, however, is out of luck. Although he wants to contribute to an Education Savings Account for Emily, he can't, at least not this year, because the overall contribution limit of $2,000 has already been reached.

As you can see, this rule can result in some problems. No national clearinghouse watches over beneficiaries, ringing an alarm when the $2,000 threshold is reached. That's something a parent or guardian must monitor. If you go over the $2,000 annual limit, you'll have made what the government calls an *excess contribution*, and you'll have to withdraw enough from the account promptly to ensure the limit is observed. Otherwise, you'll be slapped with a federal penalty on the excess contribution. How much of a penalty might you face? It's either 6 percent or 10 percent. (The language of the new law is not clear on this point, but the maximum penalty appears to be 10 percent.)

You don't have to invest right now. You have until the normal tax-filing deadline to make a contribution and have it count for the previous year.

In other words, you generally have until April 15—the usual deadline for filing your federal income tax return—to invest money in an ESA and have it count for the previous tax year.

This is a switch, by the way. The old law generally said you had to make the contribution by December 31 to have it count for that year; you couldn't delay until your April tax-filing deadline.

Don't Delay

Although the law technically gives you until mid-April to make a contribution for the prior year, why wait? The sooner you get started, the more your account may earn.

Suppose, for example, that you plan to invest in an ESA for 2004. If you invest the full $2,000 in early January 2004 and earn 5 percent interest, your account will be worth $2,100 by early January 2005.

Can't afford to invest the full $2,000 in a lump sum in January 2004? Why not instead invest each month, in 12 equal installments of about $166.67. At the end of the period, you'll wind up with about $2,055.

The point is that it's best not to delay, even though the law lets you. Start saving as soon as you can, so that your account can start earning money as soon as possible and so that you can get the benefit of compounding. Not only your principal can earn interest; your interest can earn interest, too, all on a tax-deferred basis.

For Whom May You Contribute?

You may contribute on behalf of any beneficiary. In other words, the beneficiary need not be related to you.

Just keep in mind that, in general, the beneficiary must be younger than age 18. In most cases, an ESA trustee or custodian technically cannot accept contributions "after the date on which [the] beneficiary attains age 18," federal tax law says. (The only exception: If it's a special-needs beneficiary, you may make contributions no matter what the beneficiary's age is.)

Remember that the contribution limit is $2,000 per beneficiary. You can have more than one Education Savings Account for the same beneficiary—one run by a parent, for example, and another run by a grandparent—but no more than $2,000 may be contributed in any given year on behalf of a single beneficiary.

UPON TURNING 18 . . .

How late may you contribute to an Education Savings Account on a student's behalf? There's lots of confusion over this point. Here's what the law says: "No contribution will be accepted after the date on which [a] beneficiary attains age 18."

In other words, you may make a contribution before the beneficiary turns 18, and on the day the beneficiary turns 18, but not after that. If your financial institution disagrees, refer to them to Section 530 of the Internal Revenue Code.

Multiple ESAs

You may also contribute to more than one Education Savings Account. If you're a parent, for example, you may have one ESA for each child. If you're a grandparent, you may have one ESA for each grandchild. You may also fully fund each account. If you have five children, you may contribute $2,000 a year for each of them for a total of $10,000 in annual ESA contributions. Just be sure that no more than $2,000 is contributed on behalf of each beneficiary, no matter how many people contribute and no matter how many Education Savings Accounts that beneficiary has.

In general, the shorter the time period during which you save, the smaller the potential benefit. The longer you save, the bigger the potential benefit.

Suppose, for example, that your first grandchild has just been born. You want to start saving immediately because you hope that the child will be enrolling in a private elementary school in five years—maybe the same one you went to—and you want to help pay for the cost.

If you contribute $2,000 a year for five years, earning 7 percent a year, you might wind up with about $11,500. That may be enough to pay for only one year's expenses, depending on the school. In other words, it may be a help, but not a lot of help.

Suppose, instead, that you save until the child turns 18, so that you can help with college expenses. If you start saving as soon as the child is born, you may be able to contribute $2,000 a year over 19 years. Assuming you earn 7 percent a year, you might end up with nearly $75,000. In other words, because you've saved for a longer period of time, your savings will have been allowed to grow on a tax-free basis all the while, with your interest earning interest. You'll end up with more money. It still may not be enough to cover a lot—perhaps a couple of years's college expenses—but it's a good start.

Students with Special Needs

There's one exception to the age 18 rule, and it deserves special note here: a beneficiary who has special needs.

If you have a child, grandchild, or other relative who has a physical, mental, or emotional condition that requires special services, odds are you have enough on your mind without having to worry about finances.

Nevertheless, medical, financial, and education counselors alike regularly stress the importance of developing a long-range financial plan for a child who has special needs—especially if the special needs will require years of extra care and attention.

If you're in this situation, or know someone who is, consider making an Education Savings Account part of the child's long-term financial plan. Why? The federal tax-cutting law approved by Congress and signed by President Bush in 2001 has a number of unique provisions designed to offer help to people with special needs.

- For most beneficiaries of ESAs, you may contribute to the account only until the beneficiary's 18th birthday. For a special-needs beneficiary, however, there is no such limit; you may contribute every year, and keep on contributing as long as the special-needs beneficiary is alive. In other words, you can start contributing $2,000 a year to an Education Savings Account when your special-needs beneficiary is a child, and keep on contributing $2,000 a year for that beneficiary as long as you're able. This could allow you to amass a tidy sum in the account over the years. Whatever is withdrawn from the account—original contributions as well as earnings—escapes tax and penalty, provided that it's used for the beneficiary's education expenses (which, fortunately, are broadly defined for special-needs beneficiaries).

- Normally, if any money (or other assets) is left in a beneficiary's account upon turning 30, the money must be withdrawn within 30 days—and pay tax and penalty (on the portion of the withdrawal that's attributable to earnings). Even if you don't make a withdrawal at that point, the IRS will take the position that a withdrawal has been made anyway, and the tax and penalty provisions will still apply. You generally can get around this restriction only by transferring or rolling over the money to the ESA of someone who's a member of the original beneficiary's extended family and is under age 30. In the case of a special-needs beneficiary, however, this restriction doesn't apply. As a result, you can keep money (or other assets) in the account of a special-needs beneficiary for as long as he or she is alive.

- As noted above, you can avoid the restriction for a beneficiary who turns 30 by moving the account balance to the ESA of another member of the beneficiary's family, provided that the new beneficiary is under age 30. For a special-needs beneficiary, however, this rule doesn't apply. If the new beneficiary has special needs, it doesn't matter if he or she is 30 or older. Suppose, for example, that Tom and Sarah use an Education Savings Account to help pay for the college expenses of their daughter, Melissa. When Melissa completes her education, money still remains in her ESA. Normally, you'd be able to avoid tax consequences only by rolling over the balance in Melissa's account to the ESA of another beneficiary who's related to Melissa and who is under age 30. However, if the new beneficiary has special needs, you may roll over Melissa's account balance even if that special needs beneficiary is 30 or older.

You don't have to be a genius to see the possibilities here. Saving $2,000 a year in an Education Savings Account probably won't cover all of the education and other services required by a person with special needs, especially if that person will need a lifetime of care.

Still, because of the unique benefits that an ESA offers, you'd be crazy not at least to consider using one as part of the long-term financial plan for a child with special needs. Bear in mind that, in general, you may make tax-free and penalty-free withdrawals from an ESA on behalf of a special-needs beneficiary to pay for tuition, fees, tutoring, special needs services, room and board, uniforms, books, supplies, computers, and other equipment—as well as "supplementary" items or services, such as extended-day programs—at a public or private elementary, middle, or high school. You may use the money tax-free and penalty-free for most types of college expenses, too.

What Are Special Needs?

What is a *special-needs beneficiary?* The law that created this loophole did not offer an explanation. However, a Congressional committee report gave the U.S. Treasury some guidance. As a result, whatever final regulations the Treasury eventually produces must define a special needs beneficiary "to include an individual who, because of a physical, mental, or emotional condition (including learning disability) requires additional time to complete his or her education."

That seems fairly broad and appears to give parents, grandparents, or others a great opportunity. You can save for years, potentially enough so that at least some of the educational and other expenses of a special-needs student will be taken care of.

Where to Invest Your ESA

Many banks, credit unions, brokerages, mutual fund companies, insurance companies, and other financial institutions offer Education Savings Accounts.

This is a big advantage. With some college savings vehicles, such as state-sponsored college savings plans (also known as Section 529 plans), your investment options are limited. With Education Savings Accounts, however, you have a lot of flexibility—and control. You decide how and where the money is to be invested. If you're not satisfied, you can move your money elsewhere. (The rules list only one investment restriction: an ESA can't be invested in a life insurance contract.)

Where to Invest

Exactly how you should invest the money depends on lots of factors, including your time horizon, your risk tolerance, and what the rest of your investment portfolio looks like. None of these factors is especially complicated. Here's a summary.

Your Time Horizon. One key factor in determining how you'll invest depends on how much time you have before you'll need the money. If you're saving for a newborn's elementary school education, you probably have only five or six years to invest.

As a result, you probably want to avoid stocks and other such invest-ments, because you probably won't have time to ride out an extended drop in the financial markets. Instead, you probably want to focus on more stable in-vestments, such as certificates of deposit, money market accounts, money market mutual funds, short-term Treasury securities (including inflation-indexed Treasury securities), and the like.

You won't get the kind of return you might get through stocks and other equity investments, but you won't have to worry about the market's short-term or near-term performance.

This also means you probably won't have much in the way of earnings. For example, suppose you start saving immediately, investing $2,000 a year for 5 years to help meet a child's expenses upon entering elementary school. In this example, you'll wind up with about $11,600 (assuming you earn 5 per-cent a year). That includes $10,000 in contributions, plus $1,600 in earnings. Depending on the school and the kind of expenses your child faces, $11,600 may not go very far. Still, you at least get to take advantage of the tax benefits of the Education Savings Account. Altogether, $1,600 in earnings escapes tax in this example. That might save you $400 or so in federal income tax alone, depending on your tax bracket.

However, suppose you start investing immediately and salt away $2,000 a year for 19 years to help meet a child's college expenses. In this example, you'll wind up with about $64,132 (assuming you earn 5 percent a year). That might go a lot further toward covering tuition, fees, and other costs. More-over, the longer time horizon means more tax savings. The $64,132 that you end up with in this example includes $38,000 in contributions, plus about $26,132 in earnings—all of which will escape tax if you use it for education expenses. That means a tax savings of about $6,533, depending on your tax bracket.

Your Risk Tolerance. In general, the more risk you're willing to take, the greater your potential return. The less risk you're willing to take, the smaller your potential return.

For example, if you're willing to invest in stocks (or other equity invest-ments, such as mutual funds that invest in stocks), you might be able to earn an average of 10 percent or more a year. Stick with more conservative options, such as bank CDs, and you might earn only half that (or less).

For example, if you invest $2,000 a year for 10 years in a stock mutual fund inside your Education Savings Account and average 10 percent a year, you'll end up with about $35,000.

If you invest $2,000 a year for 10 years in a bank CD or other such vehicle inside your Education Savings Account that earns 5 percent, you'll wind up with about $26,400.

In other words, you might wind up with about $8,600 more by investing in the stock mutual fund in this example. However, there's no guarantee you'll earn 10 percent a year. You could earn more or less than that; you might also lose money. If you invest your Education Savings Account dollars in a bank or credit union CD, you might not earn as much, but at least you can take comfort knowing you probably won't lose money, either.

Here's a general rule. If you have at least five to ten years before you'll need to tap your account, go with stocks or stock mutual funds (assuming you can stomach the risk). This should give your account enough time to rebound from any extended drop in the market. However, if you'll need to tap your account sooner, stick with something stable.

The Rest of Your Portfolio.   Exactly how much investment risk you can afford to take with your Education Savings Account dollars also depends on what the rest of your portfolio looks like.

If you can afford only to fund an Education Savings Account, then the factors I've already described—your time horizon and risk tolerance—will have great weight. However, if your Education Savings Account is only part of a broader portfolio that you're assembling to save for a child's college education, you may be able to take on more risk with your ESA. Your investment choices depend on whether your overall portfolio is diversified.

Suppose, for example, that you're investing for a child's college education in two ways: a state-sponsored college savings plan (Section 529 plan) and an ESA. You're putting $10,000 a year into the Section 529 plan's aggressive mutual fund (assuming the plan allows for this) and $1,000 a year into your ESA. In this example, you might want to reduce the overall risk of your portfolio by putting your ESA dollars into a short-term bond fund or another such investment that will offer some balance.

Monitor Fees, Expenses

No matter how you decide to invest your Education Savings Account dollars, watch out for fees and other expenses. Remember that $2,000 is the most that may be contributed to an ESA each year on a beneficiary's behalf, so fees play a bigger role than they would otherwise, because they can eat a bigger portion of your earnings.

Suppose, for example, that you set up an Education Savings Account at a bank and decide to deposit $2,000 into the account each year. The account earns 5 percent a year.

By the end of the first year the account might be worth $2,100—including your $2,000 original deposit, plus $100 in interest earned. However, if the bank charges you a $20 annual account maintenance or service fee, then a whopping 20 percent of what your account earns in this example will be eaten up by fees. (The bank might let you pay the $20 fee separately, instead of taking the money out of the account, but that's $20 extra dollars you'd have to kick in out-of-pocket.)

For this reason alone, it pays to shop around. Look for a financial institution that will charge you little or nothing in fees. That way, more of your money can remain in the account each year, growing on a tax-deferred basis. Even if all of the financial institutions you survey charge fees, some may agree to waive the fee under certain circumstances—if you agree to invest regularly, through direct deposit or automatic debiting of your bank account, for example, or if your balance reaches a certain threshold (maybe $5,000 or so). Some financial institutions may agree to waive the fee if all of the amounts in all your accounts—including taxable and nontaxable accounts—exceed a certain level, such as $10,000.

Keep in mind, too, that even though the law now allows a maximum annual contribution of $2,000, up from $500 under the old law, some financial institutions still may not offer ESAs. They can't earn enough—even with fees— to make the accounts profitable.

For More Information . . .

Horizon Publishing. The company that publishes the *DRIP Investor* and several other investment newsletters has launched another publication, *How To Pay For College.* It includes information about ESAs, 529 plans, and other vehicles you may use to invest for a child's or grandchild's education; details about scholarships and financial-aid packages; and tips to help a child or grandchild gain admission to the school of their choice. For more information or to subscribe, write: Horizon Publishing, 7412 Calumet Avenue, Hammond, IN 46324, or call toll-free at 800-463-6596.

The Vanguard group of mutual funds, Valley Forge, Pennsylvania. Their booklet, "New Ways to Boost Your College Savings," explains the benefits and drawbacks under the new tax law for ESAs, 529 plans, and other education savings vehicles. For a free copy, call 800-992-0855 or 866-734-4528, or see the company's Web site: <www.vanguard.com>.

Education Savings Accounts/Education IRAs
(Part 2)

8

This chapter explains the type of education expenses for which you can use your Education Savings Account, what actions may result in tax and penalty, and how to avoid tax and penalty—including the rollover option.

Using Your ESA for Education

This is the fun part. The law says you can make tax-free and penalty-free withdrawals from an Education Savings Account to pay for "qualified education expenses."

What does that include? What *doesn't* it include? It turns out that money you withdraw from an Education Savings Account can escape federal income tax (and penalty) altogether if you use it for most of the education expenses you can think of—whether for elementary school (including middle school or junior high school), high school, or college or postgraduate study.

Elementary and Secondary Education

Suppose you want to use an ESA to pay for a beneficiary's education expenses in elementary or secondary school. The law says you can make tax-free and penalty-free withdrawals from the account for any of the following items, no matter if the beneficiary is in a private, public, or religious elementary or high school (grades kindergarten through 12).

- Tuition, fees, academic tutoring, special needs services, books, supplies, and other such items (including services for special-needs students), as long as they're related to the beneficiary's enrollment or attendance "at a public, private, or religious school providing elementary or secondary education."

DOES HOME SCHOOLING COUNT?

Federal law says that you may be eligible to make tax-free and penalty-free withdrawals from an Education Savings Account if the money is used for certain education expenses at an elementary or secondary school.

What if you're teaching your children at home? In other words, what about home schooling? To find out if this would qualify, ask your state education authority; the answer may vary from state to state.

Why bother with state law? The U.S. government generally says that education expenses count if they are connected with a beneficiary's enrollment or attendance "at a public, private, or religious school providing elementary or secondary education (kindergarten through grade 12) *as determined under state law.*" [emphasis added]

In 2001, only 17 states considered home schools to be private schools, according to Sen. Tim Hutchinson (R-Arkansas). So only in those states are home schooled students eligible to take benefit from ESAs. Hutchinson has fought to rewrite federal rules so that any child who is home schooled would be eligible for ESA benefits.

- Room and board, uniforms, transportation, and "supplementary items and services"—such as extended-day programs—that are either required or simply provided by the public, private, or religious school.
- The purchase of any computer, computer technology, or computer equipment—including Internet access—as long as it's used by the beneficiary and his or her family "during any of the years the beneficiary is in school." What about computer software that mainly involves sports, games, or hobbies? Technically, the government doesn't view that as a "qualified elementary and secondary school expense" but will accept it if it's "educational in nature."

Time to Save Is Limited

One practical problem has to do with time. You probably won't have many years to save before a beneficiary reaches kindergarten. As a result, you probably won't have much time to watch your account really grow so that you'll have enough money to pay for all of a child's education expenses in the early years.

For example, suppose you start investing the maximum $2,000 a year as soon as a child is born. (Sorry, but you can't contribute to an Education Savings Account while the child is still in the womb; the child must be born before you can start saving, at least in an ESA.)

If you make five annual investments of $2,000 each and earn an average of 6 percent a year, your account will grow to about $11,950. That may be enough to cover the cost of kindergarten at a private school (depending on the school). There won't be enough, however, to cover expenses in future years.

You can keep on saving each year, but you probably won't have enough time to build up enough in the account to cover all the expenses you'd like.

That's one way to look at it—as a half-empty glass. Instead, look at it this way: every dollar you take from an Education Savings Account to pay for education is one less dollar you'll have to take from other sources to cover the same expense.

In other words, your Education Savings Account may not be enough to cover all the education expenses you have in mind, especially those in the early years. Still, it's a good way to save. The government is giving you tax incentives to save through an ESA, too. So why not take advantage of it?

Besides, who says the beneficiary will attend a private or religious school? If the child instead goes to a public school, you may not have to use as much each year of the money you've saved in the ESA. Instead, you may want to make only partial withdrawals and only occasionally—to pay for a computer and related equipment, for example—and keep the remainder in the account, so it can continue to grow on a tax-deferred basis for other education expenses later on, such as college.

College Expenses

Ever since Congress and President Bush expanded Education Savings Accounts to include expenses for kindergarten through grade 12, attention has been focused on exactly what kind of expenses count at those grade levels for purposes of tax-free and penalty-free withdrawals. It may be easy to forget that these accounts can still be used to pay for college expenses, too, at both the undergraduate and graduate level.

Here's what the law defines as higher education expenses.

- Tuition, fees, books, supplies, and equipment "required for the enrollment or attendance of a designated beneficiary at an eligible educational institution," the law says. It doesn't matter whether the student is enrolled on a full-time, half-time, or less than half-time basis. It also doesn't matter whether the student is in graduate or undergraduate work.
- Expenses for special-needs services in the case of a special-needs beneficiary that are incurred in connection with enrollment or attendance.
- Room and board up to, in general, the maximum you're allowed when you calculate the cost of attending a school for federal financial aid purposes. If the student lives in housing that's either owned or operated by

a college or university, you can count the actual room and board costs that the school charges the student.

- Amounts paid to buy tuition credits under a Section 529 prepaid tuition program, or amounts contributed to a Section 529 college savings plan, for the benefit of the ESA's beneficiary. In other words, if you save money in an Education Savings Account for your child, but later decide you want to move that money to a Section 529 plan on behalf of that child, you can do it—free of tax and penalty.

However, higher education expenses don't include expenses already covered by educational assistance that's excluded from gross income.

In other words, when figuring expenses, you generally must first subtract costs covered by scholarship or fellowship grants as well as by employer-provided educational assistance.

What about schools? In general, you may use an Education Savings Account tax-free to pay for expenses at just about any public or private college, university, or other such institution. The law lets you use ESA withdrawals tax-free and penalty-free for expenses at any "accredited postsecondary educational institutions offering credit toward a bachelor's degree, an associate's degree, a graduate-level or professional degree, or another recognized postsecondary credential."

Some specialized institutions, such as postsecondary vocational and technical schools, also count. The general rule is that the school must be eligible to take part in U.S. Department of Education student aid programs.

Tax Consequences of ESAs

If you run afoul of the rules, you run into a tax mess. Your best bet, then, is to stick to the rules, and this isn't hard to do. Just use the money that's in the account for the purposes described above (education expenses), and you're all set. The money you withdraw from the account will be free of tax and penalty.

Here's the general principle: if your withdrawal is equal to or less than the education expenses, you have no problem. If your withdrawal is greater than the education expenses, you face tax trouble.

Here are some examples to show how the rules work.

Using the ESA for Education

Suppose that Mike and Lauren save in an Education Savings Account so that their daughter, Violet, won't have to borrow as much to pay for her college education.

Mike and Lauren start saving the day the day Violet is born, make 19 annual contributions of $2,000 each, and earn 6 percent a year. They end up with about $71,600 stashed away in the ESA. (This includes $38,000 of contributions and about $33,600 of earnings.)

For convenience, let's just say that Violet attends four years of college and that each year costs about $25,000 for tuition, fees, room and board, and such, for a total of $100,000. That's far more than the $71,600 in the ESA. The family decides to use the entire $71,600 in the ESA to help pay the bill: $25,000 in each of the first two years and the remaining $21,600 in the third year.

In this example, there's no tax and no penalty. Why? In general, if the amount of expenses is equal to or greater than the amount of withdrawals, there are no tax consequences. That's what happened in each of the three years in our example above.

Even though $33,600 from the ESA represents earnings that have never been taxed, they won't be taxed now, either, because the family used the money in the right way: to pay for qualifying education expenses.

That's the beauty of the Education Savings Account, and that's why Congress created it and improved upon it. The idea is to encourage Americans to save for education.

Not *Using the ESA for Education*

Let's go back to our example but change the facts a bit.

Mike and Lauren save in an ESA for their daughter, Violet. They end up with about $71,600 stashed away in the ESA. (This includes $38,000 of contributions and about $33,600 of earnings.)

They're all set to help pay Violet's college expenses. Violet, however, has other ideas. She digs in her heels, says no to college, and decides she'll travel the world instead.

What happens? There are several possibilities. Suppose that Mike and Lauren give up and decide to withdraw the entire $71,600. There's no tax or penalty on the first $38,000, which represents original contributions. (This money has already been taxed; it can't be taxed again.)

What about the $33,600 of earnings? Violet, the beneficiary, must include the entire amount on her federal income tax return and pay tax on it. (She may also have to pay state and local income tax.) She must also pay a 10 percent penalty.

So suppose that Violet is normally in a 25 percent tax bracket, including federal and state income tax. In this example, she'll pay $8,400 in tax on the withdrawal, plus $3,360 in penalty. Altogether, she must fork over $11,760 in tax and penalty. As a result, out of the $71,600 saved in the account over the years, she's left with about $59,840.

Avoiding Tax and Penalty

Are there ways to get around this? Yes. Mike and Lauren can keep the money in the account until Violet turns 30, hoping that she'll change her mind. The money continues to grow on a tax-deferred basis in the meantime. Assuming that the entire amount in the account is withdrawn to pay for the kind of education expenses that meet the rules, it will be free of tax and penalty.

What if Violet doesn't change her mind? There are two options. Once the beneficiary turns 30, the money must be withdrawn within 30 days. Otherwise, the government will consider it to have been withdrawn at that point—even if it hasn't actually been withdrawn. In either case, there are tax and penalty ramifications. (An exception: If the beneficiary is a special-needs beneficiary, the money can remain in the account; there's no age 30 rule.)

The Rollover Option

There is an escape clause. It's the rollover option. The parents (or whoever is named as the responsible person on the account's paperwork) may roll over the money from Violet's ESA to the ESA of another beneficiary who's in Violet's extended family. Why bother? Moving the money to the ESA of another beneficiary who's in the same family lets you escape tax and penalty. And it shouldn't be hard to find another beneficiary; just about everybody in the original beneficiary's extended family counts.

ESCAPING THE PENALTY

Withdrawals from ESAs that aren't used for education expenses may still avoid the 10 percent federal penalty if they're made under any of these circumstances.

- In the event the designated beneficiary dies, the money is paid to her estate or to another beneficiary who's related.
- The beneficiary is disabled—the IRS requires proof that the beneficiary "cannot do any substantial gainful activity because of his physical or mental condition." A doctor must determine that the condition "can be expected to result in death or to be of long-continued and indefinite duration," the IRS says.
- The money is withdrawn because the beneficiary has received a scholarship or other such allowance (and the amount of the withdrawal isn't greater than the amount of the scholarship).

MEMBERS OF THE FAMILY

You generally may transfer or roll over money from the ESA of one beneficiary to the ESA of another beneficiary (free of tax and penalty) if the new beneficiary is a member of the old beneficiary's family. Who counts as family? The original beneficiary's spouse as well as the following people:

- The original beneficiary's child, grandchild, stepchild, or spouse
- A brother, sister, half-brother, half-sister, step-brother, or step-sister of the original beneficiary
- The original beneficiary's first cousin(s)
- The father, mother, stepfather, or stepmother of the original beneficiary
- The original beneficiary's aunt or uncle
- The original beneficiary's niece or nephew
- The original beneficiary's son-in-law, daughter-in-law, father-in-law, mother-in-law, brother-in-law, or sister-in-law
- Any spouse of anyone named above

For example, assuming that Violet's brother, Neil, also wants to go to college, the family can transfer the entire amount in Violet's account to an ESA with Neil as beneficiary. If he uses the money to pay for college expenses, the money will never be taxed or penalized.

What if Neil doesn't want to go to college either? The family can look for another family member to serve as beneficiary. Who counts as a member of Violet's family? Fortunately, the list is long. (See the table above for a comprehensive list of who counts as a member of the family.) The only restriction is that the new beneficiary generally must be under 30. (More about the rules for rollovers later in this chapter.)

Here, as before, the point is to use the money for the purpose that Congress intended: education. If you can't use up all the money you've saved in one beneficiary's ESA, you can move it to another beneficiary's ESA where it can be used up—without triggering tax or penalty.

Using Some of the ESA for Education

Suppose Violet uses some—but not all—of the ESA for education. What are the tax consequences? It's not the end of the world. Tax and penalty will be due (assuming that the rollover option isn't used). However, you'll need to hire an accountant to figure it all out. Back to our example.

Remember that Violet's parents have saved over the years so that there's now $71,600 in Violet's Education Savings Account. Violet goes to college for four years and uses her account to pay for her education.

For convenience, let's just say that her education expenses total $15,000 a year for each of the four years, and that there's no gain or loss inside her ESA in the meantime.

In each of the three years, she withdraws $15,000 to cover that year's college expenses. That leaves $26,600 for her fourth year. She withdraws the entire amount, using $15,000 to pay for her fourth year of college expenses, and spends the remaining $11,600 to help pay for that trip around the world she's been waiting to take.

What is the tax impact? Part of that money will be taxed (and penalized), and part of it won't. She must follow complicated formulas and complete special forms and worksheets. It would take the rest of this book to detail how all this works. The point is this: if you're using only some of your withdrawal to pay for education expenses, there will be tax consequences, and figuring out exactly how much tax and penalty you'll owe will be a nightmare. So get thee to an accountant, enrolled agent, or other tax professional.

HOPE and Lifetime Learning Credits

In general, the law said that if you withdrew money from an Education IRA to pay for a child's college expenses, you weren't permitted to take advantage, in the same year, of two unrelated tax breaks for college expenses: the HOPE Scholarship credit or the Lifetime Learning credit.

What was so bad about that? Both credits are valuable. With the HOPE credit, for example, you may claim a tax break of up to $1,500 per student per year for tuition and related expenses during the first two years of college. The Lifetime Learning credit generally allows you to claim a tax break of up to $1,000 a year ($2,000 for 2003 and later years) for education expenses incurred after the second year of study. (You can't take advantage of both the HOPE or Lifetime Learning credit in the same year; it's one or the other.)

Because of a new law which took effect in January 2002, a taxpayer may claim a HOPE credit or Lifetime Learning credit *and* get the benefits of tax-free withdrawals from an Education IRA—all in the same year, on behalf of the same student.

The only requirement is that the money withdrawn from the ESA can't be used for the same education expenses for which the credit is claimed.

Remember that you must clear several hurdles to be eligible for either the HOPE or Lifetime Learning credit. One key obstacle involves your income.

If you're single, for example, you generally may claim the full credit if your adjusted gross income is below $40,000, a partial credit on income between $40,000 and $50,000, and no credit on income above $50,000.

If you're married and filing a joint return, you generally may claim the full credit if your AGI is below $80,000, a partial credit on AGI of between $80,000 and $100,000, and no credit on AGI above $100,000. (These dollar limits may rise with inflation each year.)

How Rollovers Work

Rollovers come into play in two key ways: when you *want* to move money and when you *must* move money.

When You Want to Move

Once you open an Education Savings Account with a trustee or custodian (typically a financial institution), remember that you're not locked in. You are free to move the money to another financial institution if you want.

You may want to move if the original trustee or custodian suddenly decides to increase sharply the annual fee it charges or otherwise boosts the expenses associated with your account. You may also want to move if the mutual fund in which your ESA dollars are invested merges with another, changes portfolio managers, and suffers a performance drop as a result.

There are lots of possibilities. The point to remember is that you're not limited to just one ESA trustee or custodian; you may move your ESA from one place to another—from a bank to a brokerage, for example, or from a mutual fund company to a credit union.

You'll have to do the same sort of research you did when you first opened your account, comparing such factors as fees, interest rates, investment flexibility, and investment performance. Another factor to weigh is whether the trustee you plan to leave (and the trustee you plan to move to) will charge some kind of account-closing fee and how much you might have to pay.

When You Must Move

You may do a rollover not just to an account for the benefit of the same beneficiary, but also for the benefit of another beneficiary (who's a member of the same extended family).

For example, suppose you have a daughter, Rosemary, and a niece, Tori. You've been contributing to an ESA for Rosemary for her college education.

When she's 17, however, she tells you that she's sick of school; she wants to travel—indefinitely. Tori, however, plans to go to college to study medicine.

If you leave the money in the account, it must be withdrawn when Rosemary turns 30. Otherwise, the government will view it as a withdrawal within 30 days of that point.

To avoid tax consequences, you may transfer or roll over the money from Rosemary's ESA to another ESA for Tori. You can do this as long as the new beneficiary is a member of the old beneficiary's family and is under the age of 30.

Rules for Rollovers

You may roll over the money from one ESA to another without tax consequences. Rolling over money generally means that you withdraw it from one ESA and deposit or invest in another. But rollovers have strict limits. For example:

- You must complete a rollover within 60 days to avoid tax trouble. The clock starts ticking the day you withdraw the money; you must complete the rollover within 60 days after the date of withdrawal.
- You're allowed only one rollover per ESA during any 12-month period. This is a rolling 12-month clock, not a calendar year. If you withdraw money from an ESA on November 1 for a rollover, you can't do another rollover before November 1 of the following year.

Special Situations

There are some other special situations you should be aware of.

- If a spouse or former spouse receives the ESA under a divorce or separation agreement, there's no tax consequence. After the transfer, the spouse (or former spouse) gets to treat the ESA as his or her own. The ESA's beneficiary can be changed, and the beneficiary's interest in the account can be transferred to a spouse (or former spouse) as a result of the divorce.
- In general, you may roll over an ESA from one beneficiary to another only if the new beneficiary is under age 30. However, if the new beneficiary is a special-needs beneficiary, age won't matter; the rollover can be made without fear of tax consequences.

For More Information ...

The College Board. The College Board has lots of information about the cost of higher education, as well as information about scholarships, grants, student loans, and other sources of aid. For details, see the organization's Web site: <www.collegeboard.com>.

IRS Publications. For more information about federal income tax benefits associated with saving for college—including Education Savings Accounts, Section 529 plans, the HOPE and Lifetime Learning credits, and the deduction for college costs and student loan interest—see IRS Publications 17 and 970. For your free copy, visit your local IRS office, call the agency toll-free at 800-829-3676, or see its Web site: <www.irs.gov>.

Joseph F. Hurley. This New York accountant runs a Web site about Section 529 plans. You can compare, in detail, all the plans offered by the various states and compare Section 529 plans to Education Savings Accounts: <www.savingforcollege.com>. Hurley has also written a book, *The Best Way to Save for College: A Complete Guide to 529 Plans,* available at bookstores and at Hurley's Web site.

The National Association of State Treasurers. This organization has a Web site that includes information about state-sponsored college savings plans and prepaid tuition plans, plus links to various states's plans: <www.collegesavings.org>.

U.S. Savings Bonds. To check the current rates, call 800-487-2663. For more about the EasySaver plan, call 877-811-7283. For more about the education feature of U.S. Savings Bonds, write: Savings Bonds, Parkersburg, WV 26106, or see: <www.savingsbonds.gov>.

IRS Publications. For information on the tax aspects of using savings bonds for college, see IRS Publications 550 and 970. For free copies, visit your local IRS office, call the agency toll-free at 800-829-3676, or see its Web site: <www.irs.gov>.

9

The Roth IRA

This chapter explains what Roth IRAs are, how they work, and how you can take advantage of their benefits. It shows how you may contribute more money than ever before to a Roth IRA and outlines the rules that allow people 50 or older to save additional amounts. We also look at a new tax credit that will encourage many low-income and moderate-income people to open and contribute to Roth IRAs.

Still haven't decided whether to open a Roth IRA? Here's a point that may change your mind. Many of those who already own Roth IRAs are about to start cashing in on the Roth IRA's chief attraction: tax-free withdrawals.

That's right: tax-free.

Not just their contributions—earnings, too. In fact, they're in a position to withdraw everything in their accounts if they want, and they won't pay one cent in federal income tax.

How can this be? One of the key requirements for being able to take money out of a Roth IRA tax-free is that the account must be open for at least five years (and that you must be 59½ or older).

The earliest you could open a Roth IRA was January 1998. You needn't be an accountant to figure it out. By opening a Roth IRA in early January of 1998, for example, someone could withdraw all or a portion from the account—free of tax and penalty—as of January 2003 assuming he or she is 59½ or older.

Other people who believed in the Roth's advantages in the early years will be doing the same as time passes. Once the five-year clock stops ticking, they can pull money out of their accounts and enjoy the fruits of their savings, all without federal tax or penalty.

Now are you convinced? Then go ahead. Open a Roth IRA. It may be one of the best financial moves you'll ever make.

What's the big deal? The Roth IRA isn't really an IRA at all. It's more a savings account than a retirement account. But it's a super-duper savings account, one that offers all sorts of advantages. It's called the *Roth IRA* because

William V. Roth, Jr.

Congress wanted to honor its creator, former Republican Sen. William V. Roth, Jr., of Delaware, the tireless champion of IRAs.

No matter its origins, you should take advantage of the Roth IRA as soon as you can. When the Roth IRA first became available, some critics scoffed. They were convinced that the federal government would never allow money to build up on a tax-deferred basis, then be withdrawn entirely tax-free. Well, here we are, and the people who refused to listen to the critics, who believed in the Roth IRA and opened their own account in the early years, are poised to cash in if they haven't already.

Roth IRAs and Traditional IRAs Differ

In a way, Congress modeled the Roth IRA after the old, traditional IRA. But the Roth IRA and the traditional IRA are so different that it's hard to imagine they came from the same family.

For instance, when it made the Roth IRA, Congress stripped away one of the sweetest benefits that the traditional IRA offers—your ability to claim a federal income tax deduction for the amount you contribute. So score one for the traditional IRA.

In making the Roth IRA, however, Congress also scrapped some of the worst features of the traditional IRA. For example, with the Roth IRA, your withdrawals won't be taxed or penalized at all as long as you meet the rules. (With traditional IRAs, withdrawals are almost always taxable and may be penalized, too.)

You May Contribute after 70½

What's more, there's no requirement whatsoever to withdraw any money at all from a Roth IRA. So there's no need to start fretting when you turn 70½, no need to grind through all of the tables and formulas that come with making the required minimum withdrawals from a traditional IRA.

As a result, you can leave all your money in your Roth account if you choose, just passing it along to the next generation. Your beneficiaries generally will be able to withdraw money tax-free from the Roth account that they inherit from you.

What's that you say? You want to contribute to a Roth IRA *after* you turn 70½? Feel free. You won't have to stop making contributions just because of your age, as you do with a traditional IRA.

So score one for the Roth IRA. In fact, score lots of points for the Roth IRA, because it's simply an incredible way to save money.

How a Roth IRA Works

Okay, so what exactly is a Roth IRA? How, precisely, does it work? The answer is pretty simple. It has to do with taxes. When you contribute money to a Roth IRA, you get no immediate tax benefit. But the money inside your Roth IRA will grow year after year without being taxed. When you withdraw the money, it doesn't get taxed then, either, if you meet the rules.

That's the summary. Here are the details.

To understand the benefits of a Roth IRA, first think about how the traditional IRA usually operates. When you contribute money to a traditional IRA, you may get a federal income tax deduction. In other words, for the amount of money you contribute, you may be able to deduct an equal amount on your federal income tax return.

The traditional IRA has another key tax benefit: as the value of your IRA grows over time, the growth doesn't get taxed. As a result, all the interest, dividends, and the increase in value of whatever investment is inside your IRA— stocks, bonds, or mutual funds, for example—grow year after year without being nicked by taxes.

The only time that the money in your traditional IRA *is* taxed is when you take it out.

No Tax Deduction

The Roth IRA works like a traditional IRA in some ways but not in others. One big difference is that the money you contribute to a Roth IRA is *not* tax-deductible. That's an important point to keep in mind. You get no up-front tax break by contributing to a Roth IRA.

However, as the value of your Roth IRA grows over the years, the growth isn't taxed, the same as with a traditional IRA.

The really big difference between traditional IRAs and Roth IRAs comes at the end: as long as you meet the rules, the money you withdraw from a Roth IRA comes out free of tax.

That's the real beauty of the Roth IRA. With the traditional IRA, your withdrawals are taxable (to the extent you withdraw original *deductible* contributions and earnings; *nondeductible* contributions aren't taxed when withdrawn). Also, the withdrawals get taxed as ordinary income. The higher your income tax bracket, the higher the tax on your withdrawals.

With the Roth IRA, however, there is no tax. Your money grows tax-free while it's in your account, and it comes out tax-free when you withdraw it.

That's why experts call the Roth IRA *back-loaded* or *back-ended*, because important tax benefits come at the end.

Seems simple enough? Well, almost. As with any deal that sounds great, there's some fine print to consider.

For the Roth IRA to work best, you've got to know the rules—and you've got to follow them. Trip up and you will trigger tax problems.

How Much You May Contribute

You may open a Roth IRA at just about any bank, credit union, brokerage, mutual fund company, insurance company, or other financial institution that handles IRAs, and you must contribute only cash (stocks, bonds, and other assets aren't allowed as contributions).

As long as you have *compensation*, generally money from a job, you may contribute—and you may kick in more money than ever before. (For details on what does and doesn't count as taxable compensation, see Chapter 1.)

When Roth IRAs were created, the most you could save was $2,000 a year.

However, because of a big tax-cutting and pension-reform law enacted in 2001, the annual contribution limit is rising: $3,000 a year through 2004, $4,000 a year for 2005 through 2007, and $5,000 for 2008. After that, the limit may rise with inflation.

That's not all. In general, older people may now save an additional amount each year by making catch-up contributions to their Roth IRAs. The higher contribution limit applies to people 50 and older; it's intended to let these people catch up with other workers who had the chance to save in their younger years.

As a result, under the new law, if you're 50 or older in a given year, you'll be able to contribute an extra $500 a year through 2005, and an extra $1,000 a year for 2006 and later years.

This means that, if you're 50 or older, you'll be able to save far more than you could otherwise. By 2008, for example, you'll be able to save a total of $6,000—triple the limit under the old law. Remember, too, that how old you are doesn't matter, because there are no age limits for Roth IRAs. As long as you have compensation—such as money from a job—you may contribute.

Suppose you and your spouse turn 50 in 2008. Each of you starts saving in a Roth IRA (one account for each spouse), and you decide to sock away $6,000 a year per spouse, for a combined total annual investment of $12,000 a year for 15 years. You each earn 10 percent a year. At the end of the period, you'd have about $419,400.

What if the limit were still $2,000, so that the most you could invest (combined) was $4,000 a year? You'd end up with only $139,800. That's not bad. However, in this example, you'd be able to sock away almost $280,000 more by taking advantage of the higher limit and catch-up contribution.

Income Restrictions

Sound great? A key restriction may affect you: how much you may contribute each year is limited by your income.

- If you're single, you can make a full contribution to a Roth IRA if your adjusted gross income (AGI) for the year is less than $95,000, only a partial contribution if your adjusted gross income is between $95,000 and $110,000, and no contribution if your AGI is above that phase-out income range.
- If you're married and filing jointly, you can make a full contribution if your adjusted gross income is less than $150,000, a partial contribution if your AGI is between $150,000 and $160,000, and no contribution if your AGI is higher.

Calculating Your Contribution

What if your AGI falls within the ranges above? You may ask a Roth IRA trustee or custodian to figure how much of a contribution you may make, or you may try it yourself.

- Subtract $95,000 (if you're single) or $150,000 (if married filing jointly) from your AGI.

OLDER WORKERS CAN SAVE MORE

A new federal law means you may save more each year in a Roth IRA. If you are 50 or older, you may make an additional catch-up contribution for that year, allowing you to save even more.

Year	Annual limit (for everyone)	Catch-up (for age 50+)	Overall limit (including catch-up)
2002	$3,000	$ 500	$3,500
2003	$3,000	$ 500	$3,500
2004	$3,000	$ 500	$3,500
2005	$4,000	$ 500	$4,500
2006	$4,000	$1,000	$5,000
2007	$4,000	$1,000	$5,000
2008	$5,000	$1,000	$6,000

The maximum you may contribute in a given year is the amount listed above or your total taxable compensation for that year, whichever is less. You may contribute to a traditional and a Roth IRA for a given year, but your overall contribution cannot exceed these limits.

- Divide the result by $15,000 (if single) or $10,000 (if married filing jointly).
- Multiply the result by whatever the maximum contribution is for the year ($3,000 or higher).
- Now subtract the result from whatever the maximum contribution is for the year. (Round it up to the nearest $10. If it's more than $0 but less than $200, round it up to $200.) That's your contribution limit for the year.

Remember that these dollar limits are the *only* limits you use to figure whether you can contribute to a Roth IRA.

In other words, whether you are covered by a pension plan at work doesn't matter. As a result, if your AGI for a given year is less than the dollar limits shown here, you can contribute to a Roth IRA regardless of whether you are covered by a pension plan at work. (Pension plan coverage *does* matter if you're trying to figure out whether you can make a deductible contribution to a regular IRA.)

Limit Applies to All IRAs

Here's another key point to bear in mind.

The most you can contribute to *all* IRAs is whatever the maximum contribution limit is for the year. In other words, the government looks at all your IRAs—including Roth IRAs and traditional IRAs, deductible and nondeductible alike—and applies a single annual contribution limit across the board.

What does that mean? Suppose Sue is single and under age 50 at the end of 2003. The maximum contribution for Roth IRAs/traditional IRAs for that year is $3,000. In that case, she can't contribute $3,000 to a traditional deductible IRA, $3,000 to a Roth IRA, and $3,000 to a traditional nondeductible IRA. The overall annual limit per person on IRA contributions for that year is $3,000. Period. As a result, in this example, Sue could divide her $3,000 among the accounts or invest the entire $3,000 in just one account—the Roth IRA, for example. No matter what she chooses, however, she cannot contribute more than $3,000 in total for that year.

Some of the Roth IRA rules can work in your favor. For instance, you have up until April 15 to contribute to a Roth IRA and have it count for the preceding tax year. (Just be sure to let your Roth IRA custodian or trustee know which year your contribution is for, and remember that the April tax filing deadline is the drop-dead deadline for IRA/Roth IRA contributions.)

How to Avoid Tax

Okay, so what about all those juicy tax benefits you've heard so much about? They're available, but they come with a few strings attached.

In general, withdrawals from a Roth IRA are fully tax-free. There's no federal income tax and no penalty to pay.

However, you generally escape the tax traps only if you meet two conditions: if you withdraw money after your Roth account has been open at least five years, *and* the withdrawal occurs under at least one of these circumstances.

- You reach age 59½.
- Proceeds are paid to a beneficiary or your estate on account of your death.
- You've become disabled.
- You use the money for expenses as a *first-time homebuyer.*

The Five-Year Rule

If your withdrawal meets these conditions, the tax experts will call it a *qualified distribution,* and it will escape federal tax and penalty entirely.

How does the five-year rule work? Just count the years. If you open an account today, this year will be your Roth IRA's first tax year. As a result, you

WATCHING THE CLOCK

The five-year clock starts ticking in the year for which you made your first contribution. This is important to keep in mind, because it gives you some flexibility.

For example, you generally have until mid-April to make a contribution to a Roth IRA and still have it count for the prior tax year.

Suppose Andrea makes a contribution in April 2006 and, on the paperwork at her financial institution, makes sure that the contribution is for the 2005 tax year.

In that case, the five-year clock starts ticking in January 2005. As a result, the first time Andrea may withdraw earnings from her Roth IRA free of tax and penalty is January 2010 (assuming she's met the other requirements for a tax-free and penalty-free withdrawal).

can start making withdrawals without tax or penalty on the first day of the sixth tax year (as long as you meet the other requirements, too—you're 59½ or older, the withdrawal is made on account of your death or disability, or you use the money for first-time homebuyer expenses).

Who Can Benefit

All sorts of people can benefit by these rules, such as workers who want to provide a tax-free source of income for themselves in retirement, or elderly people who don't need the money during their lifetimes and want to provide a tax-free source of income for their children or grandchildren. (These groups meet the age requirement; all they must concern themselves with is keeping their accounts open at least five years.)

Young people who are saving for their first home may benefit, too.

Suppose Tom has just graduated from school. He's just started working, and he wants to buy a house after he's saved for several years. He saves $3,000 a year for eight years, earning 8 percent a year.

If he put the money in an ordinary taxable account each year, and is taxed at a 15 percent federal rate, he'd end up with about $32,600.

If he put the money in a Roth IRA, however, he'd end up with nearly $34,500. In other words, in this example, he'd have nearly $2,000 more simply by using the Roth.

Why? The money you earn in a taxable account (such as a bank savings account or a CD) gets taxed each year. However, the money you save in a Roth

RULES FOR FIRST-TIME HOMEBUYERS

Withdrawals from Roth IRAs generally escape taxation and penalties if you use the money for expenses as a first-time homebuyer. Here's a summary of the rules governing first-time homebuyers.

- The maximum lifetime withdrawal is $10,000 of earnings.
- The money must be used within 120 days of withdrawal to buy, build, or rebuild the first principal residence for either you, your spouse, or any child, grandchild, or ancestor of yours or your spouse.
- If the 120-day rule can't be met because of delay in acquiring the residence, you may put the money back into your Roth IRA without triggering tax consequences.
- Expenses may include "reasonable" settlement, financing, or other closing costs.
- The house need not be the first you've ever owned. A taxpayer qualifies as a first-time homebuyer if the taxpayer (or spouse) hasn't had an ownership interest in a principal residence during the two years before acquiring the new house.

IRA is generally tax-free. In other words, tax on the earnings is postponed until you withdraw the earnings. If you withdraw the earnings to help buy a house, however, and you meet the first-time homebuyer rules, the earnings come out tax-free.

In our example, the additional $2,000 saved through the Roth IRA isn't huge, but when you're borrowing to buy a house, the bigger the down payment you can make, the smaller the amount you'll have to borrow. The less you borrow, the smaller your monthly payment.

When Withdrawals Are Taxed

What if you don't meet all of the conditions for making tax-free withdrawals? Your withdrawal will be taxed.

Remember, however, that only the earnings portion of your withdrawal gets taxed, not your contributions. (This makes sense, if you think about it. You contributed after-tax dollars, so there's no reason for your contributions to be taxed again.)

Another twist here also works to your advantage. The IRS assumes that your withdrawal from a Roth IRA comes *first* from contributions, *then* from earnings. This is a great feature, because it not only saves you taxes but also saves you some paperwork.

Here's an example. Say you contribute $2,000 today to a Roth IRA. Two years from now, the account has grown in value to about $2,500. If you withdraw $1,000 at that time, none of it gets taxed.

Why? Because the IRS figures you withdrew the money from your original contribution, not your earnings. (Remember: When it comes to Roth IRAs, contributions come out first, then earnings.) Because your original contribution in this example totaled $2,000, and you withdrew only $1,000, there's no tax.

Here's another neat twist. If you have several Roth accounts to which you made contributions, and you make a withdrawal before you're supposed to, you lump together all your Roth IRAs to help you figure out what part of your withdrawal (if any) is going to get taxed.

The 10-Percent Penalty

What happens if you don't make a *qualified distribution?* In other words, what happens if you pull all the money out of your Roth IRA before you're supposed to—not just your original contributions, but also your earnings.

In that case, you'll have to report the earnings as income. The earnings will be treated as ordinary income subject to federal income tax.

For example, if you save $3,000 this year in a Roth IRA, it grows to $3,100 by next year, and you withdraw the entire amount, you'll be taxed on $100. Why? The original contribution of $3,000 isn't taxed, but the $100 in earnings are taxed. That's because, in this example, you didn't meet the rules for withdrawing earnings tax-free. (Your account must be open for at least five years, and the withdrawal must occur on or after you're 59½, on account of your death or disability, or because you're using the money for first-time home-buyer expenses.)

In this example, will the earnings also face a 10 percent penalty?

Not if an exception applies.

This means that the earnings from your Roth IRA withdrawal will not face the 10 percent penalty on premature withdrawals if the withdrawal is made under any of these circumstances.

- You're 59½ or older.
- You become disabled.
- Your beneficiary(ies) make the withdrawal on account of your death.
- The withdrawal is part of a series of substantially equal withdrawals made at least annually over your life expectancy or the life expectancy of you and your beneficiary.

- The money is for medical expenses for which you haven't been reimbursed and that exceed 7.5 percent of your adjusted gross income.
- The money pays for medical insurance premiums for you, your spouse, and your dependents, but only if you've lost your job.
- You use the money for qualified higher education expenses either for you, your spouse, or any child or grandchild of either you or your spouse.
- You use the money for expenses as a first-time homebuyer.

As a general rule, you'll want to keep your money in a Roth IRA as long as possible. That way, you'll avoid all federal income tax, no matter how much you withdraw, and your money gets to grow inside your account year after year without being nibbled away by taxes.

In other words, you'll want to keep your money in your account for at least five years to ensure that all withdrawals escape federal tax.

Okay, so maybe now you have a pretty good idea of how Roth IRAs work and some understanding of the rules. The question is, should you choose a Roth IRA? It depends.

Comparing Roth IRAs

Roth IRAs vs. Taxable Accounts

If you face a choice between contributing to a Roth IRA or investing money in a regular taxable account, the Roth IRA generally wins because of its tax advantages.

Here's an example. Suppose you put $2,000 this year in a regular taxable account, such as a bank account, and you also put $2,000 into a Roth IRA. You leave the money alone for five years. Both accounts grow at 5 percent a year.

After five years, you'll have about $2,552 in the Roth account. But you'll have only about $2,462 in the taxable account. The Roth IRA leaves you with about $90 more. Why? Because the money your Roth IRA earns each year isn't taxed, but the money your regular bank account earns each year is taxed.

This example assumes you're in the 15 percent federal income tax bracket. If you're in a higher bracket, the difference will be even bigger, because taxes will take an even bigger bite out of the regular bank account's earnings each year.

Roth IRAs vs. Stocks

But maybe this isn't a fair example. Maybe you'd like to invest in something besides a bank account, something that might earn you more over time, such as stocks.

Purely from a tax standpoint, stocks can be a better choice than regular bank accounts. Why? Because the money your bank account earns each year gets taxed each year as ordinary income, just like your salary or wages, at rates of 30 percent or more. But, if the value of your investment in a stock increases, the increase doesn't get taxed each year; it's taxed only at the end, when you sell your shares.

Even then, it doesn't get taxed as ordinary income; it gets better tax treatment at capital gains rates, which nowadays are running as low as only 8 percent (depending on how long you hold your stock and other factors).

So suppose you put $2,000 this year in a stock, and you contribute $2,000 to a Roth IRA. You leave the money alone for five years. Both investments grow at 8 percent a year.

After five years, both investments are worth $2,939. But if you cash in the stock at that time, you'll have only about $2,845 to put in your pocket. Why? Because you must pay a federal capital gains tax on the growth that's built up over the years. It's true that capital gains tax rates are lower now than they were, but you still have to pay some tax. The level of capital gains tax that you have to pay generally depends on your overall federal income tax rate.

So let's say you're in the 15 percent federal income tax bracket or higher in this example. In that case, you may have to pay a 10 percent federal capital gains tax. In this example, your $2,000 investment (consisting of after-tax dollars) grew to about $2,939. But the $939 in growth will be taxed at 10 percent. So you'll have to fork over about $94 in federal capital gains tax, leaving you with a total of about $2,845.

With the Roth IRA, however, you'll have the full $2,939 to yourself. No federal tax is due. In other words, in this example, you're almost $100 ahead of the game.

When Flexibility Is Key

This raises a crucial issue: flexibility. If this is your only goal, the taxable account wins. That's an important point to keep in mind.

True, Roth IRAs *do* have a lot going for them. But if flexibility is your main concern, then IRAs—even the much-trumpeted Roth IRAs—aren't for you. You want access to your money at all times, with no hassles and no worries. You don't want to think about tax issues. You don't want to worry whether the timing is right. You just want to be able to get at your money when you want.

If flexibility is your main goal, stick with a regular taxable account, such as a bank account or money market mutual fund.

If you have another type of taxable account, such as stocks or stock mutual funds, your life is already a little more complicated, because you must think about how long you will hold your investment: the longer you hold it, the less you'll generally have to pay in federal capital gains tax. But here, too, you don't have a lot of rules. You generally can cash in your stocks or stock mutual funds whenever you like, pay the tax, and be done with it.

The Roth IRA is more complicated. No question about it. There are tax issues *and* timing issues to consider, and the rules aren't the easiest to understand.

Of course, if you have a little bit of patience, and you can take the time to understand how the Roth IRA works, you'll easily be seduced by the Roth account's tremendous benefits.

A Look at Traditional IRAs

With traditional IRAs, you may be eligible for a big tax benefit up front. With Roth IRAs, the big tax advantage comes at the end. So, do you want to eat your cake now, or later?

It's no small matter. The same law that created Roth IRAs also expanded traditional IRAs, so that many more taxpayers each year will be eligible for at least some tax deduction for their contributions.

Keep making deductible contributions to a traditional IRA year after year, and the tax savings mount up. You can't ignore the benefit. That's one reason traditional IRAs have become so attractive once again to many more Americans. It's also one reason why it will be hard for some taxpayers to choose between the traditional IRA and the Roth IRA.

There's another reason, too. It isn't easy to pass up a tax break today for a tax break you may get in the future. Sure, Roth IRAs generally mean you'll be able to make tax-free withdrawals later on. But that may be a hard sell if you're eligible to get a tax deduction today by contributing to a regular IRA.

The General Rules

With the Roth IRA, withdrawals are tax-free, as long as you live by the rules. So, which IRA is better? There's no one-size-fits-all answer, but here are some general rules.

- If you qualify for a tax deduction from a traditional IRA, and you figure you'll be in a lower tax bracket when you retire than when you contribute, the traditional deductible IRA is generally a better deal. (In other words, go for the tax deduction you can get from a regular IRA.)
- If you expect to be in the same federal income tax bracket when you withdraw money as when you contribute money, the traditional deductible IRA may be best.

- If you expect you'll need to tap your IRA to help pay for expenses in retirement, the regular IRA is generally a better choice.
- If you qualify for a deduction with a traditional IRA, you'll reduce your adjusted gross income. Also, because of the way tax rules work, if you can cut your adjusted gross income, you may be able to claim more itemized deductions, and you may be able to take greater advantage of the HOPE Scholarship and Lifetime Learning tax credits, as well as the tax credit you may be allowed for each child you have.
- If you figure you'll be in a higher tax bracket upon retirement than when you contribute, the Roth IRA generally makes more sense.
- If you expect to withdraw money from your IRA in retirement, and your financial circumstances are such that you'll be triggering a tax on your Social Security benefits, the Roth IRA may be a better choice.
- If you don't expect to need your IRA money in retirement, and you plan to use your IRA mainly as a way to build wealth and pass it along to the next generation (or to some other beneficiaries), the Roth IRA is the better choice.
- If you simply hate the idea of plowing through all the formulas and calculations triggered by making minimum required withdrawals from a regular IRA, the Roth IRA wins easily.

Remember: These are only *general* rules. Whether they'll apply to your own financial circumstances depends on a lot of factors—and on the assumptions you use in your calculations.

Yes, all this can get really complicated, and yes, the rules involve a lot of number crunching. That's why it may be best for you to consult an accountant or other tax or financial advisor who can use computer software to run some numbers under different sets of variables. (For some software you can get on your own, see *For More Information . . .* at the end of this chapter.)

But no matter who runs the numbers, keep careful track of the assumptions they use. If you don't understand something, it doesn't mean you're stupid. Just stop the process and ask a question.

A Tax Credit for Savers

If you contribute to a Roth IRA (or a traditional IRA or just about any retirement plan at work) and your income falls below certain levels, you may also be eligible to slash up to $1,000 off your federal income tax for the year you contribute to the Roth.

That's right. Normally, you think of getting an immediate tax break only when you contribute to a traditional IRA, not a Roth IRA. For the traditional

IRA, you may qualify for an immediate federal income tax deduction. For the Roth IRA, the key tax benefit comes at the end—the opportunity for tax-free withdrawals.

Nevertheless, under a new federal law, you may be able to claim a special tax break—the *Saver's Tax Credit*—on your federal return for the year in which you contribute to a Roth or other retirement plan.

In a sense, then, you can have your cake and eat it, too. Here's how it works.

You may claim the credit only if you earn below a certain amount. However, if your overall income (from work and other sources) falls below that level, you can claim the credit on your return. That's in addition to the deduction you may get for contributing to a Roth IRA.

Who Qualifies

This option may be especially attractive if you're just starting out in the workplace and you're not quite sure whether you can afford to contribute to your plan. The tax break may provide just the extra boost you'll need.

If you clear those hurdles and qualify, you get to claim the tax credit. You may use the credit to reduce your federal income tax, dollar for dollar. In other words, after you claim all the deductions and exemptions and other such stuff on your tax return, and after you calculate your tax based on the income that remains, *then* you apply the credit. It comes right off your tax.

For example, if your overall tax for the year is $1,200 and you qualify for a tax credit of $1,000, you can slash your overall tax to just $200. That can go a long way toward helping you afford the IRA contribution in the first place.

If you're married, both spouses may claim the credit, and the tax savings can quickly add up. (See Chapter 1 for more details.)

Planning Your Estate

With all the great options a Roth IRA gives you, your beneficiaries will still need to keep in mind a few key points.

For example, Roth IRAs are still counted as an asset for purposes of calculating any federal estate tax that may be due upon your death. So, for estate-tax purposes, Roth IRAs are treated the same as traditional IRAs. In other words, the Roth IRA—along with your other assets—is counted as part of your estate and may be hit with the federal estate tax.

In addition, even though you don't have to withdraw money from your Roth IRA while you're alive, a beneficiary of a Roth IRA *must* make withdrawals from the account or face a stiff penalty.

If you're the beneficiary of an inherited IRA, keep in mind that you need not withdraw the money in a lump sum. Instead, you can choose to stretch out withdrawals over your lifetime. This can reduce the income tax impact of withdrawals and allow the account to keep growing on a tax-deferred basis.

This is no small benefit. The less a beneficiary must withdraw, the more money remains in the account to keep growing. If a beneficiary invests prudently (and maybe has a little luck to boot), the inherited Roth IRA may not only generate current income but also grow to become a source of wealth over time.

The rules that govern a beneficiary's withdrawals from a Roth IRA are the same as those that govern a beneficiary's withdrawals from a traditional IRA. These rules are spelled out in detail in Chapter 6.

When Beneficiaries Pay Tax

If you look carefully at the section earlier in this chapter about inheriting a Roth IRA, you may have seen a phrase that alarmed you. It said that the money a beneficiary withdraws from an inherited Roth IRA *generally* is tax-free. How can this be? Aren't Roth IRA withdrawals *always* free of tax?

In certain circumstances, the answer is no. It depends on when the owner of the account died. As you know, the general rule is that you must hold a Roth IRA for at least five years (and meet certain other hurdles) to be eligible to make tax-free withdrawals.

Suppose, then, that Uncle Charlie opens a Roth IRA in 2002. In January 2007, he becomes eligible to make tax-free withdrawals. A few months later, he dies. His beneficiaries inherit the Roth IRA directly from him and begin to make their own withdrawals, entirely free of federal income tax.

Great. However, suppose instead that Uncle Charlie dies in January 2005, and his beneficiary withdraws the entire amount a few months later. What are the tax consequences? The contributions that Uncle Charlie made will be free of tax. However, the money that the account earned will be subject to federal income tax, because the account wasn't held for the required five years.

For More Information . . .

Brentmark Software, Inc. Be sure to check out a Web site that keeps careful track of new developments in the world of Roth IRAs. Written for professionals as well as consumers, the site is maintained by Brentmark Software Inc., which develops estate planning, financial planning, and retirement planning software for professionals: <www.rothira.com>.

The T. Rowe Price mutual fund company. Based in Baltimore, T. Rowe Price has booklets that detail the benefits and drawbacks of Roth IRAs. For more information, write: T. Rowe Price, 100 East Pratt Street, Baltimore, MD 21202, call 800-225-5132, or see this Web site: <www.troweprice.com>.

10

Roth IRA Conversions

This chapter looks at Roth IRA conversions: what they are, how they work, and how they might work for you. We look at the advantages and disadvantages of converting a traditional IRA to a Roth IRA. We'll also look at the tax consequences as well as the long-range benefits of converting.

Let's get one thing straight: the potential benefits of converting a traditional IRA to a new Roth IRA are tremendous. No doubt about it.

With a Roth IRA conversion, you simply designate all or a portion of your traditional IRA to be a Roth IRA. Converting to a Roth IRA has a lot of advantages: the Roth IRA gives you lots of flexibility, lots of tax benefits, and a neat way to pass IRA dollars to the next generation if you want. All true.

Watch the Bottom Line

But don't be fooled. To get all these benefits, you've got to pay first. And you may wind up paying through the nose.

Sure, it could save you money—a lot of it—in the long run. But it will also cost you in taxes up front. So take a moment to think of that, and think carefully: do you want to pay taxes now or later?

Tempting Tax Breaks

For many investors, this question is crucial. The long-range tax savings you can get from converting are mighty tempting. But they're down the road. To get them, you've got to pay some taxes.

The higher the amount you convert, the more in tax you'll pay. The higher your marginal federal income tax bracket, the more you'll pay as well. If you convert a traditional deductible IRA, every dollar will be taxed. If you convert a traditional nondeductible IRA, the earnings (if any) will be taxed.

Sure, you can use some of the money you convert to pay the tax bill. But that doesn't make sense. Odds are you won't have enough years in your lifetime to make up for the money you lose by tapping your existing IRA to pay the tax. Even some of the most vocal advocates of converting acknowledge this point. So the best way in the long run to make a conversion work is to pay the tax bill with money other than retirement plan assets. In fact, it's really the *only* way that a conversion makes sense. So you've got to pay the tax out of your own pocket. That's right: You've got to write a check to the IRS.

The Price of Converting

How painful can that be? If you're in the 15 percent federal bracket and you convert a $10,000 traditional IRA to a Roth IRA, you'll have to pay $1,500 in federal income tax. If you're paying tax at a higher rate—say 30 percent or more—you'll have to pay even more, at least $3,000 in this example.

But what if you're talking about bigger numbers? Say you convert a $50,000 traditional IRA to a Roth IRA. If you're paying federal tax at an average rate of 30 percent or so, you'll have to fork over $15,000 in federal tax in this example.

That's just federal income tax. If you live in a state that levies its own income tax, your final tax bill will probably be more, maybe much more, depending on your state's rules.

Sure, you won't have to pay a penalty. In other words, if you convert a traditional IRA to a Roth IRA, you won't have to face the additional 10 percent penalty on early withdrawals, even if you're under age 59½. It's true that, for some people, at least, affordability may still not be an issue, no matter how high the tax bill is.

But let's face it: some people just hate the idea of paying a tax to the government. It's against their principles. Even though it could save them money in the long run, they'll refuse to budge. That's why Roth conversions are a harder sell than some proponents are willing to admit.

The Basics

If you decide to move ahead anyway, the future may not be so bleak. Yes, there's a tax due. But you can do some things to soften the blow a bit.

How to Convert

First the basics. If you've got a traditional IRA, you can roll over some or all of the money into a Roth IRA. There's no limit on the amount you can convert, and it doesn't get counted against the annual limit on contributions. (So you can roll over money from a regular IRA to a Roth IRA in a given year if you qualify, and you may also contribute to a Roth IRA in the same year if you qualify.)

In many cases, you can convert to a Roth IRA simply by notifying your bank, brokerage, or mutual fund company and filling out some forms.

In other words, you don't actually have to move the money or other assets from one institution to another or from one fund to another; you can simply designate a portion or all of your existing IRA as a Roth IRA. (For details and forms, contact the outfit that's holding your IRA for you, known as the *custodian* or *trustee*.) Keep in mind that if you want to convert your 401(k) or other such retirement-saving plan at work, you must first roll that money to a traditional IRA, then do the conversion; it's a two-step process.

The Benefits

Once you convert, your old traditional IRA becomes a Roth IRA, and you do, indeed, get all the associated benefits, just as you would if you had simply contributed to a Roth.

In other words, if your money is in the Roth account long enough, and if your withdrawals meet the rules, the money comes out tax-free. No tax. None at all.

What if you don't want to make any withdrawals? You just want to sit on your money for as long as possible? That's okay, too. There's no requirement to begin making withdrawals by age 70½, as with a traditional IRA. You, as the owner, need not worry about required minimum withdrawals. There's no need to check the life expectancy tables and do all that figuring. Just sit tight and let your money keep growing inside your account—tax-free.

Beneficiaries Get a Break

What happens to the account when you die? It will be included as part of your taxable estate for purposes of figuring whether any federal estate tax is due. But the money gets passed to your beneficiary, directly and automatically, bypassing the probate process, just as it would with a traditional IRA. However, unlike the traditional IRA, your beneficiary probably won't have to pay income tax on the withdrawals. So yes, the Roth IRA is sweet. Very sweet.

The Income Limits

As you might expect, however, there are limits. For example, you may convert a traditional IRA to a Roth IRA only if your adjusted gross income isn't more than $100,000 for the year in which you convert.

If your income is close to the limit, you do get a bit of a break. To see if you're eligible to convert, you figure your adjusted gross income *before* taking into account the money you plan to convert.

If you're close to the $100,000 dollar limit and you want to be sure you don't exceed it, you can take some common-sense steps to try to get yourself below the limit for that year.

Consider deferring some of your income. You may not be paid in a steady weekly or monthly salary; you may be eligible for year-end bonuses or commissions, and these count toward figuring your adjusted gross income. If you're close to the $100,000 limit, and your year-end bonus or commission might push you over the top, see if you can defer some income into the next tax year, so that you'll be eligible to convert in the current year.

If you have investments that generate taxable income, think about cashing them in and putting the money instead into investments that generate tax-exempt interest, such as tax-free money market mutual funds, or investments that generate tax-deferred interest, such as Series I or Series EE U.S. Savings Bonds.

That's the good news. By now you know the bad news. If you convert, the money you transfer from your traditional IRA to a Roth IRA (or the money or other assets in your traditional IRA that you've now designated as a Roth IRA) will be taxed as ordinary income. In other words, the IRS will view it as a taxable distribution, even if you don't actually withdraw and spend the money, even if the money never touches your hands. In fact, depending on the size of the amount you convert, you could be pushed into a higher federal tax bracket. You'll owe the tax for the year in which you convert. (In 1998, the year that Roth IRAs were first available, you could spread out the tax impact over four years. However, Congress allowed this four-year spread only for conversions that were made in or for 1998.)

Keep in mind that you can't use a deductible contribution to a traditional IRA to reduce your income below the $100,000 limit for purposes of figuring if you're eligible to convert to a Roth IRA.

Remember, too, that any minimum withdrawals you must take from a traditional IRA are counted toward the $100,000 limit right now—but they won't be starting in 2005.

If you're planning to convert, but you're not sure whether your income for the year will exceed the $100,000 limit, consider this strategy. Go ahead and convert anyway, because you generally have until October 15 of the following year, even if you file by April 15, to reverse the procedure and put the money back into your traditional IRA and still avoid tax and penalty. By that time, you're sure to know whether your income for the prior year met the $100,000 limit.

For example, suppose you figure your income for 2005 at $90,000, so you convert your traditional IRA to a Roth IRA that year. But late in the year you earn bonuses or commissions that boost your income to $110,000. As a result, your income for 2005 turns out to be too high to let you convert. Fortunately, you'll have until October 15, 2006, to undo your conversion. Just tell your Roth IRA trustee or custodian to transfer the entire amount—including any earnings—directly back to your traditional IRA (or a new one). In so doing, you escape tax and penalty.

Another reason to undo—or recharacterize—a conversion is if the market value of the account declines sharply following the conversion. In such a case, you could end up paying tax on market value that has evaporated. It's nice to know you can reverse the conversion if you need to.

Converting a Nondeductible IRA

Don't forget that these tax rules also apply if you convert a traditional *nondeductible* IRA to a Roth IRA. (And converting a nondeductible IRA to a Roth IRA is really a great idea.) Remember: With a traditional nondeductible IRA, only the earnings will be subject to income tax, not the original contributions that you made with your after-tax dollars.

Switching Over from a Traditional IRA

You also get a few options for making the conversion. You can simply rechristen your traditional IRA as a Roth IRA, as outlined earlier. In addition, you can transfer the money directly from one custodian to another (from a bank to a brokerage, for example). Or you can roll over the money from one institution to another or from one account to another.

Just remember that if you choose the rollover, you've got to complete the move within 60 days, as you would when rolling over money from one traditional IRA to another.

Withdrawals from Converted IRAs

If you convert to a Roth IRA, then withdraw money within five tax years, you'll generally pay a 10 percent early withdrawal penalty. (The five-year clock starts ticking in the year for which the conversion was made.)

For example, suppose you were less than 59½ and you converted a $25,000 traditional deductible IRA in 2002. If you withdraw $5,000 in 2004— before the five-year holding period is up—you'll pay a 10 percent excise tax, totaling $500 in this example (unless the withdrawal qualifies as an exception to the penalty under normal IRA rules).

As if that weren't complicated enough, the government also made some special rules regarding the order in which money is withdrawn when a Roth IRA conversion is involved. These rules help determine whether a tax and/or penalty apply to a withdrawal. Fortunately, all your Roth IRAs are treated as one IRA for this purpose—including Roth IRAs to which you contribute money, and conversion Roth IRAs.

In general, the government says that if you make a withdrawal, it will be treated as having come first from your annual contributions; followed by converted amounts (early conversions before later ones); then any earnings such as dividends, interest, and any price appreciation in your accounts (from stocks, bonds, or mutual fund shares, for instance.) This rule can give you a break because, for example, contributions to Roth IRAs are never taxed or penalized when withdrawn.

A word of caution: If you withdraw money after a conversion and any of the circumstances above apply to you, seek help from an accountant or other professional who is acquainted with the many IRS rulings and court decisions that are sure to arise over this complex area of tax law.

Should You Convert?

Does a conversion make sense for you? Well, it depends.
Here are some general guidelines.

- Converting may make sense if your regular IRA has been open for only a short time, and most of the money in the account is from nondeductible contributions. In this case, most of the money you convert won't be subject to tax at all, because it's already been taxed. Although the earnings will be taxed, they won't also be subject to penalty upon conversion, because conversions escape the penalty. Besides, there won't be much in earnings to convert anyway.

- If you don't expect to need money from your IRA in retirement, because you plan to have enough coming in from other sources such as pensions, investments, and Social Security, convert your regular IRA to a Roth IRA. If you're in this situation, you obviously want to pass as much money as possible to the next generation (or to other beneficiaries), and the Roth IRA is clearly a better way to do this than a regular IRA, because you don't have to make minimum withdrawals from a Roth IRA while you're alive, and your beneficiaries probably won't have to pay income tax on the withdrawals after they inherit your Roth account.
- Converting may make sense if you expect to be in a higher federal income tax bracket in retirement. If you're in a higher bracket in retirement and you withdraw money from a regular IRA, it will be taxed heavily—as ordinary income—and at a higher rate than the rate which applied when you made your original deductible contributions. (Roth withdrawals generally aren't taxable.)
- Don't convert if you expect to make withdrawals from your Roth account later that won't qualify for tax-free and penalty-free treatment. In other words, don't convert if you plan to withdraw money before your account has been open five years, or if your withdrawals won't meet the other conditions for favorable tax treatment (these conditions generally require that you be over $59\frac{1}{2}$, the money comes out on account of your death or disability, or you use it to pay for first-time homebuyer expenses). If you make withdrawals that don't qualify for favorable tax treatment, you'll suffer twice: your money won't be able to continue to grow in your Roth account to make up for the tax you had to pay upon converting, and you'll have to pay a tax (and possibly a penalty) for the withdrawals you make in this example.
- Don't convert if you expect to be in a sharply lower federal income tax bracket when you retire. If you're in a lower bracket in retirement, and you withdraw money from a regular IRA, it will be taxed relatively lightly. But, if you convert that IRA when you're in a high bracket, it will be taxed heavily.
- Don't convert if you have only a little while until you retire *and* you expect to have to make withdrawals to make ends meet. If you convert in this case, you'll have to pay tax, but your money won't have enough time to grow to make up for the tax you had to shell out in the first place.
- Look closely at exactly how much you plan to convert. Remember: You don't have to convert all the money that's in your traditional IRA; you can convert only part if you wish. If you convert a big amount, this could push you into a much higher federal income tax bracket.
- If you're collecting Social Security benefits and you're thinking about converting, look carefully at the tax impact—not only on your overall

income but also on your Social Security benefits. Remember: Social Security benefits generally aren't taxed. But they *are* taxed if your income is high enough. If you convert, you'll have to include the amount of your conversion in your income, and this could be enough to trigger a tax on your Social Security. If your Social Security benefits are already subject to tax because of your overall income level, converting could cause a greater portion of your Social Security benefits to be taxed.

Putting It All Together

Your decision whether to convert to a Roth IRA or keep your money in a traditional IRA hinges on a lot of variables. So it's hard to offer some general rules, simply because too many different factors are involved.

So enter the computer. Because that's about the only way you can tell for sure whether converting all—or even a portion—of your traditional IRA makes sense for you.

A computer program can help account for all the variables in your personal financial circumstances. Fortunately, a lot of such programs are available. Some are do-it-yourself programs, available from some big mutual fund companies. You can buy one or download one by going online. (For details, see *For More Information . . .* below.)

It also makes sense to consult an accountant, financial planner, or other financial advisor. Odds are they have their own programs and can offer you advice on whether to convert. They may also be able to point out some factors you might otherwise overlook. (And there are many, many factors to consider when deciding whether to convert.)

For More Information . . .

You can figure out whether a conversion is best for you in lots of ways. Here are a few.

T. Rowe Price. The mutual fund group in Baltimore has computer programs available that can help you decide whether to convert. For more about Roth IRAs and conversions, see the group's Web site: <www.troweprice.com>.

Brentmark Software, Inc. This Florida company that develops estate planning, financial planning, and retirement planning software (including Roth IRA and Roth IRA conversion software) maintains a Web site that has lots of information about Roth IRAs and Roth IRA conversions: <www.rothira.com>.

SEP-IRAs, SIMPLE-IRAs, SAR-SEP IRAs

This chapter looks at a special type of IRA: the employer-sponsored IRA. You may be involved in this kind of IRA—either as a business owner or employee—if you take part in a Simplified Employee Pension (SEP), a SEP with a salary reduction feature (SAR-SEP), or a Savings Incentive Match Plan for Employees (SIMPLE plan). We'll look at what each plan is, how it works, and how you're now able to contribute a lot more to these plans—lowering your tax bill and maximizing your retirement savings.

Millions of American workers who save at work for their retirement— the self-employed and people who work for small businesses—use a SEP-IRA, a SAR-SEP IRA, or a SIMPLE-IRA.

Whether you take part in a SEP-IRA, a SAR-SEP IRA, or a SIMPLE-IRA, you may now save more money each year.

If you're 50 or older, the new law allows you to contribute even more. As a result, these retirement plans have now become super–IRAs, allowing you to stash away far more than you could with an ordinary IRA. If your goal is to save a lot for retirement, now's your chance, and here's your guide.

Simplified Employee Pensions (SEPs)

These plans have long been popular among self-employed workers— everyone from carpenters and fishermen to barbers and beauticians.

What's so great about the Simplified Employee Pension (SEP)? Easy. You can sock away a lot of money into this plan, and you don't need a lot of paperwork—or professional advice—to get the job done.

CHARACTERISTICS OF HOUSEHOLDS OWNING EMPLOYER-SPONSORED IRAS

Median age of household's primary or codecision maker	45
Median household income	$70,000
Median household financial assets	$150,000
Median household financial assets in all IRAs	$48,200

Employer-sponsored IRAs included SEP-IRAs, SAR-SEP IRAs, and SIMPLE-IRAs. Figure for median household financial assets includes assets in employer-sponsored retirement plans.

Source: Survey in 2001 by Investment Company Institute <www.ici.org>

Key Points about SEP-IRAs

Here's a quick look at some key points of these plans.

- You don't set up a formal pension plan, with all the record keeping and expense that can entail. Instead, you set up your own SEP-IRA—if you have employees, you establish separate SEP-IRA accounts for them, too—and contribute money to the IRAs. For the little paperwork required, you may go through a bank, mutual fund company, insurance company, or other financial institution, which can do most of the work for you.
- You may be able to contribute far more money to a SEP-IRA than you could before. You get a federal income tax deduction for the money you contribute.
- SEP-IRAs are flexible. You need not contribute a fixed amount or fixed percentage each year, as you must for many other types of plans. In fact, if business is slow in a given year, you don't have to contribute at all—either for your own account or for your employees' accounts.
- You don't have to worry about managing the plan; a financial institution, such as a bank or mutual fund company, does it for you (as it would with a traditional IRA).
- You typically have no filing requirements with any government agencies. In other words, as a general rule, you need not make any annual filings with government regulators, as you do with many other types of plans.
- Only employers may contribute; employees cannot.
- The money the employer contributes isn't counted as income to employees and isn't taxed until withdrawn.

- Only employees decide how the money is to be invested.
- The employer has until the filing deadline of the business's federal income tax return (plus extensions) to establish and contribute to a SEP-IRA.
- Once the employer contributes, employees immediately gain the un-forfeitable right to the money in their accounts. In other words, vesting is immediate. The workers can move the money—including the employer contributions plus any investment earnings—to another IRA, for example, and can even withdraw the money (subject to tax and possible penalty).
- You (and your employees) may name beneficiaries for your account (or accounts), so that the money passes directly to them upon the owner's deaths.
- You may continue to contribute to a SEP-IRA even after you (or your employees) turn 70½.
- Participants in SEP-IRAs must start making required withdrawals from a SEP-IRA for the year in which they turn 70½. The rules are the same as for traditional IRAs.
- As a general rule, if you have employees, you must include just about all of them in your SEP arrangement. In general, you must offer the plan to all employees who are at least 21 years old, have been employed by your business for 3 of the immediately preceding 5 years, and whom you've paid at least a minimum amount for the year ($450 for 2002; this dollar figure may rise each year with inflation).
- An employer may integrate the plan with Social Security. This feature may allow the employer to contribute more money for certain higher-paid workers, recognizing that Social Security benefits favor lower-paid workers.

SEPs aren't just for the self-employed (such as the sole proprietor or partner in a limited liability company). You can set one up if you run a small business with workers, too. Remember: You, as the owner, have some flexibility regarding your contributions; you don't have to kick in contributions each year.

You May Contribute More

SEPs aren't new. A federal law created them in 1978 as a way to help the self-employed and the small business entrepreneur save for retirement. Odds are, however, that you've been hearing more about these plans lately, because you're now able to salt away more money in your account.

In 2001, for example, the most you could contribute was generally 15 percent of compensation. The most compensation you could use in the formula was $170,000. As a result, the most you could kick in to the plan for that year—on your own behalf or on behalf of a worker—was $25,500. (The formula for a self-employed person is a bit different and is mentioned later.)

Contribution Formula Changes

That maximum is scheduled to change, however. It is $30,000 for 2002. If, as expected, Congress fine-tunes the law, the government would set a new contribution limit of $40,000 per SEP participant. That would be a stunning jump, almost double the prior year's limit. It means you may stash a lot more money in a SEP-IRA.

A small business owner should check first with a financial advisor or the IRS to make sure that Congress has followed through on its intention to raise the contribution limit for a SEP. Plan participants should also keep in mind that, as with any employer-sponsored retirement savings plan, the employer need not contribute the maximum allowed by law, the employer may contribute a lesser amount—or, in the case of a SEP, nothing at all.

Limits for the Self-Employed

Unfortunately, the maximum contribution if you're self-employed is lower. That's because of the crazy formula the government requires you to use in calculating how much you may contribute. You start out with the overall income from your trade or business, then you subtract all your allowable deductions—yes, *all* your allowable deductions, including one-half of your self-employment tax as well as your retirement plan contribution.

In other words, to find out how much you may contribute, you must use a figure that factors in how much you have contributed (even though you haven't contributed anything yet.) Instead of twisting your brain into a pretzel over this, you should know that you (or your accountant, enrolled agent, or other advisor) may use a kind of shorthand formula to calculate your contribution.

Under the old rules, everybody talked about a limit of 15 percent, but it actually worked out to 13.0435 percent for a self-employed person. Under the new rules, a limit of 25 percent would work out to 20 percent for the self-employed.

(See *For More Information* . . . at the end of this chapter for ways to get more details on calculating your retirement plan contribution if you're self-employed.)

SAR-SEPs

Another type of plan, the SAR-SEP, lets workers contribute to their own accounts on a pretax basis. In a sense, these plans work like 401(k) plans. (In fact, Congress created them in 1986 so that small businesses could establish what generally amounts to a 401(k) plan without many of the administrative and other such expenses that 401(k) plans often entail.)

Ten years after creating SAR-SEPs, Congress passed another law that changed the rules. In effect, Congress created the SIMPLE plan (reviewed later in this chapter) as a kind of 401(k) plan for small businesses, one to which employees could contribute on a pretax basis.

As part of that law, however, Congress said that no new SAR-SEPs could be opened after 1996. In effect, Congress said that anyone who wants to open a salary-reduction style plan will have to open a SIMPLE plan, not a SAR-SEP.

Old SAR-SEPs Continue

Although employers may no longer establish SAR-SEPs, many such plans still exist. The law also allows new enrollees to take part in existing SAR-SEPs. For these reasons, it's important to know a bit about how these plans work.

OLDER WORKERS CAN SAVE MORE IN SAR-SEP IRAS

A new federal law means that everyone in a SAR-SEP IRA may save more money each year in their plan on a pretax basis. Also, if you are 50 or older, you may make an additional catch-up contribution each year on a pretax basis, allowing you to save even more.

Year	Annual limit	Catch-up	Overall limit (including catch-up)
2002	$11,000	$1,000	$12,000
2003	$12,000	$2,000	$14,000
2004	$13,000	$3,000	$16,000
2005	$14,000	$4,000	$18,000
2006	$15,000*	$5,000*	$20,000*

* After 2006, the maximum annual elective deferral of $15,000 for all participants in a SAR-SEP IRA will rise with inflation in $500 annual increments; the maximum annual catch-up contribution of $5,000 for SAR-SEP IRA participants age 50 and older will also rise with inflation, in $500 annual increments.

Source: U.S. Congress

Congress intended SAR-SEPs only for employers with 25 or fewer employees. Under the original rules, still in force today, the employees decide whether to have their employer put a portion of their pay into an IRA.

It is this point—giving employees the option to have their employer put some of their pay put into a SEP-IRA—that sets the SAR-SEP apart from the standard SEP-IRA.

Another key difference involves discrimination. In general, employers (or their advisors) must apply a special test to the plan at least once a year to make sure the plan isn't benefiting the highly-paid people too much. In other words, the government doesn't want all the benefits from the plan flowing only to the high-paid people on the staff; it wants the lower-paid to benefit, too.

One other key difference worth mentioning involves the way in which contributions are figured. But even here, with the SAR-SEP the big story is how high the contribution limits have gone, and how much higher they'll be going.

Contributing More to a SAR-SEP

Under the old rules, for example, the most you could set aside in your SAR-SEP account on a pretax basis was generally $10,500.

Under the new law, however, you may kick in a lot more money. The new limit, at $11,000 for 2002, rises by $1,000 each year, to $15,000 in 2006 (and keeps rising after that, based on inflation).

If you're 50 or older, you'll be able to contribute even more by making annual catch-up contributions, which are designed specifically to help older workers make up for the years in which they may have contributed little or nothing.

As a result, for workers age 50 or older, Congress set a new overall limit of $12,000 for 2002 and higher limits for later years (as much as $20,000 for 2006, for example).

SIMPLE-IRAs

Officially, a SIMPLE is a Savings Incentive Match Plan for Employees. Most people simply call it a SIMPLE plan. It's a fairly new type of retirement savings plan for small businesses. (There are two versions: one works with IRAs, the other with a 401(k). This book focuses only on the IRA version.)

Congress created the SIMPLE in 1996 out of concern that many small businesses weren't offering retirement savings plans for their workers, because the plans were too expensive and complicated to set up and maintain. Congress hoped the SIMPLE would solve these problems, and for many employers it has. Since the plans first became available in 1997 (essentially replacing SAR-SEPs), they have grown in popularity. Here's a look at how they work.

Nuts and Bolts of SIMPLE Plans

The employer sets up a plan, and the employee sets up a SIMPLE IRA. Little paperwork or regulation is involved, and you get none of the worries that come with a 401(k) or other such plan over the formulas used to ensure the highly paid don't unduly benefit.

An employer may simply use a standard form available from the IRS and can easily set up a plan by contacting a bank, mutual fund company, or other financial institution that handles such plans.

Employers contribute to the IRA on the worker's behalf. The worker may also contribute on a pretax basis, much like a 401(k) plan. (The employer gets to claim a deduction for all the money that goes into each account.)

If a worker moves to another job, the money that's been saved in the account can be brought along (although there are some restrictions, described later). In other words, the money isn't stuck with the former employer; it can be portable, moving with the employee from job to job until the worker is ready to retire and start withdrawals.

Are You Eligible?

To be eligible for a SIMPLE plan, a worker generally must clear just two hurdles.

- You had to have received at least $5,000 in overall compensation from your employer per year during any two prior calendar years.
- You must also be reasonably expected to earn at least $5,000 from your employer for the current calendar year.

The idea behind this eligibility rule is pretty basic. The law lets companies exclude from the plan people who work relatively few hours and earn relatively little pay. As a result, a company can exclude seasonal workers and others who put in only a minimal amount of time on the job over the year.

Keep in mind, however, that these eligibility requirements are the strictest allowed by law. A company needn't impose them; a company can allow for looser restrictions, allowing workers who earn even less than $5,000 to be eligible, for example.

Once you, as an employee, become eligible, you're in. Your age or years of service don't matter. There's no waiting period. This point alone sets the

SIMPLE plan apart from many other types of company-sponsored retirement plans, which may require that you be a certain age and work a certain number of years before you can be eligible.

SIMPLE Tax Breaks

One of the attractive features of SIMPLE plans is that contributions are tax-deductible—whether they're made by the employee or the employer. In other words, there's a tax break for putting money into the plan.

In this respect, the SIMPLE plan operates like its cousin, the traditional 401(k) plan, but with far fewer complications and less set-up, administration, and other costs. In addition, the money in the account grows on a tax-deferred basis. The only time tax is triggered is when the money is withdrawn, typically at retirement.

Another appealing feature about the SIMPLE plan is its flexibility. In general, you can move your account to a SIMPLE account at a mutual fund company, a bank, a brokerage, a credit union, or another financial institution. (Some other types of company-sponsored retirement savings plans strictly limit how and where your money may be invested.)

In addition, once contributions are made to your account—whether the money comes from you or your employer—it's yours. There are no complicated vesting rules to worry about.

Still another benefit of SIMPLE plans involves what pension experts call *portability.* If you change jobs, for instance, you can take the money in your SIMPLE plan with you—all of it—and invest it in another SIMPLE plan (or in a traditional IRA, if you satisfy a two-year waiting period). With some types of company-sponsored retirement plans, the money must stay in your account with the company plan for a certain time—perhaps for years.

Employer Contributions Required

How about employer contributions? An employer *must* contribute to the SIMPLE-IRA of each eligible employee. The employer has some options. Here they are in a nutshell.

- If an employee contributes, the employer may match the contribution, dollar for dollar, within certain limits. For every dollar the employee contributes in a given year, the employer can also contribute a dollar. However, the employer's total contribution for the year can't be more than 3 percent of the employee's overall compensation for the year (within a certain limit, discussed later).

- Under another option, the employer may contribute up to 2 percent of pay for all workers—regardless of which workers choose to contribute themselves, to their own accounts. In other words, under this option, the employer simply puts an amount into everybody's account.
- In rare cases, the employer can choose to contribute a smaller percentage to the employee's account than those listed above, but the amount of the contribution can't be less than 1 percent, and there are restrictions on how often your employer can use this lower figure.

No matter where the SIMPLE-IRA is located, however, remember that it can hold only contributions made through the employer's plan—whether those contributions come solely from the employer or from both the employer and employee. In other words, the SIMPLE-IRA is a vessel set up to handle only SIMPLE plan contributions; you can't throw in money from any other IRAs you have, or money or assets from other types of retirement plans.

Withdrawing Money from a SIMPLE

How do you get the money out?

Keep in mind that these plans are intended to help you save for your retirement. You can take the money out beforehand, but the withdrawal could cost you dearly.

For instance, any amount you withdraw will be taxed and treated as ordinary income. This means it will be taxed at the top federal income tax rate that applies to you.

In addition, if you withdraw money within the first two years of taking part in the plan, you'll be hit with a whopping 25-percent early-withdrawal penalty.

After the first two years, the early withdrawal penalty drops to 10 percent—the same as for traditional IRAs.

IRA Rules Apply

The penalty exceptions are generally the same as those applying to withdrawals from traditional IRAs. Keep in mind that you have the right to roll over your SIMPLE-IRA to a traditional IRA after you've taken part in your SIMPLE-IRA for at least two years.

This means that, after two years, you can move your SIMPLE-IRA money to a regular IRA. You'll then be subject to the normal IRA rules.

For example, once the money is in a regular IRA you can convert your regular IRA to a Roth IRA.

Keep in mind that these plans are truly intended for small businesses. The rule is that a plan can be established only by an employer with 100 or fewer employees who each earned at least $5,000 in compensation in the preceding year.

In addition, Congress wanted to make sure that the new plans reached workers who weren't already covered by a plan, so Congress came up with this rule: in general, SIMPLE plans can be adopted only by employers who don't have another employer-sponsored retirement plan.

Contribution Limits Are Rising

As with many other types of employer-sponsored retirement savings plans, the big story with SIMPLE plans is the contribution limit—it's a lot higher now and will move higher still in future years.

Under the old rules, the most an employee could set aside from pay into a SIMPLE-IRA was $6,500 for 2001. As a result, the maximum overall that could be set aside in the account for that year was $13,000, including $6,500 in employee contributions and $6,500 the employer could contribute as a match.

OLDER WORKERS CAN SAVE MORE IN SIMPLE-IRAS

A new federal law means that everyone in a SIMPLE-IRA may save more money each year in their plan on a pretax basis. Also, if you are 50 or older, you may make an additional catch-up contribution each year on a pretax basis, allowing you to save even more.

Year	Annual limit	Catch-up	Overall limit (including catch-up)
2002	$ 7,000	$ 500	$ 7,500
2003	$ 8,000	$1,000	$ 9,000
2004	$ 9,000	$1,500	$10,500
2005	$10,000	$2,000	$12,000
2006	$10,000*	$2,500*	$12,500*

* After 2005, the maximum elective deferral of $10,000 for all participants in a SIMPLE-IRA will rise with inflation, in $500 annual increments. After 2006, the maximum annual catch-up contribution of $2,500 for SIMPLE-IRA participants age 50 and older will rise with inflation, in $500 annual increments.

Source: U.S. Congress

Under the new rules, the limit for employee contributions starts out at $7,000 for 2002, and keeps rising, to $10,000 in 2005 (and keeps rising afterward, depending on inflation)—and the same cap applies to employer contributions.

If you're 50 or older, you're now able to stash away even more. Under the new rules, the overall contribution limit set by Congress for a worker 50 or older starts at $7,500 for 2002 and keeps rising to at least $12,500 in 2006. (An employer may also match the catch-up contributions made by older workers.)

Some Other SIMPLE Points

Here are some other SIMPLE points to bear in mind.

- In general, an employer can set up a new SIMPLE plan at any time between January 1 and October 1 of a given year.
- Although the focus here has been on SIMPLE plans for small businesses, SIMPLE plans may also be offered by nonprofit organizations. In addition, SIMPLE plans may be an attractive way to save if you're self-employed.

Points about All Plans

One of the appealing features of all these plans is that you typically get to choose where your money is invested. If, for some reason, you don't get a say on where your money is initially placed, you have the freedom to transfer it directly to another financial institution, where you can choose another type of investment vehicle. (Keep in mind, however, the limits on SIMPLE transfers described earlier in this chapter.)

For example, suppose your employer has an arrangement by which all the money from the plan flows into a certain mutual fund company. You don't like that fund company, perhaps because of its combination of high fees and expenses and its poor investment track record over the years.

What can you do? Simply arrange to have the money transferred directly to another financial institution—another mutual fund company, for example, or a bank, credit union, insurance company, brokerage, or other such organization that handles IRAs. (Ask the receiving organization what steps you need to take. Sometimes it will handle the entire transaction for you; at other times, it will ask you for some key information.)

A Special Tax Break for Employees

Don't forget that if your employer has a SEP, SAR-SEP, SIMPLE, or other such plan and you're thinking about taking an active role, you may be able to get an extra tax break—depending on how much money you earn. In other words, if your overall income (from work and other sources) falls below a certain amount, you may be able to claim a tax credit of up to $1,000.

This credit may be especially attractive if you're just starting out in the workplace and you're not quite sure whether you can afford to contribute to your plan. The tax break may provide just the extra boost you'll need. (For more information on this break, see Chapter 1.)

Protection from Creditors

Because SEP-IRAs and SIMPLE-IRAs are, technically, IRAs, the states treat them as IRAs for legal purposes. As a result, while many states protect the money in these accounts from the claims of creditors, some states do not— or the scope of their protection is not clear.

This consideration is important, especially if you're a doctor, lawyer, or other professional whose work may be more apt to attract lawsuits. You want to get the maximum protection you can for your retirement savings dollars.

The Investment Company Institute in Washington, D.C., a trade group for the mutual fund industry, does a survey from time to time that shows the state-by-state treatment of IRAs in bankruptcy proceedings under state law. This survey lists not only the impact on traditional IRAs, Roth IRAs, and Education IRAs (now known as Education Savings Accounts), but also on SEP-IRAs and SIMPLE-IRAs. You can review the latest survey at the organization's Web site: <www.ici.org>.

Keep in mind, however, that the laws are constantly changing, and the survey represents a snapshot of the treatment of IRAs at one point in time. Be sure to check with a lawyer to find out the current status of your state's laws regarding the protection of SEP-IRAs and SIMPLE-IRAs from creditors's claims.

Other Points

Here are a few other points to keep in mind.

- Some employers have a kind of payroll deduction IRA (either a traditional or Roth IRA) that doesn't technically fit the definition of an employer-sponsored plan. In effect, the employer simply gives you the convenience of payroll deduction, allowing you to contribute through your paycheck to either a traditional or Roth IRA. In this case, your IRA follows the same rules as those for traditional (or Roth) IRAs.

- A new federal law says that, effective January 1, 2003, certain types of employer-sponsored retirement plans (such as a 401(k), 403(b), or Section 457 governmental plan) may allow you to make voluntary contributions to a separate account or annuity under the plan. In such a case, the separate account serves as either a traditional or Roth IRA and is technically known as a *deemed IRA.* The effect of this law is to give you the convenience of contributing to an IRA through your employer.

For More Information . . .

The U.S. Department of Labor's Pension and Welfare Benefits Administration (PWBA). The PWBA has many booklets and other publications that spell out, in plain language, the advantages and disadvantages of retirement plans for small businesses, including the self-employed. These booklets—of interest to employees and employers—include "Simple Retirement Solutions for Small Business," "Savings Incentive Match Plans for Employees of Small Employers (SIMPLE)," and "Simplified Employee Pensions (SEPs): What Small Businesses Need to Know." For free copies, call the PWBA's publications hotline toll-free at 800-998-7542, or see the agency's Web site: <www .dol.gov/dol/pwba>.

Jordan E. Goodman. In his book, *Everyone's Money Book* (Dearborn), he provides insights and strategies on how to set up and manage a retirement savings plan (whether on your own or at work) and how to integrate your retirement plans into your overall budget. His book is a vital resource on personal finance.

The U.S. Department of Labor. This agency, as well as other government agencies and private sector groups, has contributed to a free interactive service online to help you choose a retirement plan that best suits your business. You click on the features that apply to you—whether your business is organized as a Subchapter S Corporation, a partnership, limited liability company, limited liability partnership, or sole proprietorship, for example. You also click on how you want to fund the plan—employer contributions only, employee contributions only, or a combination—as well as such items as how long you want employees to wait before they're eligible to participate and what other features you'd like (loans, in-service withdrawals). The service lets you know which plan or plans are best for you. Use this Web site: <www .selectaretirementplan.org>.

The Internal Revenue Service. The IRS has a free booklet that describes, in detail, the main types of retirement plans for small businesses and the self-employed: what they are, how they work, and the rules that govern them. For a free copy of IRS Publication 560, "Retirement Plans for Small Business (SEP, SIMPLE, and Qualified Plans)," visit your local IRS office, call the agency at 800-829-3676, or see its Web site: <www.irs.gov>.

12

Rolling Over Your Retirement Plan at Work

When you leave your job (because you're changing jobs, you've been laid off, or you're retiring, for example), you must decide what to do with the money that you've stashed away in your 401(k), 403(b), 457, or other retirement savings plan at work. In this chapter, we review your options and offer some strategies.

One of the hardest financial-planning decisions you'll ever face comes at one of the most stressful times of your life.

What should you do with that pile of money in your retirement savings plan when you leave work? It's a vital question, whether you're retiring or leaving for another job; or you've quit, been fired, or laid off; or you're taking a buyout or early retirement package.

You have lots of other things to think about at such times. However, one decision you must weigh carefully is what to do with the money sitting in your 401(k) plan, 403(b) plan, Section 457 plan, or similar retirement savings plan at your old job, because a lot is at stake.

Odds are that you've salted away a tidy sum in that plan—not only from your own contributions over the years, but also from any matching contributions your employer kicked in, as well as investment gains. It may well be your single largest asset—worth more than your car, your investment portfolio, or maybe even your house.

This issue faces millions more workers than before. Thanks to a new federal law, people who take part in government-sponsored Section 457 plans are now eligible to take their money with them when they leave their jobs. These include many of the state and local government employees who work at town halls, courthouses, and other such governmental units and agencies. Before January 2002, they had little choice; they typically had to take a lump-sum withdrawal (and pay tax), or withdraw the money in stages over time, depending on their plan's rules. Now, these workers generally face the same options as private-sector workers.

What are your choices? You typically have three:

1. Cash out, and take your money in the form of a lump sum.
2. Roll over the money to an IRA (or to another employer's plan, if you're leaving for another job and the new plan accepts rollovers).
3. Leave the money with your employer's plan.

Cashing Out

Don't do it. Tempted as you might be, don't simply withdraw the money that's in your plan. Why? One key reason is security. You saved that money for a reason. It's there to help supplement your income—and perhaps the income of your loved ones—in retirement. You owe it to yourself—and to them—not to cash out.

Worried about the future of Social Security? Wondering whether your health will allow you to work past retirement age, at least on a part-time basis? The more you have saved on your own, the better your chances of maintaining your lifestyle in retirement and having the comfort of knowing that you need not rely heavily on anyone else—or anything else—for your retirement income.

Tax Consequences

Another important reason not to cash out has to do with taxes. Remember that the government granted you all sorts of tax breaks to encourage you to save for your retirement.

For instance, odds are that you saved the money in your plan on a pretax basis. In other words, chances are that every dollar you put into your plan was a whole dollar, before taxes were taken out.

In addition, whatever your employer may have contributed, and whatever your account earned each year, also avoided tax. In a sense, you were involved in a legal tax shelter, designed to entice you to lock away money during your working years so that you'd have something to rely on in your golden years.

When you agreed to take part in your retirement savings plan at work, you agreed, in effect, to keep your end of that bargain. If you break it now, you'll pay—dearly.

For starters, your employer must, by law, withhold 20 percent of your payout. Right off the bat, then, you're out 20 cents on every dollar. Does your account hold $50,000? Your employer will hold back $10,000; you'll get $40,000.

True, $40,000 isn't peanuts. Perhaps it's enough to pay off your mortgage. Maybe it's enough to buy a car or an RV, pay off some credit card debt, and even pay for a vacation to boot. It doesn't work that way, however. You only get to hold that money temporarily; there's more tax pain to suffer.

An Advance Payment on Your Tax Bill

The 20 percent that your employer is required to withhold from your pay-out is really just an advance payment on the total tax you'll eventually owe, and that final tax bill will be a whopper.

Let's go back to our example, and forget for the moment about the withholding. You've saved $50,000 in your retirement savings plan at work, and now you withdraw it. If you're younger than 55, you'll face a 10 percent penalty for early withdrawal. That's not all. The entire sum you withdraw is also subject to federal income tax (and perhaps state and local income tax, as well, depending on where you live).

Suppose the money you withdraw is taxed by the federal government at a straight 30 percent. This means that, out of your total withdrawal of $50,000, you owe $15,000 in federal income tax. Don't forget that you may also owe an extra $5,000 to cover that early-withdrawal penalty. Your bill from Uncle Sam—including tax and penalty—could come to $20,000. That's a 40 percent bite out of your retirement nest egg. Ouch!

How about the money that your employer withholds? Where does that come in? In this example, your employer holds back $10,000, but only as a down payment to Uncle Sam to cover your eventual tax bill. In our example, your tax bill could total $20,000. As a result, you must fork over an additional $10,000—besides what your employer withheld—just to pay your federal tax bill. (And you may not be able to wait until April 15 to fess up. You may have to hand over the tax in the form of a quarterly estimated payment. If you don't, you may end up owing interest and penalties, too.)

What looked like a tidy nest egg at the start isn't so big after all, and think about it for a moment. You saved all the time you were working, paycheck after paycheck, year after year, so that you'd have a little something extra for your retirement. Maybe your employer kicked in a little bit, too, matching your contributions.

Now you're washing a big chunk of that away. You're cashing out—and you don't even get to keep the money, because you've got to pay tax and maybe a penalty, too. Do you really want to give away 40 percent of all that you've saved all that time? That's just plain dumb. Don't do it. Keep reading this chapter. Other options will suit you better.

One Exception: Ten-Year Averaging

There's one big exception. If you take a lump-sum withdrawal from your plan, you may be able to get special tax treatment—but only if you were born before 1936 and clear certain other hurdles.

This special break is known as *ten-year averaging*. Here, in a nutshell, is how it works.

Ordinarily, a lump-sum withdrawal taken in cash would push you into a higher tax bracket, forcing you to pay a potentially huge tax bill at high rates. With ten-year averaging, you may be eligible to use a special tax-rate schedule (based on rates in effect in 1986, oddly enough), which can help cushion the tax blow.

In effect, this special break lets you pay tax as if you had received the money from your retirement savings plan in ten equal annual installments, instead of just one lump sum in one year.

You still must pay the tax up front; you don't get to spread it out over ten years. However, you do get to calculate the tax on ten-year averaging separately from your regular tax—on a special form—and you can wind up paying less tax overall.

What's more, you may be able to apply favorable capital gains tax rates—a maximum tax rate of 20 percent, and maybe less—on that portion of your withdrawal that's attributable to your participation in the plan before 1974.

The problem is that ten-year averaging is available only to a relatively small number of workers, those born before 1936. In addition, the option is available only if you withdraw the entire amount from your plan in the form of a lump sum (you can't withdraw a little bit here and there).

Even if you've cleared all those hurdles and you want to take advantage of ten-year averaging, you may not get the kind of break you want. That's because of the 1986 tax rates. In general, these rates are low for small lump-sum withdrawals but high for big lump-sum withdrawals.

Even if your lump-sum withdrawal is small enough to qualify for the lower rates under ten-year averaging, keep an eye on where regular tax rates

---

FIVE-YEAR AVERAGING?

Looking around for the five-year averaging option? Forget about it. At one time, just about anyone could use this strategy to help cushion the tax blow on lump-sum withdrawals from retirement plans.

Unfortunately, it's been repealed. The last time you could have used it was for lump sums received in 1999.

are heading. Why? A big tax-cutting law in 2001 lowered federal income tax rates on ordinary income. The problem is that the law didn't make the cuts in a single step. Instead, the law lowers the rates in stages, over time.

The bottom line is that you might be better off rolling over the money to an IRA, withdrawing the money in stages over time, and paying tax on those withdrawals using current rates.

Comparing ten-year averaging with other options can get tricky, requiring lots of number crunching. If you think you may be eligible for ten-year averaging, be sure to check with an accountant or other financial advisor who can determine whether this calculation will benefit you.

Conduit IRAs

One note of caution: If you're changing jobs, and there's a chance you'll want to elect the ten-year averaging option in the future, either keep the money in your plan, move it to your new employer's plan, or—if you haven't lined up a new job yet—roll it over directly to a special purpose IRA, called a *conduit IRA*. Once your money is in the conduit IRA, seal the bottle until you're ready to pour it from the conduit IRA into your new employer's plan.

You open and maintain a conduit IRA for one purpose: to hold the money that you roll over from your plan. You don't taint that conduit IRA with other money, such as your annual IRA contributions, rollovers from other plans, or transfers or rollovers from other IRAs. (If you're planning to open a conduit IRA, talk with the financial institution that will serve as trustee or custodian of the IRA to see if any special steps must be followed.)

Instant Access—for a Price

True, there are some advantages to simply cashing out. For example, you do get instant access to your money, and once you pay the tax, you're done; there are no more tax consequences to worry about.

But that's kind of like volunteering to have your left foot amputated. Sure, you won't have to worry any more about finding matching socks. Still, spending time searching for socks is a small price to pay for keeping your feet intact.

Keep your retirement nest egg intact, too. Don't cash out. Keep reading. There are other options to consider, ones that will serve you better in the long run. (And, if your employer-sponsored retirement plan includes company stock, be sure to read the next section.)

Rolling Over to an IRA

For most people, this is the way to go. You can move the money directly from your former employer's plan to a traditional IRA. In most cases, you simply open an IRA at a financial institution of your choosing. You then direct your company plan to ship the money there. Lots of people use this strategy. Of all the households in the country that have traditional IRAs, about 44 percent of those surveyed say their traditional IRAs include rollovers from employer-sponsored plans.

If you, too, choose this option, you incur withholding, no tax, and no penalty, and your money can continue to grow inside your IRA on a tax-deferred basis. In other words, you get to move the money from one tax shelter to another.

There are other benefits. For instance, an IRA gives you maximum flexibility. Nearly every bank, credit union, brokerage, mutual fund company, insurance company, and other financial institution offers IRAs.

ROLLING OVER TO AN IRA

Nearly half of all U.S. households that own traditional IRAs reported that their IRAs include money rolled over from employer-sponsored retirement plans. The money was rolled over in many cases because of job change, in some cases because of retirement.

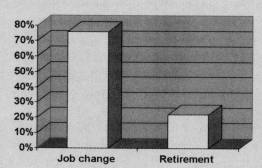

Data as of June 2001 survey, Investment Company Institute. Multiple responses included.

WELCOME TO 457 PLAN PARTICIPANTS

For too many years, a big chunk of the nation's workforce has been treated unfairly when it comes to pension rules: people enrolled in government-sponsored retirement savings plans, known as Section 457 plans.

These plans are open to millions of state and local government workers throughout the country, including people who work for courthouses, town halls, highway departments, and the like. They haven't enjoyed the same rights as have colleagues in other sectors.

Need proof? Look at rollovers. If you're in a 401(k) plan (offered by many firms in business and industry), or if you're in a 403(b) plan (offered by many universities, hospitals, and other non profits), and you're retiring, you can roll over the money from your plan account directly to an IRA. That way, you avoid tax consequences, and the money gets to keep growing on a tax-deferred basis.

However, if you were retiring from a state or local government job and had money in a 457 plan, you could not roll over that money directly to an IRA. You either had to take the money as a lump sum (and pay tax on the entire amount), or take it in the form of periodic installments (which also triggered tax consequences).

Thanks to legislation approved by Congress and President Bush in 2001, however, people in government-sponsored 457 plans now are treated in pretty much the same way as those in 401(k), 403(b), and similar plans.

So, if you're retiring or moving to another job, you'll be able to take your Section 457 money with you—rolling it directly to an IRA or to another plan (assuming the plan permits). As a result, at long last, you'll be able to keep sheltering the money you've saved from taxes. You'll also get to consolidate your retirement savings in one place.

Lots of Choices

This means you also get lots of investment options. Through an employer-sponsored retirement plan, your investment choices are typically limited. Through an IRA, you can deposit your dollars in a bank CD, for example, or invest in Treasury securities, bonds, stocks, mutual funds, or some mixture. You can let professionals manage the money for you, or you can do it yourself, even trading individual securities within your own self-directed account.

Consolidating Your Savings

IRAs allow for convenient consolidation, too. You can bring all your retirement savings together under the umbrella of a single IRA. This move can give you some peace of mind. It can also rid you of potential administrative nightmares. With a single account statement, you can keep better and more careful track of your retirement savings and how that money is invested.

This strategy is a lot easier to implement now, too. Under the old rules, you could move to an IRA money only from some employer-sponsored plans, not from others. For example, you could move money directly to an IRA from a 401(k) plan, but not from a Section 457 plan.

Now the laws are more liberal. As a result, workers have what the experts call *increased portability*. In other words, you're better able now to take the money in your retirement savings plan with you when you leave your job and move it to an IRA (or another employer's plan).

Another benefit of using a traditional IRA as a vessel to receive money from your employer-sponsored plan is that, once the money hits the traditional IRA, you can convert some or all of it into a Roth IRA.

Withdrawal Options

Another potential benefit of rolling over your retirement savings money to a traditional IRA involves withdrawals. As you know, you generally can't withdraw money from a traditional IRA before you turn 59½. If you do, you'll generally be subject to a ten-percent early withdrawal penalty.

However, withdrawals from a traditional IRA can escape the ten-percent penalty if they occur under *any* of these circumstances.

- You're 59½ or older.
- You're disabled (and you're fully disabled under the rules, which are similar to the strict rules that apply for qualifying for Social Security disability benefits).
- The money is paid out after you die.
- The withdrawal is one in a series of substantially equal withdrawals made at least annually and at least for five years or until you reach 59½, whichever is longer.
- You use the money to pay for certain medical expenses.
- You use the money to pay for health insurance premiums if you've been laid off.
- You use the money for first-time homebuyer expenses (up to $10,000) for you, your spouse, your children, or another member of your immediate family.
- You use the money to pay for certain college expenses.

For more details on how these exceptions work, see Chapter 3.

Keep in mind that, even though a withdrawal may avoid penalty under the exceptions listed above, it will still generally be subject to income tax.

Before you plan to take advantage of any of these penalty exceptions, be sure to consult an accountant or other financial advisor who's intimately familiar with the rules—especially those involving the series of annual withdrawals from an IRA before you turn 59½. These rules can be mighty tricky, and if you trip up, you could trigger the penalty.

IRA Offers Liquidity

Another factor in favor of IRAs is liquidity. Suppose you lose your job and you're strapped for cash. If you leave your money in your former employer's plan, you may have trouble getting access to it; the plan may have restrictions, and it may be some time before you can make a withdrawal.

If you move your money to an IRA, however, you can get access almost immediately. You'll pay tax on the money you withdraw (you may also face a penalty, unless you qualify for one of the exceptions listed earlier in this chapter). Withdrawing money from any kind of retirement savings plan should always be a last resort. Still, it can be a comfort to know that the money is there, easily accessible, from an IRA in case you really need it.

Move the Money Directly

If you choose the IRA rollover option, your employer may offer to let you take the money in the form of a check and bring it yourself to the IRA custodian or trustee.

Don't do it. This can trigger tax trouble if the rules aren't followed precisely. Instead, opt for the direct transfer—technically, a *direct rollover*—which moves the money directly, behind the scenes, from one place to another; the money doesn't touch your hands.

Last-Minute Rollover

Suppose you've already cashed out of your plan, and you've now changed your mind: you want to do a rollover after all.

What can you do? Don't fret; you still have the opportunity to complete a rollover yourself and have it count, as long as you do it within 60 days of having received the money from your employer.

There's one problem with this. Not knowing that you were going to roll over the money, your employer withheld 20 percent of it when cashing you out. As a result, to avoid tax trouble, you must now make up for that 20 percent in your rollover.

For example, suppose you had $30,000 in your plan when you cashed out. Your employer withheld 20 percent, $6,000 in this example. That left you with $24,000. You now want to roll it over into an IRA, within the 60-day deadline, so you'll avoid tax trouble.

That's fine. But to escape the tax trouble, you must not only roll over the $24,000 but also find an extra $6,000 somewhere so that you roll over the entire $30,000. (You'll get back the $6,000 your employer withheld when you file your federal income tax return.)

As you can see, this process can get complicated quickly. Your best bet is to stick with a direct rollover.

One Key Exception: Company Stock

Although rolling over your retirement plan money directly to an IRA has lots of benefits, think twice if your employer plan includes company stock. Here's why.

If you roll over the stock to an IRA and later withdraw it, the entire amount is treated as ordinary income, and all of it gets taxed—at your highest marginal rate.

If you don't roll over the stock but instead withdraw and sell it later on, your profit will be treated as capital gains, subject to favorable capital gains rates.

In other words, odd as it may seem, you may be better off in the long run if you withdraw the stock from your company plan and pay tax on it up front, instead of rolling it over to an IRA and postponing the tax.

How could this be?

Here's an example of how it works.

Suppose that Selena is retiring from her company. She plans to roll over the entire amount in her 401(k) account directly to an IRA. Her 401(k) includes 1,500 shares of company stock. For convenience, let's say that she bought the stock for $10 a share, for a total of $15,000. Let's also say that the stock is going to triple in value over the next several years, to $30 a share, for a total of $45,000.

Let's look at the tax impact.

Rolling Over the Stock. If she rolls over the stock today, from her 401(k) plan to an IRA, she pays no tax; tax is due only when the stock is withdrawn from the IRA.

Now let's say that several years have passed and the stock inside her IRA is worth a total of $45,000. She withdraws all of it. What's the tax impact? She treats the entire $45,000 as ordinary income. Assuming for convenience that she pays tax at a rate of 30 percent, she owes Uncle Sam $13,500 in tax.

Withdrawing the Stock. Under this option, Selena decides instead to split up her 401(k). She withdraws the stock and dumps the rest of her 401(k) into an IRA. (Either she moves the stock to a regular brokerage account or takes possession of the stock herself, perhaps by receiving stock certificates.)

She must pay tax on the stock that she's withdrawn from her company retirement plan, and the tax must be paid at the point of withdrawal. However, she pays the tax not on the market value of the stock, but rather on her *basis* for the shares—on how much she originally paid—which is $15,000 (1,500 shares times $10 a share). As a result, she must hand over $4,500 in tax.

Now let's suppose that the value of the stock triples, to $45,000, and Selena sells. What kind of a tax bill will Selena pay on her profit? Only $6,000. (Remember that, out of the total sale proceeds of $45,000, she already paid tax on $15,000, so only the remaining $30,000 is taxed—at a maximum capital gains rate of 20 percent.)

Comparing the Options. Now let's compare the impact of the two options.

In the first option, she pays $13,500 in tax. In the second option, she pays only $6,000.

What about the $4,500 in tax that Selena paid when she withdrew the stock from her employer's plan instead of rolling it to an IRA? Even when she adds that in, Selena still wins: the first option costs her $13,500, while the second option costs her $10,500.

Technically, the experts call this a tax break on *net unrealized appreciation* (NUA). If you roll the stock instead of withdrawing it, you lose the NUA break.

If your company retirement plan includes shares of company stock, be sure to meet with an accountant or other financial professional who's familiar with the rules and can show you how they fit your circumstances.

Rolling Over to a New Employer's Plan

If you're leaving one job for another and your new job allows for rollovers, what should you do: rollover to an IRA or to your new employer's plan?

The answer generally depends on your circumstances, on what's important to you now, and what may be important to you in the future. In other words, there's no one-size-fits-all answer.

Leaving It with Your Employer

Whether you're deciding to leave your retirement savings with your former employer's plan or move it to your new employer's plan, you need to consider the advantages and disadvantages of employer plans (compared to IRAs).

Advantages of Employer Plans

Borrowing. You can't borrow from your IRA. True, you can pull money out of an IRA, but only temporarily. If it's not back within 60 days, you face tax and potential penalty.

With many employer-sponsored plans, however, you may borrow from your plan account. Many plans also make the process somewhat painless from an administrative standpoint. You fill out a bit of paperwork, and you've got your loan.

If you think you're going to have to borrow from your retirement savings plan money at some point, and your new employer's plan has a loan provision, consider rolling the money into the plan sponsored by the new employer.

I don't recommend borrowing from your employer-sponsored plan. Unless you're absolutely certain that your job is secure (few people can be so sure), you'll face big tax trouble if you lose your job and can't pay back the loan promptly.

When you leave your job, your plan loan typically comes due in full. In other words, you may have to pay off the entire balance. If you don't, the balance will be treated as a withdrawal, what the experts call a *distribution*. As a result, you'll have to pay tax—and possibly a penalty—on the entire amount.

Some employers will give you a grace period, allowing you some time to scrape up enough money from other sources to pay off the outstanding bal-

---

BUSINESS OWNERS CAN BORROW

Thanks to a new federal tax law, more people are now able to borrow from their retirement savings plans at work.

Under the old rules, you generally couldn't borrow from your plan if you were a sole proprietor, a partner who owned more than 10 percent of the partnership, or an employee or officer of a Subchapter S corporation who owned more than 5 percent of the corporation's outstanding stock.

Under the new law, however, owner-employees may now borrow from their retirement savings plans at work, too.

ance on your plan loan. Others will let you continue to make payments on the installment plan, until your loan is paid off in full as called for under the original loan schedule.

In either case, however, you must find money from someplace to pay these bills. If you've lost your job through a layoff, for example, will you have the resources to pay off the loan? Maybe not.

Convenience. By moving the money from your old plan (or IRA) to your new employer's plan, you'll have all your retirement savings money in one place.

This can be handy for lots of reasons. For instance, you get the convenience of a single account statement, so there's less record keeping to worry about. Also, if you're not a do-it-yourself kind of saver, you may find bouncing ideas off of colleagues (or former colleagues) helpful.

CHOICES AT RETIREMENT

In a survey of people who took part in defined contribution plans (such as 401(k) plans, 403(b) plans, the federal government's Thrift Savings Plan, and Section 457 plans sponsored by state and local governments), 70 percent said they had several *distribution* (withdrawal) options available to them when they retired. Here's what they picked.

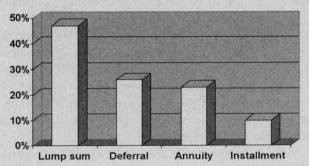

Most of those who chose the lump sum option rolled the money into an IRA. *Deferral* means that workers left the money in the plan for a certain time after retiring. Some chose more than one option.

Source: Investment Company Institute, 2000 survey.

Postponing Withdrawals. With a traditional IRA, remember, you must withdraw at least a minimum amount from your account, starting for the year in which you turn 70½.

However, if you leave the money in your 401(k) or similar employer-sponsored plan, and you keep working there beyond age 70½, you don't have to withdraw money from your plan account if the plan allows. Instead, you may have until April 1 of the year following the year in which you actually retire from that job.

This can allow the money in your account to keep growing on a tax-deferred basis for as long as you keep working—into your 70s, 80s, or beyond.

Penalty. If you withdraw money from an IRA before you turn 59½, you'll be subject to a 10 percent penalty (unless an exception applies). However, if you keep your money in an employer-sponsored plan and take withdrawals from it, you won't be subject to the 10 percent early withdrawal penalty if you're at least 55 when you leave or lose your job.

Protection from Creditors. This is tricky. As a general rule, federal law protects the money in your employer-sponsored plan from claims by creditors (such as those arising in federal bankruptcy proceedings).

However, IRAs enjoy no such protection at the federal level. Many states do shield IRAs from creditors, but some don't. (Those states that protect traditional IRAs may not extend the same coverage to Roth IRAs.) IRAs may also receive limited protection in bankruptcy proceedings, depending on where the proceedings take place and your state's rules.

If you're a doctor, lawyer, or other professional, this issue may be of critical importance to you; the nature of your profession may expose you to legal claims—from lawsuits, for example—that other people don't normally face.

Remember: The general rule is that employer-sponsored plans have federal protection and IRAs don't. However, protections at the state level for both retirement savings schemes—whether employer-sponsored plans or IRAs—vary dramatically from state to state.

So don't go by the general rule. Be sure to check with a lawyer who's familiar with the rules before you make a decision as to where to park your retirement savings.

Brand Loyalty. You may like the investment options available at your old job, and you may also feel some loyalty to your former employer. Furthermore, you may simply not be in a position to make investment decisions on your own at this point.

Downsides of an Employer Plan

Keep in mind, however, that employer-sponsored retirement-savings plans have some drawbacks. Here are a few.

Short-Changing Beneficiaries. By keeping the money in your 401(k) or similar employer-sponsored plan, you probably won't give your beneficiaries the chance to stretch out withdrawals. Once you die, the plan will probably require that your beneficiaries take the entire amount within a fairly short time.

Why? In general, a 401(k) or other such plan doesn't want to shoulder the burden of keeping track of beneficiaries—and their beneficiaries—over a period that could stretch into decades. A lot of administrative expense is involved, costs that the plan itself may have to bear.

As a result, as a matter of policy, the plan may require your beneficiaries to withdraw the money after a certain period of time, perhaps five years or less.

Bear in mind, too, that a beneficiary who is not your spouse cannot roll over the money that's in the account and treat it as his or her own. A non-spouse beneficiary must instead make withdrawals over a lifetime. (Keep in mind, however, that this is what the law allows; individual plans are free to set restrictions.)

If you roll over the money into an IRA, however, you can give beneficiaries the opportunity to stretch out withdrawals.

Roth IRA Conversion. If you leave the money in your employer-sponsored plan, you lose the opportunity to convert your retirement savings dollars into a Roth IRA. Remember the rule: you may convert to a Roth IRA only those dollars that are in a traditional IRA.

A Shocking Study by the IRS

Why bother poring through a chapter devoted almost entirely to helping you decide where to put your retirement savings? Because you need to know your rights. Sure, lots of workers already understand the options available to them once they leave their job.

If you're like most people, however, chances are you have lots of other things going on in your life; you haven't had time to devote to the scientific study of rollover rules for retirement plans. For this reason, I chose this subject as the focus for this chapter.

There's one other reason: your employer may drop the ball on this, and you need to know your rights and how they work.

In checking on some details about retirement savings plans and rollover rules, I came upon a study by the Internal Revenue Service that I found shocking.

From 1995 to 1997, examiners in IRS field offices took an especially close look at 401(k) plans. Of the 472 plans they studied, 208 plans had one or more violations. In other words, more than 44 percent showed violations of the rules.

True, tons of regulations apply to retirement savings plans, and perhaps plans can easily be forgiven for tripping up on a few of them.

Get this, though: of all the categories of rules violations, the one with the greatest number of violations involved—you guessed it—rollovers. What kinds of errors? Some plans failed outright to give departing workers the option to roll over money to an IRA or another employer's plan. In other words, because of a mix-up by the people running these plans, some workers strode out the door with cash from their 401(k) plans—and walked into a nightmare of tax problems. (In some cases, plans failed to give employees written notice about how the rollover rules work.)

Most people who run 401(k) and similar retirement savings plans at work wind up logging lots of time, not only so that they know the rules but also to get the correct information out to employees. In some cases, however, the people who run the plans drop the ball. For this and other reasons, you need to understand your rights around retirement savings when you leave your job. After all, you earned it and you saved it—it's your money.

In Summary . . .

When you leave your job, you typically face a choice about what to do with the money you've saved in your 401(k) or other such retirement savings plan at work. Remember that there's no one-size-fits-all answer.

In many cases, your best choice is an IRA rollover. However, what's best for *you* depends on your circumstances. In some cases, another option may be most suitable—if your plan includes employer stock, for example.

Before you make up your mind, talk with an accountant, financial planner, or other advisor who knows about the rules and how to apply them to your personal circumstances.

Here are some other points to keep in mind.

- In some cases, your company-sponsored retirement plan may also be your IRA. For example, many employers offer a Simplified Employee Pension (SEP) plan or a Savings Incentive Match Plan For Employees (a SIMPLE plan). Your employer may link such a plan to an IRA. If that's the case, your company plan already is an IRA, so you need not choose

whether to roll over your money from your company plan to an IRA—
it's already in one.

- This chapter assumes that you have access to the money in your
employer-sponsored plan when you leave work. Keep in mind, however, that some retirement savings plans have strict rules that generally
require you to wait until you reach normal retirement age (typically 65)
to claim your money—even if you leave for another job first.

- If you leave your job, some plans will cash you out if the balance in
your retirement savings plan is below a certain amount—generally
$5,000—even if you would prefer to keep the money in the plan. In
such cases, however, you generally may have the plan move the money
either to an IRA or your new employer's plan. (In fact, plans eventually
will be required by law to transfer such cash-outs automatically to an
IRA, if the amount of the cash-out exceeds $1,000.)

- If you're retiring, your plan may offer you another option besides the
ones listed here: an annuity. This option generally gives you the chance
to use the money in your plan account to buy an annuity (typically
through an insurance company or intermediary). Your annuity contract
probably gives you periodic payments, usually monthly, either for a
fixed period or over your life (or the lives of you and your beneficiary).

  If you're interested in this option, consider it carefully, bearing in
mind that any "guarantee" behind the annuity depends on the financial
strength of the insurer that stands behind your annuity contract. Consult a financial advisor about this option, and also check on the strength
of the insurer. Several companies provide ratings and financial reports on
insurers, including Weiss Ratings, Inc., of Florida <www.weissratings
.com>, Standard & Poor's of New York <www.standardandpoors.com>,
and A.M. Best Co. <www.ambest.com>. Your employer may also allow
you to withdraw your money at retirement in installments over time.

- Under the old rules, you couldn't roll over after-tax contributions in your
employer-sponsored plan. In other words, if you contributed money to
a 401(k) plan on an after-tax basis (so you did not get a federal income
tax break when you made the contributions), you couldn't roll that
money over—either to an IRA or to another employer's plan. If your
account was involved in a rollover, the plan administrator had to carve
out the after-tax contributions and give them to you, rolling over everything else (either to an IRA or another employer's plan).

  Under the new rules, however, you may now roll over your after-
tax contributions, either to an IRA or to another employer's plan. (This
assumes the new employer's plan will accept them. Some won't, because they're required to account for those dollars separately and the
money those dollars earn). Use this new option to your benefit. Under

the old rules, you received the after-tax contributions, probably in the form of a check, and probably spent it. Under the new rules, you can roll those dollars—along with everything else you've saved in your plan—into an IRA or another employer's plan, all in one neat package.

In other words, you can keep all those dollars together, and keep them working for you, all under the umbrella of a tax-sheltered retirement savings plan. Remember that when you finally take those dollars out, they won't be taxed, because you already paid tax on them (although you may need an accountant to help figure out which portion of a withdrawal is and isn't taxable).

- After-tax contributions held in an IRA can't be rolled over from the IRA to an employer-sponsored plan, a 403(b) plan, or a Section 457 plan.

For More Information . . .

The Investment Company Institute in Washington, D.C. A trade group for the mutual fund industry, this organization periodically surveys the states to see what kind of creditor protection they afford to IRAs. Check the organization's Web site for the latest data as a start in your decision-making process: <www.ici.org>.

Mutual fund companies. Many offer free information kits that can help you decide what to do with the money in your retirement savings plan at work. These include:

- Vanguard, at 800-523-8552; P.O. Box 2600, Valley Forge, PA 19482; or <www.vanguard.com>.
- T. Rowe Price, at 800-541-8460; P.O. Box 17302, Baltimore, MD 21297-1302; <www.troweprice.com>.
- Fidelity Investments, at 800-544-4774; 82 Devonshire Street, Boston, MA 02109; or <www.fidelity.com>.

Appendix A
Uniform Table for Calculating Minimum Required Withdrawals from IRAs by Owner

Age	Applicable divisor	Age	Applicable divisor
70	26.2	93	8.8
71	25.3	94	8.3
72	24.4	95	7.8
73	23.5	96	7.3
74	22.7	97	6.9
75	21.8	98	6.5
76	20.9	99	6.1
77	20.1	100	5.7
78	19.2	101	5.3
79	18.4	102	5.0
80	17.6	103	4.7
81	16.8	104	4.4
82	16.0	105	4.1
83	15.3	106	3.8
84	14.5	107	3.6
85	13.8	108	3.3
86	13.1	109	3.1
87	12.4	110	2.8
88	11.8	111	2.6
89	11.1	112	2.4
90	10.5	113	2.2
91	9.9	114	2.0
92	9.4	115 and older	1.8

Appendix B
Joint Life Table (to figure withdrawals when spouse is more than ten years younger than owner)

Ages	35	36	37	38	39	40	41	42	43	44
35	54.0	53.5	53.0	52.6	52.2	51.8	51.4	51.1	50.8	50.5
36	53.5	53.0	52.5	52.0	51.6	51.2	50.8	50.4	50.1	49.8
37	53.0	52.5	52.0	51.5	51.0	50.6	50.2	49.8	49.5	49.1
38	52.6	52.0	51.5	51.0	50.5	50.0	49.6	49.2	48.8	48.5
39	52.2	51.6	51.0	50.5	50.0	49.5	49.1	48.6	48.2	47.8
40	51.8	51.2	50.6	50.0	49.5	49.0	48.5	48.1	47.6	47.2
41	51.4	50.8	50.2	49.6	49.1	48.5	48.0	47.5	47.1	46.7
42	51.1	50.4	49.8	49.2	48.6	48.1	47.5	47.0	46.6	46.1
43	50.8	50.1	49.5	48.8	48.2	47.6	47.1	46.6	46.0	45.6
44	50.5	49.8	49.1	48.5	47.8	47.2	46.7	46.1	45.6	45.1
45	50.2	49.5	48.8	48.1	47.5	46.9	46.3	45.7	45.1	44.6
46	50.0	49.2	48.5	47.8	47.2	46.5	45.9	45.3	44.7	44.1
47	49.7	49.0	48.3	47.5	46.8	46.2	45.5	44.9	44.3	43.7
48	49.5	48.8	48.0	47.3	46.6	45.9	45.2	44.5	43.9	43.3
49	49.3	48.5	47.8	47.0	46.3	45.6	44.9	44.2	43.6	42.9
50	49.2	48.4	47.6	46.8	46.0	45.3	44.6	43.9	43.2	42.6
51	49.0	48.2	47.4	46.6	45.8	45.1	44.3	43.6	42.9	42.2
52	48.8	48.0	47.2	46.4	45.6	44.8	44.1	43.3	42.6	41.9
53	48.7	47.9	47.0	46.2	45.4	44.6	43.9	43.1	42.4	41.7
54	48.6	47.7	46.9	46.0	45.2	44.4	43.6	42.9	42.1	41.4
55	48.5	47.6	46.7	45.9	45.1	44.2	43.4	42.7	41.9	41.2
56	48.3	47.5	46.6	45.8	44.9	44.1	43.3	42.5	41.7	40.9
57	48.3	47.4	46.5	45.6	44.8	43.9	43.1	42.3	41.5	40.7
58	48.2	47.3	46.4	45.6	44.7	43.8	43.0	42.1	41.3	40.5
59	48.1	47.2	46.3	45.4	44.5	43.7	42.8	42.0	41.2	40.4

Joint Life Table (continued)

Ages	35	36	37	38	39	40	41	42	43	44
60	48.0	47.1	46.2	45.3	44.4	43.6	42.7	41.9	41.0	40.2
61	47.9	47.0	46.1	45.2	44.3	43.5	42.6	41.7	40.9	40.0
62	47.9	47.0	46.0	45.1	44.2	43.4	42.5	41.6	40.8	39.9
63	47.8	46.9	46.0	45.1	44.2	43.3	42.4	41.5	40.6	39.8
64	47.8	46.8	45.9	45.0	44.1	43.2	42.3	41.4	40.5	39.7
65	47.7	46.8	45.9	44.9	44.0	43.1	42.2	41.3	40.4	39.6
66	47.7	46.7	45.8	44.9	44.0	43.1	42.2	41.3	40.4	39.5
67	47.6	46.7	45.8	44.8	43.9	43.0	42.1	41.1	40.3	39.4
68	47.6	46.7	45.7	44.8	43.9	42.9	42.0	41.1	40.2	39.3
69	47.6	46.6	45.7	44.8	43.8	42.9	42.0	41.0	40.2	39.3
70	47.5	46.6	45.7	44.7	43.8	42.9	41.9	41.0	40.1	39.2
71	47.5	46.6	45.6	44.7	43.8	42.8	41.9	40.9	40.1	39.1
72	47.5	46.6	45.6	44.7	43.7	42.8	41.9	40.9	40.0	39.1
73	47.5	46.5	45.6	44.6	43.7	42.8	41.8	40.9	40.0	39.0
74	47.5	46.5	45.6	44.6	43.7	42.7	41.8	40.8	39.9	39.0
75	47.4	46.5	45.5	44.6	43.6	42.7	41.8	40.8	39.9	39.0
76	47.4	46.5	45.5	44.6	43.6	42.7	41.7	40.8	39.9	38.9
77	47.4	46.5	45.5	44.6	43.6	42.7	41.7	40.7	39.8	38.9
78	47.4	46.4	45.5	44.5	43.6	42.6	41.7	40.7	39.8	38.9
79	47.4	46.4	45.5	44.5	43.6	42.6	41.7	40.7	39.8	38.9
80	47.4	46.4	45.5	44.5	43.6	42.6	41.7	40.7	39.8	38.8
81	47.4	46.4	45.5	44.5	43.5	42.6	41.6	40.7	39.8	38.8
82	47.4	46.4	45.4	44.5	43.5	42.6	41.6	40.7	39.7	38.8
83	47.4	46.4	45.4	44.5	43.5	42.6	41.6	40.7	39.7	38.8
84	47.4	46.4	45.4	44.5	43.5	42.6	41.6	40.7	39.7	38.8
85	47.4	46.4	45.4	44.5	43.5	42.6	41.6	40.6	39.7	38.8
86	47.3	46.4	45.4	44.5	43.5	42.5	41.6	40.6	39.7	38.8
87	47.3	46.4	45.4	44.5	43.5	42.5	41.6	40.6	39.7	38.7
88	47.3	46.4	45.4	44.5	43.5	42.5	41.6	40.6	39.7	38.7
89	47.3	46.4	45.4	44.4	43.5	42.5	41.6	40.6	39.7	38.7
90	47.3	46.4	45.4	44.4	43.5	42.5	41.6	40.6	39.7	38.7
91	47.3	46.4	45.4	44.4	43.5	42.5	41.6	40.6	39.7	38.7
92	47.3	46.4	45.4	44.4	43.5	42.5	41.6	40.6	39.7	38.7

Joint Life Table (continued)

Ages	45	46	47	48	49	50	51	52	53	54
45	44.1	43.6	43.2	42.7	42.3	42.0	41.6	41.3	41.0	40.7
46	43.6	43.1	42.6	42.2	41.8	41.4	41.0	40.6	40.3	40.0
47	43.2	42.6	42.1	41.7	41.2	40.8	40.4	40.0	39.7	39.3
48	42.7	42.2	41.7	41.2	40.7	40.2	39.8	39.4	39.0	38.7
49	42.3	41.8	41.2	40.7	40.2	39.7	39.3	38.8	38.4	38.1
50	42.0	41.4	40.8	40.2	39.7	39.2	38.7	38.3	37.9	37.5
51	41.6	41.0	40.4	39.8	39.3	38.7	38.2	37.8	37.3	36.9
52	41.3	40.6	40.0	39.4	38.8	38.3	37.8	37.3	36.8	36.4
53	41.0	40.3	39.7	39.0	38.4	37.9	37.3	36.8	36.3	35.8
54	40.7	40.0	39.3	38.7	38.1	37.5	36.9	36.4	35.8	35.3
55	40.4	39.7	39.0	38.4	37.7	37.1	36.5	35.9	35.4	34.9
56	40.2	39.5	38.7	38.1	37.4	36.8	36.1	35.6	35.0	34.4
57	40.0	39.2	38.5	37.8	37.1	36.4	35.8	35.2	34.6	34.0
58	39.7	39.0	38.2	37.5	36.8	36.1	35.5	34.8	34.2	33.6
59	39.6	38.8	38.0	37.3	36.6	35.9	35.2	34.5	33.9	33.3
60	39.4	38.6	37.8	37.1	36.3	35.6	34.9	34.2	33.6	32.9
61	39.2	38.4	37.6	36.9	36.1	35.4	34.6	33.9	33.3	32.6
62	39.1	38.3	37.5	36.7	35.9	35.1	34.4	33.7	33.0	32.3
63	38.9	38.1	37.3	36.5	35.7	34.9	34.2	33.5	32.7	32.0
64	38.8	38.0	37.2	36.3	35.5	34.8	34.0	33.2	32.5	31.8
65	38.7	37.9	37.0	36.2	35.4	34.6	33.8	33.0	32.3	31.6
66	38.6	37.8	36.9	36.1	35.2	34.4	33.6	32.9	32.1	31.4
67	38.5	37.7	36.8	36.0	35.1	34.3	33.5	32.7	31.9	31.2
68	38.4	37.6	36.7	35.8	35.0	34.2	33.4	32.5	31.8	31.0
69	38.4	37.5	36.6	35.7	34.9	34.1	33.2	32.4	31.6	30.8
70	38.3	37.4	36.5	35.7	34.8	34.0	33.1	32.3	31.5	30.7
71	38.2	37.3	36.5	35.6	34.7	33.9	33.0	32.2	31.4	30.5
72	38.2	37.3	36.4	35.5	34.6	33.8	32.9	32.1	31.2	30.4
73	38.1	37.2	36.3	35.4	34.6	33.7	32.8	32.0	31.1	30.3
74	38.1	37.2	36.3	35.4	34.5	33.6	32.8	31.9	31.1	30.2
75	38.1	37.1	36.2	35.3	34.5	33.6	32.7	31.8	31.0	30.1
76	38.0	37.1	36.2	35.3	34.4	33.5	32.6	31.8	30.9	30.1
77	38.0	37.1	36.2	35.3	34.4	33.5	32.6	31.7	30.8	30.0
78	38.0	37.0	36.1	35.2	34.3	33.4	32.5	31.7	30.8	29.9
79	37.9	37.0	36.1	35.2	34.3	33.4	32.5	31.6	30.7	29.9

Joint Life Table (continued)

Ages	45	46	47	48	49	50	51	52	53	54
80	37.9	37.0	36.1	35.2	34.2	33.4	32.5	31.6	30.7	29.8
81	37.9	37.0	36.0	35.1	34.2	33.3	32.4	31.5	30.7	29.8
82	37.9	36.9	36.0	35.1	34.2	33.3	32.4	31.5	30.6	29.7
83	37.9	36.9	36.0	35.1	34.2	33.3	32.4	31.5	30.6	29.7
84	37.8	36.9	36.0	35.1	34.2	33.2	32.3	31.4	30.6	29.7
85	37.8	36.9	36.0	35.1	34.1	33.2	32.3	31.4	30.5	29.6
86	37.8	36.9	36.0	35.0	34.1	33.2	32.3	31.4	30.5	29.6
87	37.8	36.9	35.9	35.0	34.1	33.2	32.3	31.4	30.5	29.6
88	37.8	36.9	35.9	35.0	34.1	33.2	32.3	31.4	30.5	29.6
89	37.8	36.9	35.9	35.0	34.1	33.2	32.3	31.4	30.5	29.6
90	37.8	36.9	35.9	35.0	34.1	33.2	32.3	31.3	30.5	29.6
91	37.8	36.8	35.9	35.0	34.1	33.2	32.2	31.3	30.4	29.5
92	37.8	36.8	35.9	35.0	34.1	33.2	32.2	31.3	30.4	29.5

Joint Life Table (continued)

Ages	55	56	57	58	59	60	61	62	63	64
55	34.4	33.9	33.5	33.1	32.7	32.3	32.0	31.7	31.4	31.1
56	33.9	33.4	33.0	32.5	32.1	31.7	31.4	31.0	30.7	30.4
57	33.5	33.0	32.5	32.0	31.6	31.2	30.8	30.4	30.1	29.8
58	33.1	32.5	32.0	31.5	31.1	30.6	30.2	29.9	29.5	29.2
59	32.7	32.1	31.6	31.1	30.6	30.1	29.7	29.3	28.9	28.6
60	32.3	31.7	31.2	30.6	30.1	29.7	29.2	28.8	28.4	28.0
61	32.0	31.4	30.8	30.2	29.7	29.2	28.7	28.3	27.8	27.4
62	31.7	31.0	30.4	29.9	29.3	28.8	28.3	27.8	27.3	26.9
63	31.4	30.7	30.1	29.5	28.9	28.4	27.8	27.3	26.9	26.4
64	31.1	30.4	29.8	29.2	28.6	28.0	27.4	26.9	26.4	25.9
65	30.9	30.2	29.5	28.9	28.2	27.6	27.1	26.5	26.0	25.5
66	30.6	29.9	29.2	28.6	27.9	27.3	26.7	26.1	25.6	25.1
67	30.4	29.7	29.0	28.3	27.6	27.0	26.4	25.8	25.2	24.7
68	30.2	29.5	28.8	28.1	27.4	26.7	26.1	25.5	24.9	24.3
69	30.1	29.3	28.6	27.8	27.1	26.5	25.8	25.2	24.6	24.0
70	29.9	29.1	28.4	27.6	26.9	26.2	25.6	24.9	24.3	23.7
71	29.7	29.0	28.2	27.5	26.7	26.0	25.3	24.7	24.0	23.4
72	29.6	28.8	28.1	27.3	26.5	25.8	25.1	24.4	23.8	23.1
73	29.5	28.7	27.9	27.1	26.4	25.6	24.9	24.2	23.5	22.9
74	29.4	28.6	27.8	27.0	26.2	25.5	24.7	24.0	23.3	22.7
75	29.3	28.5	27.7	26.9	26.1	25.3	24.6	23.8	23.1	22.4
76	29.2	28.4	27.6	26.8	26.0	25.2	24.4	23.7	23.0	22.3
77	29.1	28.3	27.5	26.7	25.9	25.1	24.3	23.6	22.8	22.1
78	29.1	28.2	27.4	26.6	25.8	25.0	24.2	23.4	22.7	21.9
79	29.0	28.2	27.3	26.5	25.7	24.9	24.1	23.3	22.6	21.8
80	29.0	28.1	27.3	26.4	25.6	24.8	24.0	23.2	22.4	21.7
81	28.9	28.1	27.2	26.4	25.5	24.7	23.9	23.1	22.3	21.6
82	28.9	28.0	27.2	26.3	25.5	24.6	23.8	23.0	22.3	21.5
83	28.8	28.0	27.1	26.3	25.4	24.6	23.8	23.0	22.2	21.4
84	28.8	27.9	27.1	26.2	25.4	24.5	23.7	22.9	22.1	21.3
85	28.8	27.9	27.0	26.2	25.3	24.5	23.7	22.8	22.0	21.3
86	28.7	27.9	27.0	26.1	25.3	24.5	23.6	22.8	22.0	21.2
87	28.7	27.8	27.0	26.1	25.3	24.4	23.6	22.8	21.9	21.1
88	28.7	27.8	27.0	26.1	25.2	24.4	23.5	22.7	21.9	21.1
89	28.7	27.8	26.9	26.1	25.2	24.4	23.5	22.7	21.9	21.1

Joint Life Table (continued)

Ages	55	56	57	58	59	60	61	62	63	64
90	28.7	27.8	26.9	26.1	25.2	24.3	23.5	22.7	21.8	21.0
91	28.7	27.8	26.9	26.0	25.2	24.3	23.5	22.6	21.8	21.0
92	28.6	27.8	26.9	26.0	25.2	24.3	23.5	22.6	21.8	21.0
93	28.6	27.8	26.9	26.0	25.1	24.3	23.4	22.6	21.8	20.9
94	28.6	27.7	26.9	26.0	25.1	24.3	23.4	22.6	21.7	20.9
95	28.6	27.7	26.9	26.0	25.1	24.3	23.4	22.6	21.7	20.9
96	28.6	27.7	26.9	26.0	25.1	24.2	23.4	22.6	21.7	20.9
97	28.6	27.7	26.8	26.0	25.1	24.2	23.4	22.5	21.7	20.9
98	28.6	27.7	26.8	26.0	25.1	24.2	23.4	22.5	21.7	20.9
99	28.6	27.7	26.8	26.0	25.1	24.2	23.4	22.5	21.7	20.9
100	28.6	27.7	26.8	26.0	25.1	24.2	23.4	22.5	21.7	20.8
101	28.6	27.7	26.8	25.9	25.1	24.2	23.4	22.5	21.7	20.8
102	28.6	27.7	26.8	25.9	25.1	24.2	23.3	22.5	21.7	20.8
103	28.6	27.7	26.8	25.9	25.1	24.2	23.3	22.5	21.7	20.8
104	28.6	27.7	26.8	25.9	25.1	24.2	23.3	22.5	21.6	20.8
105	28.6	27.7	26.8	25.9	25.1	24.2	23.3	22.5	21.6	20.8
106	28.6	27.7	26.8	25.9	25.1	24.2	23.3	22.5	21.6	20.8
107	28.6	27.7	26.8	25.9	25.1	24.2	23.3	22.5	21.6	20.8
108	28.6	27.7	26.8	25.9	25.1	24.2	23.3	22.5	21.6	20.8
109	28.6	27.7	26.8	25.9	25.1	24.2	23.3	22.5	21.6	20.8
110	28.6	27.7	26.8	25.9	25.1	24.2	23.3	22.5	21.6	20.8
111	28.6	27.7	26.8	25.9	25.0	24.2	23.3	22.5	21.6	20.8
112	28.6	27.7	26.8	25.9	25.0	24.2	23.3	22.5	21.6	20.8
113	28.6	27.7	26.8	25.9	25.0	24.2	23.3	22.5	21.6	20.8
114	28.6	27.7	26.8	25.9	25.0	24.2	23.3	22.5	21.6	20.8
115	28.6	27.7	26.8	25.9	25.0	24.2	23.3	22.5	21.6	20.8

Joint Life Table (continued)

Ages	65	66	67	68	69	70	71	72	73	74
65	25.0	24.6	24.2	23.8	23.4	23.1	22.8	22.5	22.2	22.0
66	24.6	24.1	23.7	23.3	22.9	22.5	22.2	21.9	21.6	21.4
67	24.2	23.7	23.2	22.8	22.4	22.0	21.7	21.3	21.0	20.8
68	23.8	23.3	22.8	22.3	21.9	21.5	21.2	20.8	20.5	20.2
69	23.4	22.9	22.4	21.9	21.5	21.1	20.7	20.3	20.0	19.6
70	23.1	22.5	22.0	21.5	21.1	20.6	20.2	19.8	19.4	19.1
71	22.8	22.2	21.7	21.2	20.7	20.2	19.8	19.4	19.0	18.6
72	22.6	21.9	21.3	20.8	20.3	19.8	19.4	18.9	18.5	18.2
73	22.2	21.6	21.0	20.5	20.0	19.4	19.0	18.5	18.1	17.7
74	22.0	21.4	20.8	20.2	19.6	19.1	18.6	18.2	17.7	17.3
75	21.8	21.1	20.5	19.9	19.3	18.8	18.3	17.8	17.3	16.9
76	21.6	20.9	20.3	19.7	19.1	18.5	18.0	17.5	17.0	16.5
77	21.4	20.7	20.1	19.4	18.8	18.3	17.7	17.2	16.7	16.2
78	21.2	20.5	19.9	19.2	18.6	18.0	17.5	16.9	16.4	15.9
79	21.1	20.4	19.7	19.0	18.4	17.8	17.2	16.7	16.1	15.6
80	21.0	20.2	19.5	18.9	18.2	17.6	17.0	16.4	15.9	15.4
81	20.8	20.1	19.4	18.7	18.1	17.4	16.8	16.2	15.7	15.1
82	20.7	20.0	19.3	18.6	17.9	17.3	16.6	16.0	15.5	14.9
83	20.6	19.9	19.2	18.5	17.8	17.1	16.5	15.9	15.3	14.7
84	20.5	19.8	19.1	18.4	17.7	17.0	16.3	15.7	15.1	14.5
85	20.5	19.7	19.0	18.3	17.6	16.9	16.2	15.6	15.0	14.4
86	20.4	19.6	18.9	18.2	17.5	16.8	16.1	15.5	14.8	14.2
87	20.4	19.6	18.8	18.1	17.4	16.7	16.0	15.4	14.7	14.1
88	20.3	19.5	18.8	18.0	17.3	16.6	15.9	15.3	14.6	14.0
89	20.3	19.5	18.7	18.0	17.2	16.5	15.8	15.2	14.5	13.9
90	20.2	19.4	18.7	17.9	17.2	16.5	15.8	15.1	14.5	13.8
91	20.2	19.4	18.6	17.9	17.1	16.4	15.7	15.0	14.4	13.7
92	20.2	19.4	18.6	17.8	17.1	16.4	15.7	15.0	14.3	13.7
93	20.1	19.3	18.6	17.8	17.1	16.3	15.6	14.9	14.3	13.6
94	20.1	19.3	18.5	17.8	17.0	16.3	15.6	14.9	14.2	13.6
95	20.1	19.3	18.5	17.8	17.0	16.3	15.6	14.9	14.2	13.5
96	20.1	19.3	18.5	17.7	17.0	16.2	15.5	14.8	14.2	13.5
97	20.1	19.3	18.5	17.7	17.0	16.2	15.5	14.8	14.1	13.5
98	20.1	19.3	18.5	17.7	16.9	16.2	15.5	14.8	14.1	13.4
99	20.0	19.2	18.5	17.7	16.9	16.2	15.5	14.7	14.1	13.4

Joint Life Table (continued)

Ages	65	66	67	68	69	70	71	72	73	74
100	20.0	19.2	18.4	17.7	16.9	16.2	15.4	14.7	14.0	13.4
101	20.0	19.2	18.4	17.7	16.9	16.1	15.4	14.7	14.0	13.3
102	20.0	19.2	18.4	17.6	16.9	16.1	15.4	14.7	14.0	13.3
103	20.0	19.2	18.4	17.6	16.9	16.1	15.4	14.7	14.0	13.3
104	20.0	19.2	18.4	17.6	16.9	16.1	15.4	14.7	14.0	13.3
105	20.0	19.2	18.4	17.6	16.8	16.1	15.4	14.6	13.9	13.3
106	20.0	19.2	18.4	17.6	16.8	16.1	15.3	14.6	13.9	13.3
107	20.0	19.2	18.4	17.6	16.8	16.1	15.3	14.6	13.9	13.2
108	20.0	19.2	18.4	17.6	16.8	16.1	15.3	14.6	13.9	13.2
109	20.0	19.2	18.4	17.6	16.8	16.1	15.3	14.6	13.9	13.2
110	20.0	19.2	18.4	17.6	16.8	16.1	15.3	14.6	13.9	13.2
111	20.0	19.2	18.4	17.6	16.8	16.0	15.3	14.6	13.9	13.2
112	20.0	19.2	18.4	17.6	16.8	16.0	15.3	14.6	13.9	13.2
113	20.0	19.2	18.4	17.6	16.8	16.0	15.3	14.6	13.9	13.2
114	20.0	19.2	18.4	17.6	16.8	16.0	15.3	14.6	13.9	13.2
115	20.0	19.2	18.4	17.6	16.8	16.0	15.3	14.6	13.9	13.2

Joint Life Table (continued)

Ages	75	76	77	78	79	80	81	82	83	84
75	16.5	16.1	15.8	15.4	15.1	14.9	14.6	14.4	14.2	14.0
76	16.1	15.7	15.4	15.0	14.7	14.4	14.1	13.9	13.7	13.5
77	15.8	15.4	15.0	14.6	14.3	14.0	13.7	13.4	13.2	13.0
78	15.4	15.0	14.6	14.2	13.9	13.5	13.2	13.0	12.7	12.5
79	15.1	14.7	14.3	13.9	13.5	13.2	12.8	12.5	12.3	12.0
80	14.9	14.4	14.0	13.5	13.2	12.8	12.5	12.2	11.9	11.6
81	14.6	14.1	13.7	13.2	12.8	12.5	12.1	11.8	11.5	11.2
82	14.4	13.9	13.4	13.0	12.5	12.2	11.8	11.5	11.1	10.9
83	14.2	13.7	13.2	12.7	12.3	11.9	11.5	11.1	10.8	10.5
84	14.0	13.5	13.0	12.5	12.0	11.6	11.2	10.9	10.5	10.2
85	13.8	13.3	12.8	12.3	11.8	11.4	11.0	10.6	10.2	9.9
86	13.7	13.1	12.6	12.1	11.6	11.2	10.8	10.4	10.0	9.7
87	13.5	13.0	12.4	11.9	11.4	11.0	10.6	10.1	9.8	9.4
88	13.4	12.8	12.3	11.8	11.3	10.8	10.4	10.0	9.6	9.2
89	13.3	12.7	12.2	11.6	11.1	10.7	10.2	9.8	9.4	9.0
90	13.2	12.6	12.1	11.5	11.0	10.5	10.1	9.6	9.2	8.8
91	13.1	12.5	12.0	11.4	10.9	10.4	9.9	9.5	9.1	8.7
92	13.1	12.5	11.9	11.3	10.8	10.3	9.8	9.4	8.9	8.5
93	13.0	12.4	11.8	11.3	10.7	10.2	9.7	9.3	8.8	8.4
94	12.9	12.3	11.7	11.2	10.6	10.1	9.6	9.2	8.7	8.3
95	12.9	12.3	11.7	11.1	10.6	10.1	9.6	9.1	8.6	8.2
96	12.9	12.2	11.6	11.1	10.5	10.0	9.5	9.0	8.5	8.1
97	12.8	12.2	11.6	11.0	10.5	9.9	9.4	8.9	8.5	8.0
98	12.8	12.2	11.5	11.0	10.4	9.9	9.4	8.9	8.4	8.0
99	12.7	12.1	11.5	10.9	10.4	9.8	9.3	8.8	8.3	7.9
100	12.7	12.1	11.5	10.9	10.3	9.8	9.2	8.7	8.3	7.8
101	12.7	12.1	11.4	10.8	10.3	9.7	9.2	8.7	8.2	7.8
102	12.7	12.0	11.4	10.8	10.2	9.7	9.2	8.7	8.2	7.7
103	12.6	12.0	11.4	10.8	10.2	9.7	9.1	8.6	8.1	7.7
104	12.6	12.0	11.4	10.8	10.2	9.6	9.1	8.6	8.1	7.6
105	12.6	12.0	11.3	10.7	10.2	9.6	9.1	8.5	8.0	7.6
106	12.6	11.9	11.3	10.7	10.1	9.6	9.0	8.5	8.0	7.5
107	12.6	11.9	11.3	10.7	10.1	9.6	9.0	8.5	8.0	7.5
108	12.6	11.9	11.3	10.7	10.1	9.5	9.0	8.5	8.0	7.5
109	12.6	11.9	11.3	10.7	10.1	9.5	9.0	8.4	7.9	7.5

Joint Life Table (continued)

Ages	75	76	77	78	79	80	81	82	83	84
110	12.6	11.9	11.3	10.7	10.1	9.5	9.0	8.4	7.9	7.4
111	12.5	11.9	11.3	10.7	10.1	9.5	8.9	8.4	7.9	7.4
112	12.5	11.9	11.3	10.6	10.1	9.5	8.9	8.4	7.9	7.4
113	12.5	11.9	11.2	10.6	10.0	9.5	8.9	8.4	7.9	7.4
114	12.5	11.9	11.2	10.6	10.0	9.5	8.9	8.4	7.9	7.4
115	12.5	11.9	11.2	10.6	10.0	9.5	8.9	8.4	7.9	7.4

Joint Life Table (continued)

Ages	85	86	87	88	89	90	91	92	93	94
85	9.6	9.3	9.1	8.9	8.7	8.5	8.3	8.2	8.0	7.9
86	9.3	9.1	8.8	8.6	8.3	8.2	8.0	7.8	7.7	7.6
87	9.1	8.8	8.5	8.3	8.1	7.9	7.7	7.5	7.4	7.2
88	8.9	8.6	8.3	8.0	7.8	7.6	7.4	7.2	7.1	6.9
89	8.7	8.3	8.1	7.8	7.5	7.3	7.1	6.9	6.8	6.6
90	8.5	8.2	7.9	7.6	7.3	7.1	6.9	6.7	6.5	6.4
91	8.3	8.0	7.7	7.4	7.1	6.9	6.7	6.5	6.3	6.2
92	8.2	7.8	7.5	7.2	6.9	6.7	6.5	6.3	6.1	5.9
93	8.0	7.7	7.4	7.1	6.8	6.5	6.3	6.1	5.9	5.8
94	7.9	7.6	7.2	6.9	6.6	6.4	6.2	5.9	5.8	5.6
95	7.8	7.5	7.1	6.8	6.5	6.3	6.0	5.8	5.6	5.4
96	7.7	7.3	7.0	6.7	6.4	6.1	5.9	5.7	5.5	5.3
97	7.6	7.3	6.9	6.6	6.3	6.0	5.8	5.5	5.3	5.1
98	7.6	7.2	6.8	6.5	6.2	5.9	5.6	5.4	5.2	5.0
99	7.5	7.1	6.7	6.4	6.1	5.8	5.5	5.3	5.1	4.9
100	7.4	7.0	6.6	6.3	6.0	5.7	5.4	5.2	5.0	4.8
101	7.3	6.9	6.6	6.2	5.9	5.6	5.3	5.1	4.9	4.7
102	7.3	6.9	6.5	6.2	5.8	5.5	5.3	5.0	4.8	4.6
103	7.2	6.8	6.4	6.1	5.8	5.5	5.2	4.9	4.7	4.5
104	7.2	6.8	6.4	6.0	5.7	5.4	5.1	4.8	4.6	4.4
105	7.1	6.7	6.3	6.0	5.6	5.3	5.0	4.8	4.5	4.3
106	7.1	6.7	6.3	5.9	5.6	5.3	5.0	4.7	4.5	4.2
107	7.1	6.6	6.2	5.9	5.5	5.2	4.9	4.6	4.4	4.2
108	7.0	6.6	6.2	5.8	5.5	5.2	4.9	4.6	4.3	4.1
109	7.0	6.6	6.2	5.8	5.5	5.1	4.8	4.5	4.3	4.1
110	7.0	6.6	6.2	5.8	5.4	5.1	4.8	4.5	4.3	4.0
111	7.0	6.5	6.1	5.7	5.4	5.1	4.8	4.5	4.2	4.0
112	7.0	6.5	6.1	5.7	5.4	5.0	4.7	4.4	4.2	3.9
113	6.9	6.5	6.1	5.7	5.4	5.0	4.7	4.4	4.2	3.9
114	6.9	6.5	6.1	5.7	5.3	5.0	4.7	4.4	4.1	3.9
115	6.9	6.5	6.1	5.7	5.3	5.0	4.7	4.4	4.1	3.9

Appendix C
Single Life Expectancy Table (to figure required withdrawals from inherited IRA)

Age	Divisor	Age	Divisor	Age	Divisor
35	47.3	60	24.2	85	6.9
36	46.4	61	23.3	86	6.5
37	45.4	62	22.5	87	6.1
38	44.4	63	21.6	88	5.7
39	43.5	64	20.8	89	5.3
40	42.5	65	20.0	90	5.0
41	41.5	66	19.2	91	4.7
42	40.6	67	18.4	92	4.4
43	39.6	68	17.6	93	4.1
44	38.7	69	16.8	94	3.9
45	37.7	70	16.0	95	3.7
46	36.8	71	15.3	96	3.4
47	35.9	72	14.6	97	3.2
48	34.9	73	13.9	98	3.0
49	34.0	74	13.2	99	2.8
50	33.1	75	12.5	100	2.7
51	32.2	76	11.9	101	2.5
52	31.3	77	11.2	102	2.3
53	30.4	78	10.6	103	2.1
54	29.5	79	10.0	104	1.9
55	28.6	80	9.5	105	1.8
56	27.7	81	8.9	106	1.6
57	26.8	82	8.4	107	1.4
58	25.9	83	7.9	108	1.3
59	25.0	84	7.4	109	1.1
				110	1.0

Bibliography

Allen, Jr., Everett T., et al. *Pension Planning*. Irwin, 1992.

Beam, Jr., Burton T., and John J. McFadden. *Employee Benefits*. Dearborn, 1996.

Bogosian, Wayne G., and Dee Lee. *The Complete Idiot's Guide to 401(k) Plans*. Alpha, 1998.

CCH, Inc. *2001 U.S. Master Tax Guide*. CCH, Inc., 2000.

CCH, Inc. *Law, Explanation, and Analysis [of the] Economic Growth and Tax Relief Reconciliation Act of 2001*. CCH, Inc., 2001.

Choate, Natalie B. *Life and Death Planning for Retirement Benefits*. Ataxplan, 1996 (and 1998 supplement).

Combe, Cynthia M., and Gerard J. Talbot. *Employee Benefits Answer Book*. Panel, 1998.

Downing, Neil. *Maximize Your Benefits*. Dearborn, 2000.

Downing, Neil. *Maximize Your IRA*. Dearborn, 1998.

Employee Benefit Research Institute. *Fundamentals of Employee Benefit Programs*. Employee Benefit Research Institute, 1997.

Ferguson, Karen, and Kate Blackwell. *The Pension Book*. Arcade, 1995.

Goodman, Jordan E. *Everyone's Money Book*. Dearborn, 2001.

Kaster, Nicholas, et al. *2000 U.S. Master Pension Guide*. CCH, Inc., 2000.

Leimberg, Stephan R., and John J. McFadden. *The Tools & Techniques of Employee Benefit and Retirement Planning*. The National Underwriter Company, 1997.

Leimberg, Stephan R., et al. *The Tools & Techniques of Estate Planning*. The National Underwriter Company, 1992.

Levy, Donald R., et al. *Individual Retirement Account Answer Book*, Fifth edition. Panel, 1999.

Lochray, Paul J. *Financial Planner's Guide to Estate Planning*. Prentice Hall, 1992.

McCormally, Kevin. *Kiplinger's Cut Your Taxes*. Kiplinger, 1999.

RIA Group, Inc. *RIA's Complete Analysis of the Economic Growth and Tax Relief Reconciliation Act of 2001*. RIA Group, 2001.

U.S. Congress, *Economic Growth and Tax Relief Reconciliation Act of 2001 [H.R. 1836, Conference Report]*. U.S. Congress, 2001.

Index

A

Active participant, 12
Adjusted account balance, 53
Adjusted gross income (AGI)
  conversions, 148
  Roth IRA, 131–32
  traditional IRA, 11–13
  withdrawals and, 50
Administrative fees, 29–30
Age rule, 10
Alimony, 18
A.M. Best Co., 183
American Association of
  Individual Investors, 26
Annuity, 63, 183
Automatic investment plan,
  26

B

Back-loaded/back-ended,
  130
Beneficiary
  changing, 70
  education savings
    account, 107–10
  form, 68–70
  401(k), 181
  grace period, 91–92
  of inherited IRA, 92
  multiple, 89–92
  naming, 67–71
  nonspouse, 86–89
  Roth IRA, 142, 147
  rules, 44, 45–46
  separate accounts,
    89–91
  SEP-IRA, 155
  special needs, 108–10
  spouse as, 54–55
  state law and, 71
  tax break, 92–96

  trust, 64–65
Brand loyalty, 180
Brentmark Software, Inc.,
  66, 142, 152
Bunching, 49–50

C

Capital gains, 41
Cash out, 168–71, 183
Catch-up contribution
  Roth IRA, 130–31, 132
  SAR-SEP, 158
  SIMPLE-IRA, 162
  traditional IRA, 6–8
Charitable gifts, 79
Choate, Natalie, 79
College Board, 125
College expense, 38, 117–18
Compounding, 4–5, 19
Conduit IRA, 171
Consolidation, 174
Consumer Reports, 26
*A Consumer's Guide to the
  Retirement Distribution
  Rules*, 66
Contingent beneficiary, 68,
  102
Contribution
  after-tax, 183–84
  age rule, 10
  annual, 21
  catch-up, 6–8, 130–31,
    132, 158, 162
  deductibility of, 12, 130
  education savings
    account, 97–98,
    99–100, 101–6
  401(k), 21, 183–84
  403(b), 21
  married couples, 14, 18
  nondeductible, 19, 21,
    39, 130

  Roth IRA, 127, 129–33
  SAR-SEP, 158
  SEP-IRA, 154–56
  SIMPLE-IRA, 159–61,
    162–63
  tax benefits, 3
  tax deduction formula,
    13–14
  timetable, 17–19
  traditional IRA, 1,
    5–8
  two-part test, 10–13
Convenience, 179
Conversions, 145–52, 181
Coverdell, Paul, 100–101
Creditor protection, 72, 164,
  180
Custodial fees, 29–30
Custodian, 17, 23–24

D

Death, 37, 136, 174
Death designated
  beneficiary, 102
Death tax. *See* Estate tax
Deferral, 179
Deferred benefit plans, 11
Defined contribution plans,
  11, 179
Designated beneficiary, 64,
  82
Direct rollover, 175
Disability, 37, 136, 174
Distribution, 178, 179
Diversification, 25, 28–31
Divorce, 39, 124

E

Early withdrawal penalty,
  31
Earned income, 8–9, 21

Earnings, 3
Education expense, 137, 174
Education savings account
    (ESA), 97
    beneficiary, 107–10
    contribution, 97–98,
        99–100, 101–6
    education credits and,
        122–23
    education useage,
        118–19
    family members, 121
    fees, 112–13
    income limits, 102–4
    investment of, 110–12
    multiple, 107–8
    noneducation useage,
        119–20
    partial use, 121–22
    qualified education
        expenses, 115–18
    rollovers, 120–21,
        123–24
    special needs student,
        108–10
    tax benefits, 98
    tax consequences,
        118–23
    time horizon, 110–11
    withdrawal penalty,
        119–20
Elementary education,
    115–16
Employer-sponsored plans,
    153–65
    advantages, 178–80
    disadvantages, 181
    IRS and, 181–82
    saver's tax credit and,
        16
    traditional IRA and,
        10
    withdrawals, 63
Estate planning
    beneficiary, 67–71
    death tax, 74–79
    liquidity, 76
    Roth IRA and, 141–42
    stretch IRA, 72–74
    trust, 71–72
Estate tax, 74–75
    basis, 77–78
    charitable gifts, 79
    exemption, 78
    phase out, 75, 93
    relief, 76
Excess contribution, 106

F

Federal insurance, 24–25
Fees, 29–30, 31, 112–13
Fidelity Investments, 32, 184
First-time homebuyer,
    38–39, 134–35, 137, 174
Five-year averaging, 170
Five-year rule, 83, 127,
    133–34
Flexibility, 138–39, 154, 160
Form 1099, 2
Form 8606, 19
401(k), 21
    after-tax contributions,
        183–84
    beneficiary, 181
    conversion, 147
    IRS and, 182
    rollover, 176–77
    withdrawal, 180
403(b), 21

G

Gift tax, 103–4
Goldberg, Seymour, 66, 79
Goodman, Jordan E., 165
Government-sponsored
    plan, 167, 173
Grace period, 49, 56, 91–92

H

Health insurance, 38, 137,
    174
Higher education expenses,
    117–18
Home school, 116
HOPE credit, 122–23
Horizon Publishing, 113
Hurley, Joseph F., 125
Hutchinson, Tim, 116

I

Income, 3
Income limits, 13, 131–32,
    148–49
Income tax
    on conversions, 145–46
    federal rates, 50
    Roth IRA and, 151
    on withdrawals, 35, 36,
        50–51
Inheritance, 81–82
    direct, 84–89
    indirect, 82–84
    of inherited IRA, 92

multiple beneficiaries,
    89–92
nonspouse, 86–89
special tax break, 92–96
spouse, 84–86
Insurance companies, 27
Interest, 2
Internal Revenue Service
    (IRS), 22
    college expenses, 38
    disability, 37
    education savings
        account penalty, 120
    publications, 125, 166
    rollovers, 31
    series of withdrawals,
        37
    small business plans, 63
    taxable distributions,
        148
    transfers, 30–31
    withdrawals, 44
Investment
    company, 25
    diversification, 28–31
    options, 25–28
    time horizon, 29
Investment Company
    Institute, 32, 164, 184
IRA Advisor, 65–66
Irrevocable life insurance
    trust, 78

J

Joint-and-survivor annuity,
    63
Joint Life and Last Survivor
    Expectancy table, 54, 55

K

Kiplinger's, 26

L

Last-minute rollover, 175–76
Life expectancy, 47
Lifetime Learning credit,
    122–23
Liquidity, 76, 175
Loan provisions, 178–79

M

Maintenance fee, 29–30,
    112–13
Married couples
    contribution, 18

saver's tax credit, 16
special benefit, 14
Medical expense, 38, 137,
174
Minors, 10, 18
Miscellaneous itemized
deductions, 30
Modified adjusted gross
income, 13
Money, 26
Morningstar, 26
Multiple IRAs, 59–61
Mutual fund companies, 184
Mutual funds, 25–26

N

NASD Regulation, Inc., 80
National Association of
Securities Dealers, 74, 80
National Association of
State Treasurers, 125
Net unrealized appreciation
(NUA), 177
No-Load Stock Insider, 33
Nondeductible IRA
contributions, 39
conversion, 149, 150
required minimum
distribution, 61–62
value, 21
withdrawals, 19–21

P

Payroll deduction, 164–65
Pension plan, 10–11
Pension and Welfare
Benefits Administration
(PWBA), 165
Per capita, 69
Percentages, 53
Per stirpes, 69
Portability, 160, 174
Precious metals, 27–28
Premature withdrawal
penalty, 36
Probate, 67, 82–83
Professional management,
25
Prospectus, 26
Provisional income, 40

Q

Qualified distribution, 133
Qualified education
expenses, 115–18

R

Required beginning date,
46, 83
Required minimum
distribution (RMD)
advance withdrawals
and, 65
annuities, 63
calculations, 51–58
employer-sponsored
plan, 63
first withdrawal, 48–55
five-step plan, 47–58
grace period, 49, 56,
91–92
magic age, 47–48
multiple IRAs, 59–61
nondeductible IRA,
61–62
penalty, 46–47
Roth IRA, 64
rules, 45–47, 58–59
SEP, 63
SIMPLE, 63
spouse exception, 60–61
trusts, 64–65
when not required, 65
Responsible individual,
101–2
Retirement plan, 10–11, 16
Rights, 23–24
Risk tolerance, 25, 111–12
Rollover
education savings
account, 120–21,
123–24
employer-sponsored
plans, 172–77, 183
spouse beneficiary,
84–85
traditional IRA, 23–24,
31, 39
Rotenberg, Marvin, 79
Roth IRA
age limit, 10
background, 127–28
contributions, 21, 127,
129–33
conversion, 145–52, 181
earnings, 22
estate planning and,
141–42
first-time homebuyer
rules, 134–35
five-year rule, 127,
133–34

flexibility, 138–39
income restrictions,
131–32
required minimum
distribution, 64
saver's tax credit, 16,
140–41
stock comparison,
137–39
taxable account
comparison, 137–39
traditional IRA
comparison, 128–29,
139–40
withdrawals, 22, 127,
130, 133–37, 147
Roth, Jr., William V., 128

S

SAR-SEP, 157–58
Saver's tax credit, 2, 15–17,
22, 140–41
Savings account, 2
Savings Incentive Match
Plan for Employees
(SIMPLE), 63, 158–63,
182–83
Secondary education,
115–16
Section 457 plan, 167, 173
Section 529 plan, 100, 102
Securities brokerage, 26–27
Self-directed IRA, 26–27
Self-employed, 153–56
Separate maintenance
decree, 39
Series of payments, 37–38
Simplified employee
pension (SEP), 63, 153–56,
182–83
Single Life Expectancy
Table, 83, 85
Slott, Ed, 65–66, 96
Small business plans, 153–65
Social Security benefit, 40,
151–52
Special circumstances, 37–39
Special needs beneficiary,
108–10
Spouse
as beneficiary, 54–55
inheritance, 84–86
required minimum
distribution and,
60–61
Standard & Poor's, 183

State income tax, 50–51
Stepped-up basis, 76
Stock, 26–27
    rollover, 176–77
    Roth IRA comparison,
        137–39
Stretch IRA, 72–73
Strong Funds, 22
Successor beneficiary, 68

T

Taxable account, 2, 137–39
Taxable compensation, 8–9,
    21
Tax credit, 2, 164. *See also*
    Saver's tax credit
Tax deduction
    formula, 13–14
    SIMPLE-IRA, 160
    traditional IRA, 3, 21,
        129
    two-part test, 10–13
Tax-deferred compounding,
    4–5, 19
Tax payments, 39
Tax Reform Act of 1986, 10
Ten-year averaging, 170–71
Threshold exemption, 78
Time horizon, 29, 110–11
Timely withdrawals, 39
Traditional IRA
    contribution, 1, 5–8
    conversion, 145–49
    eligibility, 8–10
    growth, 4–5
    investment options,
        25–28
    rollover, 23–24

Roth IRA comparison,
    139–40
    saver's tax credit and,
        140–41
    tax benefits, 3–4, 129
    tax credit, 2
    value, 3, 4
    withdrawals, 24, 130
Transfer, 30–31, 39, 87–88
T. Rowe Price, 143, 152, 184
Trust, 64–65, 71–72
Trustee, 17, 23–24

U

Uniform table, 54
U.S. Department of Labor,
    165
U.S. Savings Bonds, 125

V

*Value Line Mutual Fund
    Survey*, 26
Vanguard Group, 113, 184

W

Weiss Ratings, Inc., 183
Withdrawal
    adjusted gross income
        and, 50
    advance, 65
    annuities, 63
    between 59½ and 70½,
        35, 40–41
    cash out, 168–71
    converted IRA, 150
    employer-sponsored
        plan, 63

five-step plan, 47–58
formula, 20–21
401(k), 180
grace period, 91–92
income tax and, 50–51
lump sum, 170
multiple IRAs, 59–61
nondeductible IRA,
    19–21, 61–62
nonspouse beneficiary,
    88–89
over 70½. *See* Required
    minimum
    distribution (RMD)
penalty, 31, 36–39,
    136–37, 150, 174, 180
penalty-free, 37–39
postponement, 180
required beginning
    date, 46, 83
Roth IRA, 22, 64, 127,
    130, 133–37, 147
rules, 24, 44–47, 58–59
SEP-IRA, 63, 155
series of, 136, 174
SIMPLE-IRA, 63, 161
special situations,
    37–39, 59–65
spouse beneficiary,
    85–86
stock, 177
stretch out limits, 83
tax-free, 61–62, 127
timely, 39
traditional IRA, 128,
    130
trusts, 64–65
under 59½, 35, 36–39

The New IRAs

For special discounts on 20 or more copies of *The New IRAs and How to Make Them Work for You,* please call Dearborn Trade Special Sales at 800-621-9621, extension 4455.

Dearborn™
Trade Publishing
A **Kaplan Professional** Company